THE SELF-SUFFICIENT GLOBAL CITIZEN

THE SELF-SUFFICIENT

GLOBAL CITIZEN

A GUIDE FOR RESPONSIBLE FAMILIES AND COMMUNITIES

ATTA ARGHANDIWAL

Paperback ISBN 978-0-9978870-2-0
Library of Congress Control Number: 2017949584

This resource guide is designed to provide generic definitions, best practices, and helpful tips based on extensive hands-on experience and knowledge of the author as a refugee and an immigrant. The book is being published with the understanding that the author and the distribution company have not and will not be engaged in providing legal, professional, or financial advice. Readers must seek any legal, financial, and professional advice or services they require through appropriate professional resources.

Editor: Nina Shoroplova
Typeset: Greg Salisbury
Book Cover Design: Marla Thompson
Portrait Photographer: Edreece Arghandiwal
Published by Attamoves
Visit www.attamoves.com

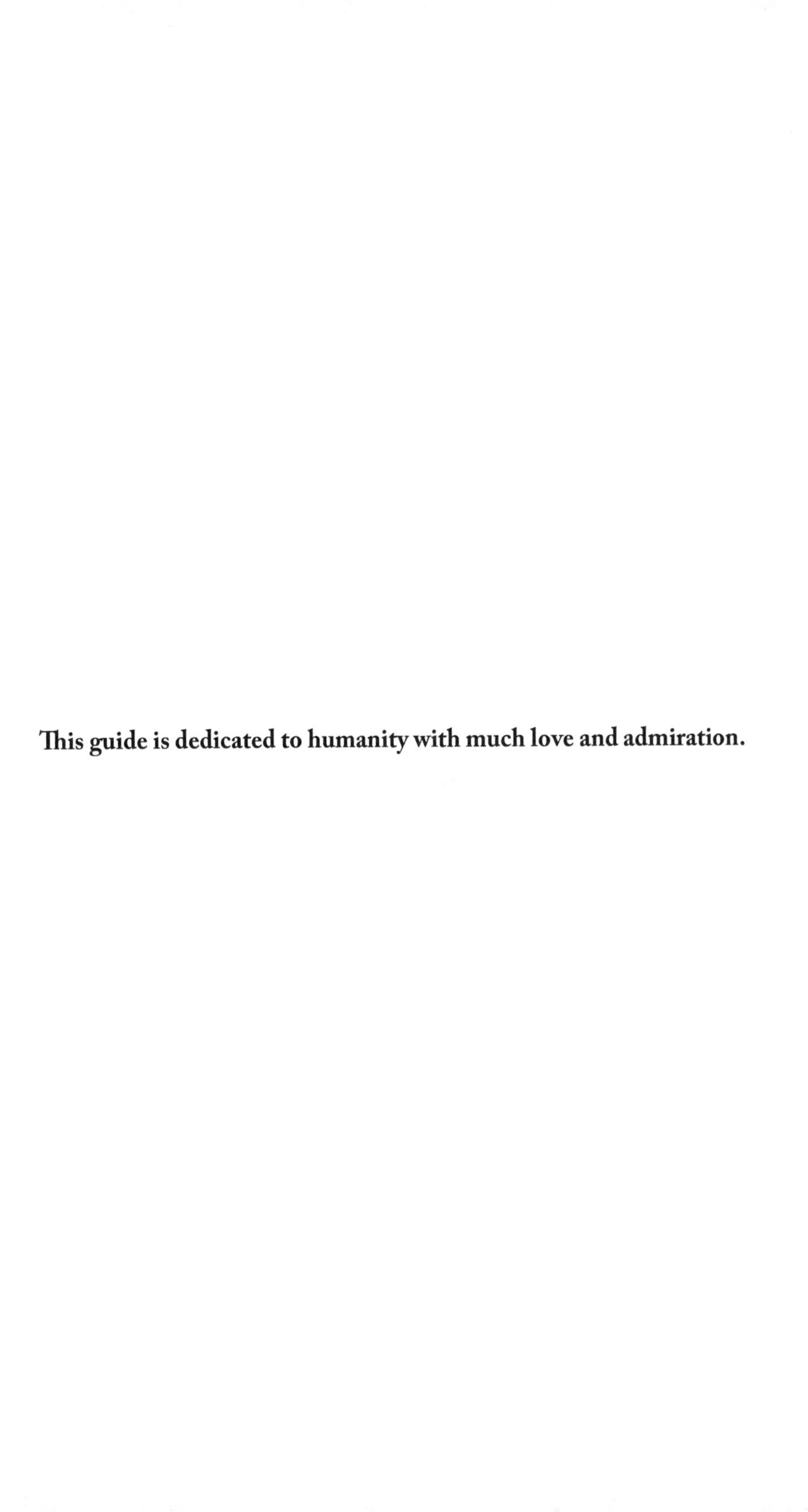

This guide is dedicated to humanity with much love and admiration.

CONTENTS

FOREWORD

This incredible encyclopedia of resources affecting every dimension and decade of life provides guidelines leading to eventual success as global citizens, whether as refugees and immigrants or in our native countries. Atta Arghandiwal, a remarkable Afghan-American visionary, once a refugee himself who became a bank vice-president, inspires the reader to not just endure terrible hardships but to flourish during the many challenges of their new world, hopefully a kinder world.

Atta knows firsthand how to start over with nothing, to build a new life in a new country with basic English. He knows it because he's lived it. Wanting to spare the reader his experiences and mistakes, he guides us through every aspect of life, from the first breath to the last. He helps refugees and immigrants negotiate the complexities of a country's systems from banking and insurance to education and health care. Please refer to Atta's site www.attamoves.com for access to resources and links.

This book serves as a step-by-step blueprint for a successful transition whatever your path. This brilliant, compassionate, and practical leader has given all of us the gift of resources and support systems that enable the suffering to overcome the many challenges they face and to grow and thrive to be good citizens.

In addition to his humanitarian work, mentoring of youth, devotion to family, and business successes, Atta has provided training to governments, the United Nations, and businesses globally in best business and government practices, ethics, and humanizing the workplace.

Atta walks side by side with us from the moment we first think of leaving our home to seek a safer, better life for ourselves and our family. He helps us figure out, assuming we have time, how to get our affairs in order, saving what we can. Of course, if we leave under gunfire, running for our lives, hopefully some pre-packing has happened and we have grabbed what is most important.

What papers will you need? What to pack? What if we get stuck in a camp for refugees? Who should go and who must stay? Maybe you're pregnant or have a child whose health is fragile, maybe too fragile to bring along but whose very life is at stake if you stay. What about your grandfather who can barely walk and frequently wanders off? If you have a choice in where you go, how do you decide? What to do if you end up incarcerated? When you get to your host country, how do you survive?

Atta offers all kinds of little tips to make your journey easier. He encourages you to turn what you may see as a tragedy into a new adventure once you're on your way. This book should be with you at all times if possible. Some days you might need one part of it; another day, other sections.

Many immigrants start out and thrive as entrepreneurs, eventually becoming successful business people. In the process they've learned the ways and laws of their new land and have filled out all the necessary paperwork and licenses if needed, paying appropriate taxes.

The changing role of women provides many challenges to entering a new world where those who wear scarves or full concealment are suddenly faced with half-naked girls and women walking around the streets, acting as if they are really dressed.

Men's fashions also leave a lot to be desired with their droopy pants and underwear showing. These fashions can cause a lot of stress in immigrant families where the generations clash and the authority of the patriarchal father is eroded.

Sadly, there is a lot of anti-immigrant hatred in our world and Atta believes that our community kindness circles as outlined in *Global Kindness Revolution* should be held in all organizations dealing with refugees and immigrants in particular. The directions are in "Appendix A: Stress Survival Skills for Refugees and Immigrants." Instructional videos can be screened on YouTube, so give it a try. Also included there is the "Kindness at Noon for Refugees and Immigrants, Everywhere, Every Day," the KAN Technique.

These techniques of Vibrational Social Change are at the forefront of a new view of our challenges to discipline and contain our primitive MEAN MINDS while we nourish and encourage our more evolved KIND MINDS, aligning globally every day at noon as alerts go off on our devices. By 2020, more people will have smartphones than have indoor plumbing or electricity, so this is the first time we have the chance to align our minds in unison, powerfully neutralizing the negative energy that so dominates these times.

These are new things we can try, to change our heritage from planetary destruction to one where we acknowledge our common humanity and how we ARE capable of lifting each other up so we ALL succeed in healing ourselves and our Mother Earth. This book helps make us better people, more confident of the possibility of a better world for our children and our grandchildren's children still to come.

I plan to gift everyone I care about with a copy of this truly unique and valuable book.

Judith Trustone, author, *Global Kindness Revolution: How Together We Can Heal Violence, Racism and Meanness.*

PREFACE

The idea for this resource guide—*The Self-Sufficient Global Citizen: A Guide for Responsible Families and Communities*—evolved over a long period of time, as a matter of fact upon my arrival in Germany as a refugee in August 1980 and my subsequent migration to the United States. Like every other refugee and immigrant, I needed a lot of information to start life in my new environment. I looked for a simple guide that would help me navigate my way through my new life and home, but I could never find one. In the first couple of years, the best things I could put my hands on were brochures and pamphlets. Eventually I was able to find some self-help books but most of them focused on just one or two topics, while others focused on such complicated matters that it was discouraging rather than helpful to read them. In addition, because this was before the Internet, it took a lot of time and patience to find out what I needed to know.

I often thought about creating a condensed lifestyle guide geared toward immigrants—a road map, if you will—but over time I got busier and busier. A couple of years ago, I succeeded in creating a comprehensive resource guide for immigrants to North America—*Immigrant Success Planning: A Family Resource Guide*. Honestly speaking, I really wanted to write a global guide but I was persuaded to write a guide for immigrants to North America first.

So I am now delighted to have finally succeeded in creating a pragmatic global best practices and success resource guide that can be used anywhere around the world. This guide is the product of years of knowledge, real life practices, and proven ideas. It expands and builds on the knowledge and success of *Immigrant Success Planning*, while also providing updated and new information. More importantly, this guide was developed based on core principles and input from various focus groups of refugees and immigrants from all walks of life, including parents, students, teachers, social services experts, entrepreneurs—in short, anyone I've met who had best practices to share.

The result is a self-sufficiency guide that focuses on individuals and entire families, as well as communities. Chapters include useful details, best practices, and success tips that can be used throughout the life cycle, from the birth of a child through retirement and beyond. You could say that the information it contains never expires, always providing the foundation for a successful and powerful way of life.

Due to the ongoing fast pace of change today, I have made a decision to limit the use of online links and references throughout this book and instead I will provide up-to-date links and resources through my website, www.attamoves.com. I am also committed to providing tables, worksheets, and helpful checklists through this website.

Despite the amazing life full of joy, hard work, love of family and friends, and successes I have enjoyed, I truly consider this book to be my ultimate achievement in life and my personal gift to humanity. I hope it gives you as much pleasure.

Atta Arghandiwal

ACKNOWLEDGEMENTS

This book could not have been written without all the wonderful people who comprise various chapters of my life. I have been extremely blessed.

I wish to express my sincere thanks and profound gratitude to the following people without whose invaluable assistance and generous contribution this book would have not been successfully accomplished. I hold you all so close to my heart.

My children, Edreece and Hailai, I am so grateful for your unwavering trust in me as you simply remind me every day to not give up and stop. Your willingness and amazing ability to play the game (soccer) I loved, for all those long trips in the wee hours of the day and the invaluable conversations during long drives, romancing wins and losses, and then back at practices the next day. My special thanks go to Edreece, my son, who devotedly assists me and stands firm by my side in branding, marketing, and ultimately completing my book projects. He has been my closest companion and coworker.

My amazing mom for her daily dose of well wishes and constant prayers and words of advice (my friends all say, She is not only your mom but everyone's mom.).

My close-knit family for their unconditional support and ongoing belief in me, putting up with my emails and reminders and follow ups. You have and continue to energize me to serve.

Enayet jon, finding you back after thirty years has been a true blessing and source of inspiration. Thanks for your unmatched human kindness and spirit. Your long and difficult journey to make it to safety while raising children with such grace and a sense of responsibility provided me with so much inspiration and energy to write this book. You simply bring out the best in humanity.

Farid jon and Masuda jon, you two have been with me for the longest time and the most important moments in life. You have defined "friendship" better than anyone in my life.

Judith Trustone, for listening and for your spirited guidance and friendship. Your unmatched stamina and relentless drive to promote Global Kindness has reenergized me since the first day I met you. I would love to have the energy you have at your stage in life, when I turn eighty.

Joy Pittel, your commanding, determined wisdom and drive have been such influential forces. You don't take no for an answer. Your ability to not let any negativity get through has instilled in me a different style of drive and passion to move forward.

Doug Warwick, you are so bright, so witty, and so willing to share and you never hesitate to speak your mind. You have inspired me better than anyone during the last couple of years. I had to save your messages and go back to them to review, learn, and adjust myself to your challenging words of advice.

My amazing mentors, coaches, manager, and coworkers, everything I have learned and become is due to your support, guidance, and motivation.

Marla Thompson, my amazingly talented book cover designer. Marla is brilliant at capturing the essence and theme of a book title's purpose, and she recommends and makes quick work of things. She made my book cover designs and work smooth and easy. Thanks for the wonderful work.

Nina Shoroplova, my expert editor, thanks for your brilliant work and creativity. You have truly provided much-needed guidance and support in formatting and restructuring these topics with a pragmatic sense of understanding and appreciation for making this resource guide easy to use. I am truly grateful for your amazing work.

Shafiq Ahamdi, your professional and caring work in creating great brand and marketing ideas is truly appreciated. Your thoughtful and practical ideas have laid the foundation for the solid branding of my work. I will always be grateful.

Humaira Ghilzai, your wisdom is priceless in reminding me about the meaning and impact of the term "Global Citizen." Your reminder provided further motivation to challenge refugees and immigrants to not only lead a more productive lifestyle but to raise themselves to the highest standards of excellence worthy of each global citizen's responsibilities.

My amazing players, you all trusted me to bring out the best in you in playing soccer, despite my lack of playing capability or notable background. Coaching soccer was only a vehicle, but a truly rewarding experience, to mentor and help you develop as responsible members of communities. I am also very grateful for the opportunities to have so much fun in celebrating our club wins and chemistry and proudly representing the Afghan community. Thanks for listening and following my advice and mentorship. Your growth and development and particularly your pursuit of advanced education have been the biggest rewards back to your coach and parents.

Nahid Aria and Ahmad Aria for your friendship and consistent reminders about the value of community service and opportunities in order to reach out and make a difference. Thanks for your service and true friendship.

Parwana Kahkeshan, your drive, passion, and courage for self-sufficiency as a scholar and a student away from home served not just as an example of self-sufficiency but as further motivation to point out the important attributes of self-sufficiency, and to never give up. Your drive in finding your way, a new home, and answers to many challenges served to model great human resilience.

Tamana Ansari for taking time to review this book's table of contents and for providing encouragement about its potential impact on others.

Zamarud Amini for providing and reminding me of some very important elements and reminders for refugees and potential future community-based workshops and trainings.

Mariam Atash for your willingness to not hesitate in sharing your ideas about this guide. Your family contribution and overall proud representation of Afghan-American communities are matters of pride for all of us.

Aria Shiva for your upbeat and positive response and for sharing your thoughts about European refugee status and needs.

There is no way to mention everyone's names. You all make me keep going.

Life is indeed a team game. Your wisdom is priceless.

This book came to life as a result of humanity's perseverance.

My amazing focus groups for your highly professional skills and input in making it possible for all immigrants to understand and easily digest the book's substance and purpose, my sincerest thanks to all of you.

Chapter One: Humanity Is on the Move

Do You Know Where You Are Headed and Why?

I remember holding my breath, afraid the Russian soldiers walking past the shadow in which I was trying to hide myself would smell my fear. I was on my way to Kabul's international airport through back streets and rugged roads, eluding the Russian troops that had invaded my beautiful country, Afghanistan. I was escaping, afraid for my life. I'd secretly gotten a plane ticket and was desperate to get on that plane, a memory that has never left me, even after thirty-seven years. I've learned that life's successes, and failures with their misfortunes and tragedies bring about transformation that can either be positive or negative. Truth, honesty, and integrity, at times elusive, will always guide us toward the right path, even when we may be feeling uprooted and powerless.

Imagine you and your family are living quietly and going about your life. However, suddenly, through no fault of your own, the situation changes. Your country, like mine was, is invaded, or a civil war breaks out, or a big tsunami hits your region. Or a new government or a large group of terrorists or religious demagogues decide that your ethnic or religious group or even social class presents a problem that can only be cured through the destruction of all individuals and groups and even dwellings in that social class. Or a hurricane or other natural disaster destroys your whole way of life.

In my case, Russians had invaded my beautiful country of Afghanistan. Fearing for my life, I escaped in the dark of night, leaving behind my family, friends, and colleagues for guaranteed uncertainty.

You are now on your way out, maybe running for your life! I'll never forget that feeling of being on the run. Cross a border, board an unsafe boat, or, if you can, buy a plane ticket, and off you go. Think about simply moving across unfamiliar places, cities, and countries, maybe not even knowing the languages. I was fortunate to have learned English from Peace Corps volunteers during my high school days in Kabul.

Leaving home is no longer about moving across short distances in search of food, gas for your car, or fare for a bus or taxi. Rather, it is life on the move, maybe carrying all you can of your worldly possessions, for an uncertain future. Now imagine doing that over hundreds and thousands of miles, with people actively trying to find you, prosecute you, search you, incarcerate you, and even take your life. Also, flights may not exist if and when you get to the airport, or the shortest way to a new country may be impossible. You are suddenly a migrant refugee! You are forced to flee across international borders with fear for your life. But simply wanting to move to a different country does not make you a refugee. Instead, having your whole life depend on getting away is what makes you a refugee.

Sadly, your home could have been in any number of places in the world. Forced movements of human beings are nothing new. From the Jews' escape from slavery in Egypt through the parting of the Red Sea to Muhammad's followers finding safety in Ethiopia, all have been seeking to escape persecution! The potato famine in the 1800s brought the Irish to America and other shores. The desertification of Africa left Africans adrift in search of arable land and water. Millions were taken by force from their families and lands to serve the profitable slave trade, still existent today in some places. Modern-day slavery exists through the horrendous numbers of women, boys, and girls stolen from their families or the streets by sex traffickers today.

Native Americans are considered to be non-immigrants, even though they are said to have crossed the land bridge connecting Asia and North America thousands of years ago. But in recent history, we are all immigrants, though our ancestors may have immigrated two hundred and fifty years ago, fifty years ago, or just a few months ago. In America, immigration began when the *Mayflower* arrived with roughly a hundred Pilgrims in 1620. Millions of Europeans migrated here in the centuries that have followed, seeking freedom from starvation and persecution, and a better life.

In general, thousands of similar forced movements have existed throughout ancient and modern history. In countries like Australia, we saw the movement of convicts and indentured servants seeking freedom from another form of slavery. All separated by time and place, refugees and migrants, just like all of us, have the same goals in mind—we are simply trying to find a safe place to live out their lives with their families.

It is, however, important to know our world is beginning to feel the impact of this unprecedented mass movement. Humanity is starting to feel the food insecurities and water shortages—realities millions of innocent people face on a daily basis. Although mass migration is not unknown, it is now becoming normalized, expected yet resented by some. In reality, it is unfortunately a complicated aspect of modern life.

This recent crisis of mass movement due to wars, economic poverty, climate change, overpopulation, and political and social unrest has forced over sixty-five million (9 percent of the world's population) refugees to seek shelter and opportunities away from their original homes, both inside and outside their countries of birth. As a result, millions of families and their innocent children are left with feelings of worthlessness, of not belonging in this world as human beings.

Most recently, anti-immigrant sentiments and senseless fears of losing jobs to foreigners have arisen. These feelings in host nations are stronger now than they were over thirty years ago when I first left home. They follow in the wake of terrorism. These sentiments dehumanize refugees and migrants as "aliens," not as human beings who are the victims of war, political posturing, climate change, and natural disasters.

Some people are being forced into unacceptable and inhumane conditions with no real chance to exercise their basic human rights or be part of a shared planet. This wave of human suffering is certainly changing the world while presenting an enormous challenge for us as humans to open our hearts to embrace and welcome everyone. Forced out, not by their own intention, most end up as "aliens," often perceived as threatening to the rights and economics of the native populations of their host countries. They are now subject to all of life's potential challenges while also being looked upon as burdens and threats to the local security and endangering its way of life. In reality, forced migrants are simply in search of safety and basic human rights as true victims of common enemies' atrocities and other political factors.

Atta's Take on the Refugee Crisis

Today's charged world and the influence of incompetent, corrupt politicians and uninformed citizens—even within settled populations of host countries—try to transfer the "issue of refugees" from universal human rights into that of "homeland security." Turning the tide while being rough and tough on foreigners in the name of security from potential terrorists is obviously generating more political currency than appealing for benevolence and compassion for people in distress. Regardless of all these challenges, the best way to deal with migrants and refugees is to look at injustices as opportunities and tests for humanity. I believe we have a chance to unlock the potential inside all of us for the better and to move on with a sense of accountability, human dignity, and resilience. As humans, we all naturally play a zero-sum game with ourselves while thinking of the past. Our ultimate goal should be to end wars and pave the way to safety and economic opportunities within conflict zones. Thinking about what happened six months ago takes space and energy that could be redirected elsewhere or to a project in the new chapter of our lives.

Refugees, Immigrants, and Migrants

The word "refugee" applies to a displaced individual who is forced—due to fear of danger or persecution for reasons of race, nationality, religion, political affiliations, or membership of a social group—to cross her or his national boundary and seek shelter and protection elsewhere. The term "immigrant" refers to a person who has been able to enter a new country and has been granted residency and the potential for naturalization. The term "migrant" refers to people who migrate either into ("immigrant") or out of ("emigrant") a country. Immigration today is more common than ever it was in the past. In reality, the line and meaning between these two categories of migrant—refugee and immigrant—is quite different. People can easily fall within both categories at once and shift from one to the other depending on their conditions while being victim to potential acts of terrorism, humanity, and trafficking.

Due to mass displacement and the lack of governance of millions of people, many refugees turn to migration as a key livelihood strategy. This has created enormous challenges for governments and policymakers to draw realistic distinction between those moving to seek protection from persecution and those moving for better economic opportunities.

No matter what, how, and where they are, migrants make and reshape the world!

According to the Office of the United Nations High Commissioner for Refugees (UNHCR), displaced people surpassed sixty million for the first time in 2016. Here is a list of the top ten source countries of refugees (not counting Palestinian Refugees) according to Amnesty International (May 2017 report).

1. Syria
2. Afghanistan
3. Somalia
4. Sudan
5. South Sudan
6. The Democratic Republic of the Congo
7. Myanmar
8. Central African Republic
9. Iraq
10. Eritrea

These are the top ten refugee host countries.

1. Turkey (more than 2 million)
2. Pakistan (1.5 million)
3. Lebanon (1.5 million)
4. Iran (950,000)
5. Ethiopia
6. Jordan
7. Kenya
8. Chad
9. Uganda
10. China

The current number of refugees worldwide is estimated at 19.5 million; there are 1.15 million vulnerable refugees who need resettlement; 86 percent of refugees are hosted by developing countries.

Challenges

Reflecting on my own and many others' experiences, today's migrants by far have more serious challenges to deal with than our ancestors endured. Our world is dealing with more multiple challenges now than in the past: the forced migrations and exodus of millions as a result of wars, the rise of terrorism, economic and financial uncertainty, the erosion of traditional pension plans, poverty, unemployment, income inequality, climate change, overpopulation, and the lack of a concentrated effort or funded plans and policies by local, state, and federal governments. Refugees and migrants go through various types and levels of fear, anxieties, and challenges, many of which cause severe psychological results:

- constant mental risk for entire family
- fear of adjustment to new environment
- loss of confidence

- loss of contact with family and friends
- loss of contact with original ethics
- loss of homeland
- loss of mother tongue
- loss of social status
- social failure

Cultural Barriers

Cultural barriers impact each and every aspect of life for refugees and migrants. It is frankly very common for cultural misunderstandings to take place. But despite all the challenges, human beings are incredibly strong and grateful for the opportunity to be in their new homes. They have the same basic desires as others, such as having their children succeed in school and being able to put a roof over their heads. After everything they have already been through, they do all that they can to keep their families afloat in this new, scary place.

My challenge to residents of host countries is to ask them a simple question: "What if you had to pack and leave your country without any warning due to fear of the unknown? Of possible death, rape, or starvation? How would you like to be treated if this were to happen to you?"

Language and Communication

Language and communication challenges comprise the most significant issue. It is not just about language within a new environment but rather the entire process of communicating from the beginning of travel plans to the late stages of settlement. Don't forget that non-verbal clues and body language are crucial parts of communications. Problems may arise between different cultures, for instance, direct eye contact—acceptable in some cultures as forthright and honest—may be taken as a form of aggression in another culture; whereas a lack of eye contact suggests the person has something to hide.

Here are some key examples of communication issues:

- the lack of proper research and knowledge about the general life conditions, potential challenges, and expectations within new environments
- the lack of proper family communication and expectations

- the lack of understanding and proper communication resulting in constant arguments or disputes about roles and responsibilities within the family, especially when cultural customs like the role and treatment of men, women, children, and elders are challenged
- the disruption of the parent-child relationship when parents must rely on their children for translation and communication

Let's be honest, not many Western countries are known for being multilingual. Imagine being in a foreign land, unable to speak the language of your host nation, and trying to get a job, make friends, or even complete such basic tasks as filling out various forms and buying food. There is more in the next chapter about what to do to overcome these challenges!

The biggest obstacles refugees and migrant parents have is raising their children in an unfamiliar culture and environment. Parents find that their children quickly adjust to the new culture, which may be totally at odds with their own old culture. Besides, kids tend to pick up languages much faster than their parents do. Teenagers especially use this proficiency with language to their advantage, hurting the dynamics between themselves and their parents, as they often have to serve as their parents' translators.

Impact on Children

In spite of their ability to learn the new language more quickly than their parents, some migrant and refugee children are vulnerable to anxiety and a tendency toward drug use. Seeking refuge in a new land has a severe impact on children:

- social life fragmentation (home and school are polar opposites)
- refugee children are five times more likely to be out of school
- socio-economical deficiencies
- parents are overwhelmed due to life and investment destabilization
- emotional cost of sharing housing with other families and strangers

Transportation

Similar to cultural and communication challenges, troubles with transportation is a big issue that affects almost all aspect of life for millions. Most cities have complicated routes for buses, trains, and other methods of transportation. Fortunately, most cities and municipalities do a very good job in providing their residents with up-to-date information and options through their websites and in print. This guide also provides more information on transportation in chapter five.

Finding Work

While most newcomers are eager to take whatever job becomes available when they first enter the country, that job may not be the best fit long term. It is, however, important to start a job, learn and gain experience, evaluate your progress, and look for future potential options. Read chapter eight, "Finding Employment," to understand some of the steps you can take to improve your position.

Finding Housing

Affordable housing is becoming increasingly expensive in all Western countries. Just imagine trying to obtain housing with low-paying jobs. For that reason, large families often choose to live together, creating stressful, at times noisy environments that are hardly conducive to studying or resting.

Refugees and immigrants may fall victim to exploitation at the hands of their landlords. Having to move from one location to another because of language difficulties, unfamiliarity with laws, and falling victim to exploitation or scams can be quite expensive.

Please refer to chapter eleven for housing solutions and options.

Accessing Services

Newcomers fail to take advantage of many available services due to a lack of proper guidance and tools required to utilize the services, such as a computer connection. This book offers the widest range of service providers for a wide variety of needs along the life cycle.

Human Trafficking

Human trafficking is one of the most devastating but hidden current phenomena. It technically means the purchase or sale of another human being for potential labor or sex. Simply stated, it is an exchange of anything of value for sex. Human trafficking is taking place in every corner of the world, and in some areas—such as Eastern Europe and South America where the vulnerability of mass migrant and refugee movement makes people prey to victimization—more than others. There is more on this topic in chapters three and six.

The Diverse Values of Migrants and Refugees

Historically, the diverse values of migrants and refugees in general has proven to be good for all host countries, since, in part, newcomers bring different perspectives, experiences, and values to the table.

- Migrants often bring high educational standards and work ethics into their new country.
- They reflect a deep diversity of life experiences and personal beliefs due to their very diverse life histories and economic backgrounds.
- Migrants' tragedies and triumphs serve their new countries well.
- Migrants connect people across different groups by demonstrating common humanity. They prove the fact that people from all over the world have a lot in common even while also proving that not all cultural beliefs and practices are equal.
- They become entrepreneurs and start businesses. Worldwide in general, more migrants start their own businesses than non-migrants.
- They are also more likely to create their own jobs. According to the US Department of Labor, 7.5 percent of foreign-born residents are self-employed compared to 6.6 percent among the native-born.
- They develop cutting-edge technologies and companies. According to the National Venture Capital Association, migrants have started 25 percent of the public US companies backed by venture capital investors. This list includes Google, eBay, Yahoo Sun Microsystems, and Intel.
- They are the world's engineers, scientists, and innovators. According to the United States Census Bureau, despite making up only 16 percent of the resident population holding a bachelor's degree or higher, migrants represent 33 percent of engineers, 27 percent of mathematicians, statisticians, and computer scientists, and 24 percent of physical scientists (physicists, chemists, astronomers, and geologists).
- Additionally, according to the Partnership for a New American

Economy, foreign-born inventors were credited with contributing to more than 75 percent of patents issued to the top ten patent-producing universities in 2011.

Refugees and Migrants Make the World Go

Early day immigrants have set examples for "how to be" by learning host nations' values and laws, and by the fact that they earned the respect of everyone based on the contributions they made, rather than solely on their backgrounds. It is really important to understand that human beings, no matter where, should be treated equally under the law. I believe it is important to cherish traditions, heritage, and culture; I believe it is equally important to adapt and enjoy new environments quickly and to learn the values and principles practiced there, despite how uncomfortable they make us.

There is nothing wrong for a first-generation grandmother, for example, to speak in her native language at home, but the grandchildren born in the new country must learn to speak the language of that new country. First-generation immigrants may have a difficult time questioning authority, but (to the dismay of the first-generation immigrants) that becomes second nature for younger generations due to their awareness of the contrasting values between their country of origin and the new land!

People continue to pass on their value system to the next generation. Adapting to a new environment is the hardest thing for anyone and with that come uncertainties that could be very uncomfortable; there is nothing wrong with asking questions instead of trying to reinvent the wheel all over again. We have a responsibility to do our part to follow the right path of happiness and to pursue success with responsibility and optimism. The majority of the countries of the Western world allow for freedom of speech, freedom of the press, and are under the rule of law, enabling citizens to question any authority and speak up when needed.

Despite the fact that their journeys are almost never easy, immigrants' adaptability, creativity, and strengths make the world go! Immigrants historically have made up the population in many countries and communities around the world while in search for their ideal new home in place of the one they left behind

You Are Not Alone

The hearts and minds of many refugees remain gripped with fear and desperation, many suffering from post-traumatic stress disorder (PTSD), even while living inside the rich countries of the world. Migration today is a global phenomenon, a life-changing event with enormous implications not only for those who migrate but also for those who remain behind in the country of origin and for some natives of host countries. This latest exodus of many millions of families further destabilizes world communities. Many people have to leave relatives and even their children behind to keep them safe.

I personally witnessed many parents leaving Afghanistan in the summer of 2015 in hopes of finding a future home for themselves and the children they had left behind. In recent years, the world has also witnessed the exodus and heartbreaking journeys of millions of children leaving their homelands without their parents. These children need extra help, especially protection from predators.

In general, the needs of migrants are far greater than those of native-born citizens.

Lead the Way and Explore

That's right, don't just lead, but explore as well. Regardless of any of the conditions that are forcing you to move, whether it is your decision or someone else's that is moving you into a new part of your journey, you are in reality taking a leadership position. You are now responsible for showing or helping pave the way for yourself, your family, and others. You are actually now a tour guide, a trailblazer. You must learn to help, navigate the challenges, so that everyone on this journey can thrive.

Do you have curiosity about life? A sense of adventure? Why not explore and look for more opportunities and something new? Check out the world around you and find things that may be waiting under the rock.

Successful human beings have curiosity and they love to turn over stones and find new things. We may not always find something, but we improve our chances by a big margin when we try leading the way and exploring. Try to instill a sense of exploration in yourself and those with you as you move forward. Don't sit around and drink lemonade, but rather look over the fence and find out what is out there.

Build Your Future on Your Values

The great thing about human beings is that we are all free to build our future. But our life is always about establishing our own personal code and deciding exactly what we consider to be the most important values in our life. Values are the gold that exists in each and every one of us. They are the real fortunes of our lives.

To start finding your gold, take a piece of paper and write out your five most important values and attributes. Write down the five qualities that are most important to you (values such as freedom, family, success, creativity, music, creativity, music, generosity, and honesty).

In order to become an outstanding human being, you must be completely clear about the values that will serve as your own personal philosophy. But know that no one's values are any better or more important than anyone else's. It is, however, important to realize good values like honor and compassion are key to enhancing life while poor values like greed and jealousy destroy lives. But let's first do an honest analysis of your life's existence and contributions.

Your legacy is a sort of symbolic immortality. You can dodge the questions for quite some time, but eventually you start to ask them of yourself. Take a long-term view now and consider how your legacy will impact the next generations! Write down your answers.

- What will people say about me when I die?
- What is my story?
- What is my legacy?
- Is my world a smaller world or a bigger world?
- Am I isolated or connected?
- Why am I here?
- What do I want to do with my life?
- Why do I exist?
- How can I contribute?
- What will I leave behind?
- What example am I setting for my family and future generations?
- What are the things I should be grateful for, despite my suffering?
- How should I explain my life experience?
- What sacrifices have I made in my life?

- Have I stayed true and committed to my decisions?
- Have I defined my boundaries?
- What are my most important values in life?

Your Priorities

It's important to prioritize the activities in your life. Other than ensuring you have the basics for survival, focus on spending time productively. If you like big families, have them, but recognize up front that kids require time and effort, and you'll have to choose a lifestyle that supports quality time with them for you to feel satisfied and for them to grow up with the best opportunities. It currently costs an average of $250,000 dollars in the US to raise one child, so don't have more than you can afford. List your priorities based on the lifestyle you wish to have.

Now the Big Question

The big question is "Have you stayed true and committed to the most important decisions in your life?" Deciding and acting are not the same thing. We know this to be true, but how many times have you decided to learn something different but then found a year or two later, that you had made no progress? That's the bad news.

The good news is that your success in life has surprisingly little to do with the things that happen to you, and has everything to do with how you *respond* to what happens to you. Everyone faces difficulties and challenges in life, some more than others. What separates the winners from the losers is how we choose to deal with our challenges. Oftentimes, we become easy targets of skepticism when we are bold enough to share our stories with others.

The Main Reasons Why Humanity Suffers

There are many reasons why humanity suffers. Here are some of the main ones:

- living in poverty and with disease
- not having a well-defined purpose in life
- not having a core or central purpose in life

- having no goal to aim for
- not having ambition to aim beyond mediocrity
- lacking in self-discipline and self-control, which control all negative qualities

There cannot be any hope for people without a core, central purpose in life.

A Turning Point

Key to making change in life is commitment toward action and the legacy you wish to leave behind. The question is not whether you will leave a legacy but rather what kind of legacy will you leave. I am a firm believer that to be successful, one must establish a solid purpose in life. Our purpose will serve as the basis for creating and sustaining our legacy. I can say this with confidence based on personal and professional experience while working with people who struggle to find and know their purpose. On the other hand, people who have a grasp of their purpose and engage with it succeed in leading fulfilling lives.

Three Stages in Life

Our lives consist of three stages (early growth years, middle age, and retirement). Here are the main questions as you prepare and think of the three stages in your life. It is important to think of our strengths and vulnerabilities as we grow, age, and mature; these changes do not occur overnight.

- Are you ready to define your purpose in life?
- Are you willing to embrace life and reinvent yourself?
- What things in your life excite you?

So what are you waiting for? Get out and show the world what you can do. And while you're working toward your success, you'll also improve the skills you need for success.

The biggest challenges facing humanity are lack of focused, achievable, realistic goals and actions to achieve them. It is therefore important to establish goals in the following manner:

Stage One—Early Growth Years
Short-term goals

____

____

____

Medium-term goals

____

____

____

Long-term goals

____

____

____

Stage Two—Middle Age
Short-term goals

____

____

____

Medium-term goals

____

____

____

Long-term goals

____

____

____

Stage Three—Retirement and Beyond
Short-term goals

____

____

____

Medium-term goals

____

____

____

Long-term goals

____

____

____

Leading Life through Efficiency

No one can do everything well. The things we do well usually give us greater satisfaction and require less time than the things we don't do well. Don't take on something with a big learning curve if you don't have the available energy or resources. It is best to design your life to meet your wants, and recognize when to say no to opportunities that are outside the scope of your desires or capabilities. Building lifestyles without design and letting things happen by default are mistakes. Your life and example will continue in some way to have an impact on the lives of others when you are gone. Just what will your future generations' lives look like!

Live an Efficient Lifestyle

Here are some tips for living an efficient lifestyle.

- Tackle a challenge that you can manage without trying to solve the world's problems.
- Tackle that challenge honestly, sincerely, and with determination and dreams.
- There is nothing wrong with working hard, single-handedly, but we have to think of the world. It is a big world. No matter how good you think you are, there is someone bigger and better than you.
- In reality, there is no such thing as burnout. It occurs when we lose our curiosity, dreams, and drive. You probably just need to rest for a while and then gain momentum for going forward again.
- Our actions have very little to do with what the situation; they have everything to do with our attitudes.

Empowerment does not mean just handing responsibility to someone else. Empowering is about mentoring, coaching, and enabling others to accomplish and succeed.

The Need for Self-Sufficiency

In order to succeed in this day and age, you simply have to learn to become self-sufficient and not rely on others to carry you. Here are the reasons why so many around the world are failing while depending on others.

Discipline

Discipline comes through self-control. This means that we must control all our negative qualities. Before we can control conditions, we must first control ourselves. Self-mastery is the hardest job we will ever tackle. If we do not conquer ourself, someone else will conquer us, period. We may see at one and the same time both our best friend and our greatest enemy, by stepping in front of a mirror.

Growing up in a large military family of nine siblings was probably the best lesson for me and my family. Structure, discipline, and established expectations set the tone for all of us for the rest of our lives.

Accountability

We live in a world with lower moral codes than the ones once established by past generations who had amazing human values and much higher expectations. Our systems are broken. Corrupt politicians, leader pretenders, warlords, profiteers, and greedy business leaders destroy millions of lives by deceit, fraud, and illegal actions. They continue to escape any kind of punitive action themselves and instead reap massive profits and end their tenures only to go to another financially lucrative position with golden parachutes that are equally obscene.

This unfortunately translates into our younger generation having less trust and a lack of confidence in a hopeful future. Look around. It's everywhere, unfortunately, even very close to us. Some societies have become so accustomed to this low level of accountability that they glorify it instead of condemning it. Many politicians no longer seem to feel shame, if ever they did.

Accountability in my view has important components: a sense of duty and, more importantly, a willingness to take responsibility for our actions both in words and in how we conduct ourselves. Another important aspect is taking responsibility and having respect for the trust people place in us. In essence, we become accountable and responsible for our own actions and doing the right thing with courage to stand up to wrongdoings and evil.

Accountability also requires us to do away with ego and self-importance, and to maintain ourselves selflessly in all areas of our lives.

Keys to Accountability

Here are some keys that will move you toward accountability—being responsible for your actions.

- Put accountability to practice and don't just speak about it.
- Avoid covering up errors, brushing things off.
- Avoid quick fixes and think of long-term ramifications.
- Do away with bad habits that do not add value.
- Don't let any challenge exist for a long time.
- Don't shut others out when they try to correct you or give you a new idea.
- Good intentions are just not enough; accountability is about action.
- Don't fall in love with the picture you have painted for yourself, but rather let others paint a picture of you.
- Accept the fact that we all need new skills in life to be successful.
- There's never anything wrong with saying "It is my fault." Accept responsibility for errors and mistakes with dignity and a human touch.
- Envision what you want for your children and share your dreams with them, while also encouraging theirs.

Accountability and responsibility, therefore, are the work of a lifetime. They are ongoing, requiring that we commit to strengthening the central part of our character by developing, maintaining, and growing ourselves. Accountability should be truly every individual's top attribute, but it requires courage, diligence, and vigilance. It requires continual self-examination. It requires continual change. Much of the time, maintaining accountability requires the ability to stand alone.

Turning Your Dreams into Reality

Whether we are planning for a wedding, the purchase of a home, or a visit to a loved one, we all have dreams. What is important and exciting is to turn our dreams into reality. As mentioned earlier, there will always be challenges in life but it is important that we not let them hold us back. Continuing to move forward may require a change of perspective and mindset.

Turning our dreams into reality is about keeping our eyes on both the goal and what is present at the moment. Think of driving at night when you can see only what the headlights reveal; you are able to make the entire trip that way, just seeing a little way ahead.

Tips for Achieving Your Dreams

There's nothing wrong with dreaming big but it's important to be realistic about possibilities and dreaming within our limits. Here are some tips for achieving your dreams.

- If you believe it is worth talking about something, it may be worth doing it. This is your first step toward achieving a lifelong dream. Prepare your initial plans by writing down your dreams and start talking to friends and loved ones, and ask for advice about how to start.
- When appropriate, seek out someone you respect to serve as your mentor.
- It's important to remain confident. This is of course doable and there's no need to show your fears as they do not reflect reality. You must capitalize on your fears and convert them to your weaknesses. Say to yourself loudly and clearly that you can in fact make your dreams into reality.
- Nothing happens without a sense of urgency and passion. The biggest problem facing many people is procrastination and doubt. It's important to take care of priorities and responsibilities right away and treat them as if they are on specific deadlines.
- Life is all about improvement. No matter what or how big your accomplishments have been, keep applying new skills and experiences to your future endeavors.
- Dreams will not be accomplished without resilience. Dreams don't get

accomplished simply through luck. They happen as a result of hard work and persistence. It is important to know that you are not the only tired one.

Create Your Own Opportunities

You must go out and seek your own opportunities but if you can't find some, create them while embracing challenges, as in most cases your challenges become your opportunities.

- That's right! Waiting for someone else to knock on your door with a solution is not the way to go.
- Take care of yourself by sleeping enough. It is believed that 90 percent of the world's problems could be solved if everyone were able to get a good night's sleep. So get enough good, deep sleep to keep going and accomplish your goals.
- And, of course, nourish your body with healthy food and exercise.

Keys to Leading a Successful Life

Let's be honest, leading a successful life does not occur without a lot of hard work. Here are some real keys:

- You have to have ambition to put yourself in a future you desire, and never allow yourself to think you are undeserving of a better future.
- You have to compete. We live in a very competitive world where people must compete for everything at every stage. It is an advantage to have a competitive spirit in order to go through the obstacles in life.
- You must continue to learn no matter when, where, and how far you have come. Successful people never stop learning, even at the highest positions and with the greatest achievements.
- Keep learning by reading books, asking for advice, and finding solutions to your challenges.
- Learn from your failures and move on.
- Never let change impact you negatively.
- You have to really love what you're doing and see the next steps toward progress. Being in love with the process will help you achieve your goal.
- One of the keys to success is knowing when to find a new opportunity but also knowing when to get out.

- Another key is listening to your gut instincts.
- You have to learn to remain calm during critical situations. Successful people don't lose their sense of purpose in the face of any crisis. They instead become the rock so that those around them can lean on them and look for direction.

Atta's Lesson on Being Above Average

While grateful for the opportunity to be granted asylum as a refugee in Germany after being forced to leave my homeland in 1980, the thought of just waiting there with no opportunity to improve my education and my prospects for employment really bothered me. After witnessing Western society's progress and prosperity firsthand, I started to question myself about not being average. Why should any of us settle for being average? Therefore, while waiting in Germany, I decided to seek immigration opportunities to the United States right away, as I had no plans for leading an average lifestyle and waiting for things to happen to me. That move was indeed the best decision I have made in my life, not only so that I could help myself, but also so I could rescue my parents, siblings, and several others and help us all lead a better-than-average lifestyle.

The world is populated with average people and of course exceptional people. Which one are you? Do you want to be average?

I always wonder why people allow themselves to be average. I have a keen interest in helping others grow. While coaching and mentoring many clients during my career, I witnessed many of them being content with living an average life and work style. As a matter of fact, I have made a habit of asking people questions while noticing their potential capabilities were clearly not being put to proper use. It is important more than ever nowadays to understand that, at our core, most of us have the same goals to be self-determined, to be part of the social fabric of family and friends, and to pursue lives of enduring value.

Why settle for an average life, education, work, health, relationships, death, everything?

In all honesty, it does not take a lot to be above average. It really just requires a stronger desire, passion, effort, thinking, and a little bit more time. So much more can be accomplished with a little bit more effort.

"Awesome" is a great word, isn't it? It is a word that lifts us up at any given time. It means that something is beyond all expectations and that something has just been performed beyond all expectations. Let us not call every accomplishment "awesome" but we should all try to lead an awesome life. No, don't just wish for it. Make it happen. Do more! Go higher! How about you? What are you going to do to be more than average, to be awesome?

Chapter Two: The Logistics of Migrating

Being fortunate to have traveled much of the world over the course of the last forty-plus years, I have witnessed and experienced many of the challenges people face. I love sharing some pragmatic tips and checklists that will make your future travels easier and more efficient. Traveling abroad and away from home under certain conditions—especially under stressful and time-sensitive situations—can be a lot different from traveling domestically. Millions flee wars and poverty, risking their lives in the hope of finding a better life away from their homelands. Conditions will of course be very different for those risking their lives through perilous conditions.

Moving Preparations

It is important to prepare for any journey but particularly for migrant refugees who may have no idea about the distance, location, and duration of their journeys. Your main goal should always be to pack less and travel light. The majority of people pack too many unnecessary items but still neglect to carry the most important ones. So it is always helpful to take an inventory before traveling in order to be as well-prepared as possible.

To avoid this challenge get a piece of paper and ask yourself the following questions:

- How many days will I be in the same place?
- Will there be any side trips (birthday party, meet-up, vacation, etc.)?
- What weather am I going to be dealing with?

Once you provide answers to these questions, begin by picking the right outfits:

- Start with shoes first. Based on what you are going to be doing on this trip, pick the shoes that fit the color of your clothing choices and put them at the bottom of the suitcase.
- Clothing: some people simply forget basic stuff such as pajamas, underwear, workout clothes, and socks.

Keep All Important Items in Your Daypack

Just imagine losing your luggage! It is advisable to carry your most important items and some of your valuables in a daypack. Make sure to keep it by your side or on your body at all times.

"Important items" include these:

- a debit card
- a flashlight
- camera
- external hard drive
- laptop
- passport
- some spare cash

Also useful to keep in your daypack are these:

- business cards
- electronics, chargers, GPS
- glasses (and a spare pair)
- neck pillow
- notepad, travel plans, book
- toiletries, vitamins, medicine, toothbrush
- tote bag
- water bottle

Make Your Bank Aware of Your Travel Plans

It is fair to say you will be dealing with multiple challenges as you travel, starting with time changes, jet lag, and waking up at different times. It's quite frustrating to hear from your bank about the suspension of your card. This can happen as banks and card issuers monitor account activity and usage. It is quite a hassle to establish connection and get your card reinstated. So call your bank ahead of time and make them aware of the places and countries you will be visiting.

A Credit Card with No Transaction Fees

It's important to review and research your credit card details before usage. Some credit card companies waive 1 percent to 3 percent foreign transaction fees, but most apply these charges.

Obtain Fee-Free Credit Card

Quite a few big-name popular credit cards with point values waive foreign transaction fees. Again, it's important to research and identify these card carriers before traveling.

Obtain a Smart Chip Card

The majority of developed countries now offer credit cards with smart chips in them. These cards are less vulnerable to fraud. In reality, many payment machines in other countries simply cannot (or merchants refuse to) process a magnetic strip card. It is best to call your credit card company issuer or carefully review details through their disclosures before you travel.

Avoid ATM Fees

I use my automated teller machine (ATM) card often to withdraw money while traveling, because the exchange rate my bank gives me is usually better than those offered by most currency exchange bureaus. You should, however, look for fees charged by banks and ATMs. The majority of banks and card issuers charge either a flat fee of up to about five US dollars or a percentage of the total withdrawal, usually between 1 percent and 3 percent.

It's a good idea to use ATMs located inside bank kiosks and secured areas, and avoid isolated outside and street ATMs.

XE.com's free app for live exchange rates between many currencies is an ideal application for the most up-to-date conversions and features like simultaneous currency monitoring, and you can even use it offline.

Register with the Nearest Embassy

It is important to register with the proper embassy of countries you will be visiting and vacationing in before leaving home. Embassies appreciate advance notices before emergencies occur, especially in the case of stolen or lost passports. They will also be in a better position to help in the case of a natural disaster.

Vaccinations

Research the vaccination requirements that are specific to the regions you will be traveling through.

Take Care of Your Bills and Payments Ahead of Time

There will be no time and opportunity to take care of a payment once you are enroute. Pay all bills including rent, utilities, credit cards, and so on., ahead of time so you don't have to worry about them until you settle down. The other option is to designate a trusted member of your family to process your payments or, better yet, set up automatic payments ahead of time and ensure there will be enough in your bank account to cover the payments.

Avoiding Crimes and Falling Victim

To avoid being a target of crime when traveling, do not wear expensive clothing and jewelry, and do not carry excessive amounts of money, more than you would normally spend in a day or two.

- While making sure you have your passport, laptop, camera, money, phone, and external hard drive with you at all times in your daypack, know that you will be fine if you leave anything else behind.
- Establish routines while arriving and leaving places. Having a routine that you go through every single time will help you keep track of everything.
- It's a good idea to check in the bathrooms and under the beds and desks to not leave anything behind.
- Never leave unattended luggage in public areas.

- Do not accept packages from strangers.
- Search out and retain instructions from your country's consular personnel at embassies and consulates abroad; some provide 24/7 (twenty-four hours a day, seven days a week) emergency assistance to their citizens.

Expect Things to Go Wrong

No one travels without gathering some stories of mishaps, misfortunes, or at times falling victim to uncontrollable circumstances. No matter how prepared you are, it is possible to get lost, get scammed, miss your bus, get food poisoning, or injure yourself.

It is good to be prepared and not be surprised. Don't lose your temper when something unexpected does happen, especially if your children are observing you. It achieves absolutely nothing and makes you look bad. Instead, calm down, put a smile on your face, think of how this will make a great story one day, and rationally figure out an alternative plan.

Notes, Notes, and Notes

Make a note of the address of your accommodation before you arrive. It is a very good idea to keep a hard copy on hand of all the important information about your travel, in addition to having it on your laptop or phone. The information can include complete names of accommodation(s), address(es), email confirmation(s), and reservation number(s).

Back Up All Your Records in Multiple Locations

It is a very good idea to back up all your personal and business records. One of the worst feelings is the sense of loss from parting with your valuable records.

- Back everything up, in multiple places.
- It's a good idea to back up all your photos to an external hard drive. I use CrashPlan to back up the entire contents of my laptop to the cloud. I highly recommend using it!

Global Satellite System

This satellite-based navigation system is really a remarkable technology that is rapidly becoming available and instrumental for use worldwide.

In this day and age, devices equipped with Global Satellite System (GPS) are available as talking maps mounted on our dashboards in our cars to chips in our smart phones that help us find nearby restaurants.

Grocery and retail stores even equip their shopping carts with GPS to track consumers' movements and scrutinize their shopping habits.

Take your unit with you whenever you leave your car.

Changing Currency

Changing currency at the airport is a bad idea. It is where exchange rates are the highest, so exchange your foreign currency and travelers checks through banks and other exchange bureau locations if possible. It is also important to carry coins and smaller-denomination notes, as purchasing with larger bills is often a hassle.

Unlocking Phones

An unlocked phone allows you to use your phone without being tied to a specific carrier, and it can work with more than one network or service provider. You'll be able to buy local SIM cards and access cheaper data from available local networks as you travel to other countries. Cheap data means getting to use Google Maps when you want to find a destination or when you're lost, being able to Snapchat your way around a city, and being easily contactable by your local friends. It's a good idea to consider options before you travel.

Start a Journal

Looking back I always regret not starting a journal early. It is natural to think you will remember everything. You won't remember the name of that lovely person you met or the place you visited a few years ago. Reflecting on all good and even undesirable events in life can be a rewarding experience.

Carry the Google Translate App

Download the Google Translate app to your cell phone before you travel and use the camera feature for translating menus, signs, posters, and anything else you need to read. You simply press the camera icon, aim your phone at the text, and the Google Translate app translates it for you in real time. This is unbelievably convenient when you have no understanding of the signs around you.

Make Your Luggage Stand Out

It happens in all locations at all times that people accidentally take someone else's luggage at the baggage reclaim. Put some stickers on your luggage, attach some duct tape along one side, tie some ribbons to the handle—make sure it stands out in a sea of similar luggage!

Charging Your Devices

It's still quite common to turn up in a room and find you only have a couple of power sockets to share between eight laptop-toting backpackers. Bring a power strip to ensure you can charge what you need to, while allowing everyone else to charge his or her equipment too.

Learn a Few Tips about Local Customs

It's a good idea to do your research, brush up, and learn about the local customs and behaviors of your travel destination before you arrive. You don't want to offend anyone while you travel, so make sure you're aware of offensive behaviors before you arrive. For example, in some countries it is not customary to shake a woman's hand; stretching your feet toward people can be observed as disrespect.

Trusting People

Some people will want to take advantage of you, but the vast majority of people you meet when you travel are good and decent, and will want to help you. Don't let bad experiences prevent you from trusting again. It is a matter of making a proper connection, and getting to know a person before sharing. One easy and common-sense practice is to ask lots of questions. A person who comes up to you with amazing English and wants to be your best friend for no reason at all is out to scam you. Be the most wary of people approaching you in places frequented mostly by tourists.

Protecting Your Equipment

People have disastrous experiences with equipment, but now there are cases to protect everything. It's worth getting a shell for your laptop, a keyboard cover for accidental spills, a sturdy case for your Kindle, and a waterproof case for your phone. Replacing electronic equipment can be quite expensive and spending a day trying to figure out which island you need to fly to in order to get your laptop repaired can be frustrating.

Tracking Your Expenses

It's annoying and time-consuming to track your expenses, but you'll be better off financially if you're aware of how much money you're going through and how it compares with the amount you've budgeted. You can make adjustments if you're spending too much or allow yourself a small treat if you're doing better than planned.

Be Cautious about Taking Photos

Be cautious when you take photos. Just imagine if someone turned up around you and your household and started randomly taking photos. It's a great idea to find the right spot and be ready to ask for permission before taking pictures of locals. It is the polite and respectful thing to do.

Airline Mileage Programs

It's a good idea to join airline mileage programs to earn miles for all the flights you take.

- Research recommended airline programs to find which could be your favorites, and enroll.
- If you are taking a flight and the airline company does not partner with

your main airline mileage programs, simply create an account with that airline. It's important, however ,to avoid sharing your personal information with too many companies. In order to be sure you get all your mileage points, keep a copy of your boarding pass; the mileage program will ask for a copy if you have to call them to find out why they have not yet credited your account.

Know Some Common Phrases

Prepare a list of common phrases for the language of the countries you'll travel to. It's a good idea to obtain a guidebook; they usually have this information in them. Knowing how to say "thank you," "hello," "I'm sorry," and a few other phrases is a necessity whenever you are visiting a country.

Avoid Travel Theft

Thieves often perceive females as easier targets for theft than men. (After all, aren't they the weaker sex? Not!) The most obvious solution is to stick to the safer parts of town, but you'll certainly miss some adventures if you do. Make sure to wear comfortable shoes so you can run if need be!

Be sure to read "Protecting Data against Identity Theft" at the end of this chapter.

In the Case of Theft, Let the Bag Go

Most experts say not to resist—let your bag go and then shout for help rather than risk being assaulted. Opening your wallet and handing over your money might be enough for the thief and you can keep your bag. But, it also might make a thief think you're reaching for a weapon. Better to hand over the bag.

Safety Tips for Women

I'm not a paranoid traveler, but I do travel by myself often, and I take a lot of precautions. To travel without fear, we need to be savvy. I learned these tips from a woman who recently took a self-defense class. The instructor who taught the class had interviewed a group of rapists in prison and learned what they look for when scoping out a woman.

Here are some interesting facts:

- The number one thing men look for in a potential victim is hairstyle. They are most likely to go after a woman with a ponytail, bun, braid or other hairstyle that can easily be grabbed. They are also likely to go after a woman with long hair. Women with short hair are not frequent targets.
- They also look for women on their cell phone, searching through their purse, or doing other activities while walking, because they are off guard and can be easily overpowered.
- The time of day men are most likely to attack and rape a woman is in the early morning, between 5 a.m. and 8:30 a.m.
- The number one place women are attacked and abducted from is grocery store parking lots. Number two is office parking lots and garages. Number three is public restrooms.
- These men are looking to grab a woman and quickly move her to a second, secluded location where they don't have to worry about getting caught.
- Only 2 percent of the rapists interviewed said they carried weapons because rape with a weapon is fifteen to twenty years. Therefore, if you put up any kind of a fight at all, they get discouraged because it only takes a minute or two for them to realize that it will be time-consuming to go after you.
- These men said they would not pick on women who have umbrellas or other similar objects in their hands that can be used from a distance.
- Keys are not a deterrent because the victim has to get really close to the attacker to use them as a weapon.
- So, the idea is to convince these guys you're not worth it.

Airline and Airport Ethics

Avoid Airport Hassle

This is a huge ongoing challenge for millions of travelers. No matter how experienced and well-traveled they are, millions of people continue to repeat and face the same mistakes they have made in the past. Here are some real facts and challenges you must be aware of before embarking on your journey. Dealing with all the hassles and anxieties these days at airports is a fact of life and simply unavoidable in light of various concerns throughout the world. You can take the following steps to make life easier for yourself, airport personnel, and authorities:

- Never ever be late. You must check in and be ready to stand in line for your flight two hours before departure for domestic flights and at least three hours for international flights. Make this your rule, no matter what, where, and how.
- Add at least half an hour or more to your commute to airports. I have witnessed and actually experienced several road closures and delays traveling to airports.
- Take note of special holidays as more and more people travel then, causing longer delays.
- You have absolutely no control over that next accident on the road.
- Check the road and weather conditions the night before, hours before your departure, and then turn on your local radio for updates from the moment you leave your home or hotel.
- Most airports around the world are now equipped with many amenities such as ongoing sports games and news coverage, so why not relax and enjoy your time?
- Never wait until the last second to call your family or friends. I feel sorry for people who are trying to talk on their cell phone while maneuvering their way to the gates.
- If walking is a problem for you, request a wheelchair to meet you at the airport entrance when you order your ticket. This also enables you and those with you to avoid long security lines. The procedure varies from country to country so make sure to do some research.

Overbooked Flights

In the case of overbooked flights, most airlines offer vouchers for future use. Never settle for the lowest one.

- Listen and watch for volunteers, as airlines will increase their offer by attracting passengers to give up their seats.
- Insist on cash compensation instead of a voucher first. Airlines will issue even a check at the airport if volunteers step up to take their offer.
- The US Department of Transportation rules say you may be entitled

to as much as thirteen hundred dollars in cash in lieu of your seat, depending on your ticket price and how long you are delayed.

Lost Luggage

It is extremely important to report lost luggage right away even if the lines to do so are long. Most airlines require passengers to fill out forms within a short period of time so you don't want to miss the deadline and have your claim denied.

Flight Cancelation

Flight delays and cancelations occur for a variety of reasons (weather, equipment, and security). Be realistic and don't expect everything to be perfect.

- Get in line right away.
- While you are waiting in line, get on the phone right away. Airline websites are not price-comparison sites. Try your best to reach an airline phone agent before you approach a tired and frazzled agent behind the counter.
- No matter what, it's extremely important to not get angry and raise your voice. with the agents. You simply will not win that battle. Agents who are nice, humorous, and polite in general will accommodate you in the best way possible.
- Don't get angry if your flight gets cancelled. The airline will offer to put you on another flight even if you have a non-refundable fare.

A One-Way Ticket Is Better

A one-way ticket is better because it simply gives you more flexibility and will save you money unless you are sure of exactly when you will be returning to your home or office destination. There are never any guarantees in life or travel. With more airlines providing discounts and last-minute deals, it is very easy to get a plane ticket these days.

Important Personal Documents

Wherever you are, there are a number of documents you need to have and to safeguard carefully. Some of these documents should remain in your immediate possession, while others can be stored in a secure location, like a safe deposit box at the bank, a fireproof box in your home, or a locking file cabinet. It's also important to think about where the best place is to keep your originals and the copies of documents before leaving home temporarily or permanently. Here is a description of the various documents you need for both day-to-day and occasional use.

- birth certificate
- personal identification card, including a student ID if you have one
- passport and travel visa(s), including business visa(s); double check that your passport and visas haven't expired
- citizenship card
- green card (US)
- work permit
- contract work
- education scholarship acceptance document and permit
- frequent flyer card(s) and other loyalty program cards such as those from hotels

Birth Certificate

This document is used to prove your identity, age, and citizenship. It is issued by the country or city in which you were born and is commonly required when you apply for various services such as a driver's license and a passport, as well as when you apply for admission to a college or university, or for a job. Here are some suggestions in order to avoid confusion and challenges:

- It is always helpful to maintain copies of your original birth certificate translated into English or into the language of your known host country. It should be translated word-for-word and certified to verify its accuracy. Too many people around the world have had challenges translating their certificates in unfamiliar and new environments.
- The naturalization services in most countries will not accept a document that's not in their language.
- You will also need your original birth certificate when you apply for

citizenship. Until then, protect it in a secure area (safe, bank safe deposit).

- Keep a copy of the translated document with your original birth certificate for easy reference.
- Never carry the original with you; instead, make a few photocopies of it. You may also wish to purchase a couple of extra certified copies to have on hand in case the need arises.
- Don't give those copies out to anyone. In this age of identity theft, passing out a document with your name and birth date on it is like giving thieves the key to your house. Read more about identity theft in chapter four, "Being Organized and Prepared."
- You may find it helpful to create a worksheet with birth information for every member of your family. Include the full name of each person; the birth certificate number; the issue date; the issuing country, city, and state or province; the name and address of the hospital or home where the birth occurred; and the date of registration. Print copies of this worksheet and store the original with your other important papers.

Personal Identification Card

The personal identification card (IC) is issued by several Western countries. If you don't plan to drive, you should apply instead for an IC, a non-driver identification card, or another similar state identification card.

- This card may be presented as official proof of identify when boarding an aircraft, opening a bank account, making a credit card purchase, and in other situations.
- The card is issued by the state the same way a driver's license is issued. In fact, the card looks a lot like a driver's license, with a unique identification number, a photograph, and the name and address of the individual carrying it.
- Also like a driver's license, a personal identification card has an expiration date.
- You will apply for an IC at your local department of motor vehicles or other licensing authority. Typically you will be required to produce two or three pieces of identification to obtain it, such as your Social Security card in the US, proof of citizenship or naturalization, birth

certificate, passport, income tax documents, military identification card, or other materials.

- Generally, if you are not a citizen of the country in which you live, you can still obtain an IC by showing proof of residency.
- Acceptable forms of proof of residency are utility bills, a state certificate of title for a motorized vehicle, a mortgage statement for your residence, a property tax bill, and some other documents. Again, check with your local department of motor vehicles for a complete list of acceptable documents.

Passport

If you expect to travel internationally, you will need a passport. This is also true for children; they have to have their own; this includes infants.

In addition, if and when you decide to seek citizenship in certain countries like the US, you will have to apply for a passport, something that is often done as part of the naturalization process.

- Each country's proper authority (such as its ministry of internal or foreign affairs) issues passports.
- Locate the closest passport agency to your residence.
- There are different agencies and facilities in various countries also designated to accept passport applications on the country's behalf. They include certain post offices; clerks of court; public libraries; and state, county, township, and municipal government offices.
- To find the appropriate authority close to you in the US, use the passport acceptance facility search page at iafdb.travel.state.gov/.
- Passports have different expiration dates. For example, US passports are good for ten years.

Travel Visa Information

It's always important to obtain visa information for the country you are traveling to. Check to find out whether you need a pre-visa for the particular country you are visiting. Certain countries do not require a pre-visa for shorter lengths of time or for citizens of certain countries. Each country's requirement is different, so never assume the same rules apply to every country. It's a good idea to inquire and research well in advance and avoid potential personal and business visa challenges.

Death Certificates of Close Family Members

It's helpful to keep copies of the death certificates of close family members in case proof is needed, as in the case of insurance claims. Contact your local vital records department to request a death certificate.

Marriage Certificate

This is the most important document next to your birth certificate and citizenship papers.

- Marriage bureaus, other similar offices, and provincial or territorial governments issue marriage certificates.
- Many jurisdictions will allow you to request a copy of a marriage certificate online, so search the Internet (also known as "the world-wide web" or "the web") for information.
- It's very important to have a certified word-for-word translation created if the document is not in English.

Driver's License

Every person who operates a motorized vehicle on a public roadway must have a valid driver's license.

- Generally speaking, you can use your foreign driver's license for a year in North America. Getting a new license in your new state, province, or territory should be a priority.
- Every state and province in Western countries require drivers to be licensed to drive a passenger vehicle. Even if you were licensed in your homeland, you may not be able to drive elsewhere with just that license.
- Americans and Canadians may drive in both countries using their state, provincial, or territorial license; an international driving permit is not necessary. However, Americans do need a passport, enhanced driver's license, or identification card to enter Canada, and Canadians do need a passport, enhanced driver's license, or identification card to enter the US.

More information on holding a driver's license can be found in chapter eleven.

International Driving Permit

An International Driving Permit (IDP) serves as an identity document that allows an individual to drive a private motor vehicle in many countries. This document must be accompanied by a valid driver's license. Make sure to check with your local authorities or your insurance company about rules and details.

Immigration Documents in the US

As you know, dozens of documents may be required before you emigrate to and after you land in a new country. If you are immigrating to the US, you will find that all these forms are available free of charge at the US Citizenship and Immigration Services website at uscis.gov/forms. Make sure to always use the most up-to-date forms as forms and requirements change constantly.

These forms provide a record of your journey from your homeland to your new country and should be retained indefinitely. As with other records discussed here, you should make copies of these forms and file a complete set in a safe place like a safe deposit box.

Packages to apply for residence in other countries vary, but they may include the following common ones:

- skilled workers application package
- skilled trades program application package
- selected skilled workers application package
- experience class application package
- investors, entrepreneurs, and self-employed application package
- family sponsorship application package
- live-in caregiver's application package
- refugee's application package

Information about each of these application packages can be found on government websites.

Naturalization Documents

Your naturalization papers will be among your most important possessions. As soon as you are eligible for citizenship in your new host country, you can fill out proper forms on the road to naturalization.

Your naturalization papers are one-time documents that must be carefully safeguarded. Since the only time you'll need to show these papers is if you apply for a passport, you should make copies of the originals, then place the originals in a safe deposit box or a fireproof file cabinet.

Social Security Card in the US

Every person who lives legally in the United States has a Social Security Number. This includes US citizens, permanent residents, noncitizens who are authorized to work in the US, and children.

- The nine-digit number, which appears on an official Social Security card, is unique to you. You'll use it when filling out employment paperwork, your income tax return, and a credit card application, car loan, and government benefits.
- This number is also needed when people apply for city, county, and state welfare benefits.
- Your children need their own Social Security number so you can claim them as dependents on your income tax return, and so your children will be eligible for free and low-cost health insurance, if needed.
- If you don't have a Social Security card yet and you're eligible, apply at your nearest Social Security office.
- When applying, provide proof of identity, citizenship, or immigration status.
- Documents that are acceptable include a certified original copy of your birth certificate, your passport, and your certificate of naturalization, among others. A noncitizen will need current, unexpired US immigration papers, and a foreign passport when applying. These documents will be returned to you after your application is processed.
- Despite the fact that your Social Security card is so important, you won't have to show it very often. For this reason, you shouldn't carry it with you. Rather, protect it by tucking it away somewhere safe, such as in a locking file box or safe deposit box.

Social Security Card Elsewhere

Check and apply in your new host country about similar programs or numbers to these that the US uses.

Health Insurance Card

Health insurance companies commonly issue identification cards to their policyholders. You'll definitely want to carry this card with you at all times, since you usually have to show it when you use health care services, from doctor's appointments to medical tests, and when you pick up prescriptions. Even so, make a couple of copies of your card and keep them with the copies of your other personal papers.

Money as Cash

Cash is king. It is really important to carry some foreign money as cash on hand before landing in a destination country, although you can usually find an ATM at the airport and at train stations. I can, however, remember quite a few occasions even inside a major airport terminal when the ATM machine was out of cash or there was a problem with the machine reading my card. This can be quite frustrating as many taxis and even public forms of transport like buses and shuttles will only accept cash. Despite the amazing possibilities for easy-to-use services and goods through the use of mobile banking, credit cards, and payment systems, it is always possible for the unexpected to happen (loss of power and natural disasters), so it is a very good idea to carry enough cash while traveling. "Enough" is a very subjective description that depends on the person's standard of living, but enough for a couple of days.

- It's a good idea to split up your cash and store it in various places in your daypack, and also at times in your shoes or in hidden anti-theft body bags.
- In the worst-case scenario, with some cash left, you will then be able to pay for some food, a dorm bed, and a Skype call or a reverse-charge phone call to your family to get an emergency wire transfer of funds until you can get back on your feet again.
- US dollars are the most widely accepted currency around the world and easy to change.

Travel Checklist

Make a copy of this checklist. Then start collecting all your important personal documents and items in one place. This will help ensure you have all you need to travel. Add a date for future reference.

Item	Check
Passports. It's a good idea to check for the expiration months in advance	
Travel visas	
Personal ID cards	
Required vaccinations	
Cash	
Credit cards	
Health insurance	
Travel insurance	
Airline tickets	
Other transportation tickets	
Emergency contact numbers	
Banking notices for credit card use and/or other potential transfers in advance such as pre-authorizations	
Phones	
Tablet and other electronic devices	
Chargers for all devices	
Headphones	
Electronic-device adapters for use with other wall sockets	
Travel pillow	
Blanket	
Eye mask	
Ear plugs	
Pens and pencils	
Notepads	
Guidebooks	
Maps	
Language guides	
Hand sanitizer	
Wet wipes	
Medications and prescriptions for a minimum of your intended time away or ninety days	
Eyeglasses and cases	
Toiletry bag	

Item	Check
Toothbrush and toothpaste	
Floss	
Mouthwash	
Hairbrush or comb	
Sunscreen	
Face wash	
Mirror	
Lip balm	
Personal hygiene items, including feminine hygiene items	
Perfume or cologne	
Hair care products	
Shaving kit and extra razors	
Sewing kit	
Nail clippers, scissors, tweezers (these items must be placed in your checked luggage if they are sharp)	
First aid kit (gauze, bandages, adhesives, etc.)	
Cold medicine	
Throat lozenges	
Diarrhea medicine	
Allergy medicines	
Antibacterial ointment	
Multivitamins	
Sunburn relief	
Insect repellent, mosquito net, sting reliever	
Motion sickness pills	
Eye drops	
Check for proper rules in carrying items such as the following in your daypack inside the plane. In some countries, you must place them in clear plastic bags: • Liquids • Gels • Aerosols • Pastes • Creams However, having these items wrapped in plastic inside a suitcase would also help protect the other things you have packed from any spills and breakages.	

Items to Carry

There are many items that are best carried with you, whether on paper or scanned and emailed.

Medical Records

Medical information is considered private, and there's even a US law called the *Health Insurance Portability and Accountability Act* that protects you against discrimination due to medical conditions. It also protects your privacy. So you'll want to do the same by safeguarding your medical records. Do keep copies of documentation from doctors and dentists for at least three years or scan them and, in order to save space, shred the original documents.

Keep the following:

- all immunization and vaccination records
- dental records
- a 90-day supply of your prescribed medication
- your eyeglass prescription and at least one extra pair of glasses

First Aid Kit

A first aid kit may be useful if you're going off the beaten track or taking part in high-risk activities. For minor injuries, assemble a kit of antiseptic with gauze squares, non-adherent dressings, bandages, fabric plasters, adhesive tape, scissors, tweezers, and safety pins. You can buy bottles or sprays of standard antiseptic from all major chemists, or get ready-prepared antiseptic wipes. Kits available from pharmacies that include sterilized and sealed syringes, sutures, and needles can be useful when visiting developing countries where hospitals and dentists may not have properly sanitized equipment.

Insect Repellent

Insect repellent may be a necessary item to bring with you.

- Mosquitoes usually bite between dusk and dawn, and are attracted to humans by our body heat, smell, and the carbon dioxide we breathe out.
- Research shows that products containing the chemical diethyltoluamide

(DEET) are the most effective insect repellents and are safe when used correctly. DEET products are available in sprays, roll-ons, sticks, and creams.
- Your family doctor, any general practitioner, or your travel health clinic will tell you whether the area you are going to is malarial and what protection is advised.

Copies of Important Documents

Scan your important personal documents (see list above). In particular, make a copy of your passport, any credit cards you will be bringing, your driver's license, and receipts for travelers checks. I usually keep one set of copies of these important documents with me and also scan a set to send to my email and to a trusted member of my family, as I mention under "Moving Preparations." Then if things are lost or stolen, I will be able to take copies to my embassy and authorities.

Carry Around Spare Passport Photos

Carrying spare passport photos of you and your family members can be incredibly useful and save you a lot of time and hassle in certain instances. You can use them to apply for visas, to get a new passport if yours expires, and you never know when and where you may be required to submit a passport-type photo. Having spares means that you won't have to waste a day researching and then wandering around a city to try and find someone who takes passport photos.

Medical Travel Insurance Card

Be sure to obtain overseas medical travel insurance coverage if you know your plans. Ask your medical insurance company if your policy applies overseas, and if it covers emergency expenses such as medical evacuation. If it does not, consider buying a foreign supplemental insurance.

When possible, it is always a really good idea to purchase a travel medical insurance policy before traveling to foreign countries. Travel medical insurance covers important things like emergency medical evacuation, trip cancellation, and baggage delivery.

Protecting Data against Identity Theft

All the personal documents described in this chapter share one thing in common: they can be stolen and used to commit crimes like fraud and identity theft. Identity theft is a growing problem worldwide. In 2012, around 12.6 million people were victims of identity theft in the United States alone, according to a survey by Javelin Strategy and Research.

Identity theft can cost you a great deal of money, time, and stress, and recovering from the effects of the crime isn't easy. At best, it can take years to unravel the damage caused by an identity thief; at worst, it can destroy your credit and ruin your good name.

All a thief needs to impersonate you and open accounts in your name, access your bank accounts, or make fake-but-convincing-looking documents with your name on them is your full legal name, your date of birth, and your Social Security Card or Social Insurance Number. It is important to know that the data we carry and our Internet habits can easily put our data security and individual privacy at risk. These include Internet browsing, email messages, telephone calls, and fax transmissions.

Here are some best practices that you can exercise before, during, and after traveling to secure your privacy and data. These tips may seem cumbersome, but they provide really important protection to ensure data security and privacy while traveling abroad.

Preparations before Traveling

Preparations before traveling will cut back on the potential of being a victim of identity theft.

- Update data protection software on your devices that use operating systems, such software as anti-malware, anti-virus, security patches, and others.
- Install full-disk encryption on laptops.
- Obtain as much information on the country of travel as possible, as security testing and hacker tools are forbidden and illegal in some countries.
- Update device passwords; use passwords that are at least four digits long (longer if supported).

- Use a different password on each device.
- Configure automatic wiping settings to wipe the device's data after a pre-determined number of passcode entry failures.
- Do a full backup of your devices and secure them with a strong password.
- Inform your credit card company and banks about your travel plans, including dates, locations, and any special instructions. International transactions are most often flagged as fraud, and purchases may be delayed or your card is cancelled because you haven't given advance travel notice.
- Minimize the number of cards you carry.
- Take only your identification card, credit card, and debit card.
- **Scan important documents and save them to a flash drive that is used only for that purpose.** (Don't save the information on to your laptop's hard drive because it can be hacked when you're on the Internet.) Password-protect the file so only you know how to access it. Just remember to memorize or write the password down in a secure location so you can open the file again when you need to.
- Shred financial documents you don't need any more, if they contain personal information, your own or a client's. Never just toss these documents into the trash or a dumpster. Identity thieves find most of the personal information they need in exactly those places.

For more information on avoiding identity theft, read the recommendations listed in chapter four under "Effective Electronic Organization."

Protection of Data While Traveling

It is fair to say you cannot reasonably expect privacy in some countries while you are traveling.

- Your electronic communications and phone calls and even hotel rooms may be monitored as a standard practice. Sensitive or confidential conversations, transactions, or data transfer should be kept to a minimum until you return home.
- Be prepared to turn on and off devices, and present all removable media for customs officials. You may be asked to decrypt data for inspection at international borders. In some countries, withholding your password is a criminal offense.

- Understand the difference between sharing a photo on social networking versus connecting to your bank or credit card company.
- Use the safest-available ATMs in visible public areas and only during daylight. It's important to cover your hand as much as possible when you're entering your personal identification number (PIN) and when you're taking out cash from an ATM.
- Determine the availability and cost of purchasing a local cellphone, or buy local SIMs. Prepaid local phones limit costs by not working after exceeding a maximum number of minutes. They are cheaper for local calls and have better connectivity.
- Internet connections in cyber cafes, public areas, and hotels may not be safe; it's a good idea to limit your usage.
- Never lend your device to anyone, and never attach unknown devices such as thumb drives. Unknown thumb drives are notorious for infecting computers.
- Disable Wi-Fi when not in use. Wi-Fi ad-hoc mode or unsecured file sharing enables direct access to other devices.
- Disable Bluetooth when not in use (or set it to "hidden," not "discoverable").
- Report lost or stolen devices as soon as possible to whomever it concerns. This might include your company, mobile provider, hotel, airline, insurance company, and local authorities. Local authorities have a better chance of finding stolen property if it is reported stolen as soon as you know it is missing.
- Limit the number of personal items you carry with you when you leave the house. Naturally, you need your driver's license or personal ID card, as well as a credit or debit card if you're going shopping. Leave all the others you have at home for safekeeping.

Atta's Lesson on Preparing Carefully

My personal experience in watching thousands of travelers during my lifetime is that quite a few people simply do not prepare well. Lack of proper preparation and planning may easily cause frustration and anxiety. I think of travel and movement that—due to a lack of preparedness—come and go as wasted opportunities. Why not do it intentionally and daily so that you are prepared when the opportunity comes? It may be too late if you are unprepared.

Chapter Three: Your New Neighborhood

Settling In

You have arrived in your new environment! In fact, it's a place with new opportunities and energy for your life! It is now your responsibility to embrace and make the best of the opportunities in this new stage of your life.

The visibility of this human movement and its unprecedented magnitude is obviously drawing a lot of attention to fears that we are trying hard to hide inside us, fears forced upon not just the immediate victims but on humanity in general through weak governments, incompetent leaders, and political theatrics. As immigrants, possibly deprived of our homes, possessions, security, cultural values, our basic human rights, and our entitlement to feel accepted and respected as human beings, it is easy to feel victimized.

Don't Allow Yourself to Be Demonized

The majority of migrants today are leaving their homelands to escape the devastating impacts of wars and unrest, rather than for economic reasons. Yet, the majority of people in Western societies do not understand or have adequate knowledge of the root causes of all these forced movements. So it is quite easy for migrants to feel demonized by some Westerners while being referred to as "refugees and/or migrants"; not many understand the distinction that migrants have a choice to stay or leave their homeland; refugees do not—they must flee to stay alive.

Honestly speaking, I believe the world is now in need of a new vocabulary in order to establish a meaningful human response to these conditions that force millions of inhabitants out of their homelands. But as migrants, we are just given a gift of opportunity to chart our own course with the strong wind of experience and wisdom on our backs.

After the most challenging and fearful experience of leaving my country of birth Afghanistan in August 1980, the longest most tearful flight, and an excruciating interview process with German police, I was finally out and allowed to walk on the streets of Frankfurt as a refugee. I felt a strange mixture of freedom, safety, hope, and opportunity to look forward to the future. Frankly, it was a feeling of being challenged to rely on my own perseverance. I realized at the time that the world was not about me but rather others; I would have to persevere now to do my part.

There are times when we have to do things that are difficult without even realizing how that difficulty might be the key to getting things done, no matter what. I started to move on to the next stage of life with a sense of personal responsibility to embrace and prosper while telling myself, "Things can't get any worse than what I have witnessed!"

Crisis, Shock, and New Ways of Life

Migrants can suffer crisis and shock as they live life in new ways. We live in a time of the most dynamic changes that have ever been seen or experienced in human history; these changes are more unpredictable, faster, and probably more radical. Expect the impact of such change in every aspect of your life with any choice and decision that you make. No matter how fast and big the changes, there has to be a core to your existence. That is you at the center—you have to maintain balance and stability in your life while enjoying inner peace and self-control.

Here are some of the basic and most important challenges and areas of focus for anyone coming to a new environment.

Risks and Denial, Resistance and Fear

While we may feel that we are controlled by risks, fears, and other circumstances, the fact remains that our lives are largely determined by our own personal decisions and choices . You are where you are because of choices, decisions, and the forced circumstances of the past. It is now up to you to make a decision as to where, what, and how you live your life. It is no longer about past decisions but rather about what you do from here on.

Some people cling desperately to the past. They hang on to what is familiar, snuggling more deeply into their comfortable routines while avoiding dangerous and chilling thoughts of dealing with change. They defend the old way of doing things to maintain personal stability and feel more in control.

They fight against change and what could happen, resulting in unpleasant results.

My Advice

I firmly believe there are always opportunities that lead to new discoveries for you and your loved ones, even when you think everything seems to be working against you. But the key is to being open to change and more importantly to commit to understanding, embracing, and looking at new opportunities. Blaming and complaining are indeed draining and are clear wastes of time and energy. I have learned to never ever hold a grudge. We all are guilty of grousing as at some point someone may have crushed our ego or undermined our pride, but holding onto the hurts will do nothing but hurt us. Forgiveness is the key to mental well-being. Socrates said something along the lines of "Any unjust harm we do to others will only harm our own souls." Rethink whose time is being wasted if you hold onto old grudges that the other person has forgotten. What does not kill you makes you stronger. We have got to reframe our ideas about the universe and how we fit into it. If we want to accelerate our rate of achievement rapidly, we must reach out and vigorously employ new behaviors.

I want you to succeed in life and say no to every excuse or blame. Go out and embrace your new world while celebrating small successes, always being grateful. Surround yourself with people who are kind to you and love you. Other people will make you unhappy, unkind, and unsuccessful. Say no to everything that is going to impact you in a negative way. Say yes to things that really matter, such as time to read, sleep, and reach out to family and friends. Live a loving life.

Open Your Gifts of Life

Treat life as a precious gift—it is important to value life and create a fire of success. It is not actually easy to move forward from a troubled today, and that can create doubt, cynicism, and disillusionment. Many things may kill people's faith in the future, but if you can identify your purpose, never underestimate its power to rebuild your faith in life. Believe in your purpose.

Open Your Mind and Withhold Your Judgment

If you don't like a country's customs, remain open-minded, rather than immediately jumping to judgments and conclusions that you're right and the custom is wrong. Ask questions, research more, and listen to other peoples' points of view. And don't let your bad experiences taint your opinion of an entire country—if you had a crappy time somewhere, it doesn't mean that the country sucks or it's not safe. Maybe you just had bad luck that once.

Be Polite and Smile Often

You'll be more approachable, you'll find it easier to make travel friends, and the locals will warm to you if you are polite and smile often. Being rude and looking grumpy will bring nothing good your way. It is your responsibility to prove that you are worthy of space and sharing. And respect.

Every one of us wants respect; the question is not whether it should be given but the question is, Are we earning it? You cannot ask for respect or demand it. We earn everything the hard way through trust, but we have to learn. You've got to prove you are worthy of respect.

Atta's Message on Settling In

After spending a couple of very difficult and emotional months inside a refugee camp close to Frankfurt, Germany, in 1980, I was assigned to live in a remote area called Bad Münstereifiel, Euskirchen where no refugee had ever lived before. As our busload of first-time refugees moved toward the beautiful hilltop village of Mahlberg, the entire community's front doors and gates appeared closed, a clear sign of rejection; we were not welcome. We made it through to our new home rented by the city with much anxiety and total frustration.

The next morning, I ventured out and approached a middle-aged neighbor as she stood sending her son off to school. I started a conversation by saying good morning in German. She extended her hand with a big smile and said, "Ich Elizabeth," meaning "I am Elizabeth."

Right away, I looked at her son and asked if he knew any English. He smiled and said, "A little." I then asked if he could tell his mother to help us refugees to organize a meeting with the villagers. Elizabeth was a very kind woman and right away she said, "Of course."

That was an amazing beginning to allow our group to not only have a very productive meeting with the villagers but to share our journey and why we were there. But more importantly, we offered to help our new neighbors in any and every way possible. At the end of that week, our entire Afghani refugee group were active participants in a launch of the biggest Oktoberfest celebration there. That was an experience that allowed us to become active participants in our new environment. Mahlberg became a village that none of us wanted to leave when we eventually embarked on our ongoing refugee journeys throughout Europe and other parts of the world.

I honestly believe right now is the real-time opportunity more than ever in history to voice courageousness, positivity, and inclusiveness in order to make a difference in the lives of others. Most of us are simply not grateful enough for opportunities handed to us. Gratitude simply does not even exist in many minds, and it is all about more for me, me, me.

Nothing should come easily. Who said life is easy? Why should it be? Are you doing your part to make it easy? Adversity and difficulty are and will always be part of our lives, whether we like it or not. It is how we respond and honor struggle. We can use struggle as a mirror to learn through or look the other way.

The Need for Self-Sufficiency

You and your household must find the ability to meet your basic needs (including protection, food, water, shelter, personal safety, health and education) with dignity through self-sufficiency and sustainability. You have to approach life through this process and should always pursue self-reliance while reducing your vulnerability and long term reliance on others and organizations. We must remember and consider initial support as short term and never as a long-term solution.

Learn the Language

It is incumbent on the migrant to learn the language of his or new country.

- To address this big language challenge, many refugees and immigrants take language classes, but finding the time between caring for kids and finding jobs can be quite difficult. This is particularly difficult if you weren't literate in your native tongue to begin with.

- The results show that people with better host-country language skills are more satisfied with their jobs and education and have a better understanding of their culture.
- Unfortunately the assumption many times is if you are living in a new country, you will come into contact with people and over time learn the language; it actually happens the other way around: when you learn the language, you will meet more people in your new country.
- It is important to know that newcomers cannot expect to learn simply through contact only with host-country speakers.
- The bottom line is that language skills are needed before meaningful contacts can be made and that this in turn increases well-being.

Overcome Language Deficiencies

Here are some ways to overcome language deficiencies:

- Obtain a solid pocket dictionary and carry it with you at all times or better yet download an electronic application and carry the device with it on.
- Pay attention to the real meaning of words.
- Write down the words you cannot fully understand to check the meaning in the dictionary or in other resources.
- Read newspapers, novels, books, magazines, and other printed materials.
- Listen to talk shows and discussions that are related to your field.
- Jot down and write newly learned words to register in your long-term memory.
- Set up a goal of learning a certain number of new words each day.
- Create flashcards of the new words and review them periodically.
- Try forming sentences using the new words and incorporate them into your vocabulary-building process.
- Listen carefully. Most newcomers tend to talk and respond quickly without listening carefully. This often results in not understanding, asking questions, and repeating conversations.
- Interact with others and use the language you wish to enrich.
- Never speak fast to impress others. Remember this is not your original

language and you may have a strong accent that is hard for others to hear and understand.
- Remember to pronounce words distinctly and clearly.
- Concentrate on the real matter being discussed. Ask for others to repeat themselves if you don't understand. It is wise to interact and have the right conversation rather than pretending you know and causing challenges for yourself.
- Ask for help about slang and variations that are common in your region.

Stay Mentally Strong

Stay mentally strong while you are living in your host country by considering the following:

- Believe and evaluate your core values and evaluate them often.
- Embrace change with open arms.
- Never stop moving.
- Staying happy should be your goal 24/7.
- Think and stay productive all the time.
- Be prepared to work and succeed based on your own merit.
- Enjoy your time when alone too.
- Celebrate other people's success always.
- Take responsibility for your behavior.
- Be kind, always realizing all humans face challenges.
- Maintain both mental and physical energy.
- Learn from your failures; it is okay to fail.
- Take calculated risks.
- Always reflect on your progress.

Human and Civil Rights

The majority of refugees and immigrants arriving in various parts of the world are often treated as passive beneficiaries of aid who should be grateful to receive the basics necessary for survival. In fact, they should be guaranteed the same human and civil rights as the established residents of the places where they arrive, but often some are denied from claiming these rights. Naturally certain rights should be reserved for citizens of each country, especially rights of institutional political participation and representation.

Based on my extensive experience while working with diverse groups from pretty much all over the world, I have found engagement and participation in society are the keys to success. I have found engaged migrants to be the most successful ones within their new environment rather than the happiest ones. In my honest opinion, social responsibility is all about a human being's moral obligation to represent oneself properly within a society. It is also about our responsibility to participate and be accountable while representing our community and its dynamics.

Contribute

Here are some ways you can help to do your part as a member of your new community:

- Get to know your neighbors and community. It's easier for any host country residents to hold anti-refugee and immigrant views when they don't personally know you. I firmly believe it is only by creating personal connections with those we don't know that we begin to change our hearts and minds. This is the single biggest way you can bridge the gap.
    - Participate in your neighborhood; communities act together.
    - Learn to identify your local politicians and representatives while following their lead, agenda, and topics of interest regardless of any affiliation or parties they represent.
    - Attend local, city, and other important town halls, meetings, and events. Plan to donate, fundraise, or volunteer your time.
    - Educate yourself on refugees' and immigrants' rights by attending workshops.
- Plan ahead by creating safety plans for your families to be better prepared for emergency events and other unforeseen dangers.
- Take part in local initiatives and start working with different non-profit organizations. Engage with the people in your community. Helping one another is really helpful for your future, their future, and for the future of society. Working in civil society organizations or working in various initiatives to help others can open many new doors for you.
- Consider providing the list of some non-profit organizations along with their contact details to other immigrants so they can start working as interns or volunteers. This will be helpful and then, once things

improve and immigrants start working on some amazing things, thc conflict will slowly vanish among citizens, refugees, and immigrants.

- Get in touch with your sponsor and find out about support organizations; learn about these organizations and their information:
    - full name of organization
    - address of organization
    - phone number and websites at earliest possibility
    - contact name for inquiries

Managing a Household

Once you're in your new home, you'll have many responsibilities—and expenses. This chapter covers general household activities.

Welcome to the Neighborhood

Although it won't be one of the first things you do when you enter your home for the first time as a newcomer, part of the fun and excitement of moving into a new neighborhood is getting to know the people and places around you. In particular, kids like to know who lives nearby because they'll be looking for instant friends in their new neighborhood. But unfortunately, many societies today are very insular; people tend to mingle only with those they know very well, like family members and friends. But you can break through the barrier if you make the effort to get to know your neighbors and become part of "the 'hood," as the kids say.

There are many ways to get to know your neighbors.

- For example, the Welcome Wagon, a group of volunteers who drop in on new neighbors to welcome them, will probably arrive at your door after you've moved in, but don't wait for them. Instead, go out and meet people yourself and make sure your family comes with you.
- Shake a few hands, make small talk, and exchange phone numbers or email addresses.
- Offer to look after your neighbors' homes when they're away—maybe pick up the mail, look in on pets, or keep an eye on a vacant house to head off mischief—and they'll probably feel compelled to do the same for you.
- Take a gift to your next-door neighbors. It can be something

small—maybe a favorite homemade pastry, or a small token from your homeland, like a scarf or an inexpensive piece of jewelry. The idea is to reach out to the people around you.

- Walk around the neighborhood. That way, you can introduce yourself to anyone who happens to be outside. When you meet someone you like, invite them over for a drink. They'll be as interested to know about you and your lifestyle, as you'll be to know about theirs. Drinks can include coffee, tea, and soft drinks—you don't have to serve alcoholic beverages.
- Arrange a play date. Mothers love having a place to take their kids for a while, and offering your backyard for a play date with their kids could make you instant and fast friends forever.
- Organize a block party. This kind of party is open to anyone who wants to come. It's held outside, sometimes right in the street if there's not too much traffic (like on a cul-de-sac). Just crank up some music, set out some soft drinks and coffee, and invite people to bring their favorite dishes (a process known as a potluck).
- This is a good time to showcase a favorite dish or two from your own culture. Be sure to enlist the aid of a couple of neighbors to help, since you'll be the new person on the block and you'll want to meet as many people as possible.

Getting Organized

When you first move into your new home, a little household chaos is to be expected. But once you've had time to get settled, you'll probably find that you won't have any patience with clutter. To keep your home and life organized and tidy, try these tips.

- Set up a schedule to deal with routine household chores. For instance, always run the dishwasher at night, and then empty it the next morning (this is a great chore to assign to your kids).
- Do the laundry on Saturday mornings, followed by the vacuuming.
- Get the kids' lunches, gear, and schedules sorted out on Sunday night so everyone can grab and go on Monday morning.
- Sit down with your kids at the same time each day to help with homework.
- Activities like these add up to an efficient, well-run home. You don't

have to be fanatical about keeping to a schedule, but adopting one will keep your household on track and your environment stay clutter-free and clean, even if you have little ones.

- And speaking of the little ones, even the youngest (say, two years old and up) can take some responsibility for keeping the house tidy. Your toddler may only be capable of dropping his toys into the toy box before bedtime, so assign that task to him and work with him to make it happen, even if he fusses. Gently emphasizing the need for tidiness will set up good habits that will last a lifetime.
- Establish a central place for posting family messages. This can be a simple write-on-wipe-off board or calendar on which everyone can mark his or her activities. This will keep the counters free of notes and loose papers and will keep everyone on time. Assign a different colored marker to each family member so you can see at a glance who needs to be where and who needs what done when it comes to school project due dates, appointments, and deadlines.
- Place a box or other receptacle somewhere handy where all the incoming mail can be deposited. Then once a day, go through the box and weed out the bills from the junk mail. Immediately toss or shred the mail you don't want, and put the bills and other mail you need to keep in a folder so they can be handled properly.
- File important papers right away. You'll recall from chapter two that there are a number of different immigration and citizenship documents that should be filed away indefinitely. This goes for other important paperwork, too, like tax-deductible receipts, doctor's bills, and your children's artwork—in short, anything you may want or need again later.
- Don't let the paperwork get out of control because there never will be enough time to deal with it if the pile gets too large. A good way to file bills is to use an accordion-style folder with twelve slots so you can file paperwork by the month.
- You might also consider buying a sheet-fed scanner like the Neat Desk or Fujitsu ScanSnap. Both allow you to place a pile of paperwork—even papers of different sizes—into the hopper all at once; the scanner then turns it into beautifully sorted and retrievable documents. Once it's scanned, immediately recycle or shred the paper.
- Designate a central place where keys can be dropped when someone

enters the house. A simple basket will do the trick and will eliminate those frustrating searches for keys when you're on the way to work.

- Hang up coats, hoodies, and other outdoor gear the moment you come in the door. Install a coatrack (a board with a series of hooks screwed into it), or make some space in the closet nearest the main entry so everyone is encouraged to hang, store, and put things away before they go any further.

Caring for Your Home

There's nothing like a neat, clean, sweet-smelling living environment to keep your spirits high and give you a sense of accomplishment. You'll be surprised how much you can get done in small increments each day. So here are some tips for making that happen.

- Clean as you go. Don't let dishes pile up in the sink; wash them immediately or stack them in the dishwasher.
- Wipe the mirror and shower door in the bathroom after every shower you take so they look clean at all times.
- Put away laundry as soon as it comes out of the dryer or in from the laundromat.
- Do a more intensive spring-cleaning once a year. If you use the incremental approach all year long, you'll find that this deep cleaning will go much faster.
- See if your community has a recycling program, then use it faithfully. Recycling aluminum cans, bottles, and paper (newspapers, junk mail, and loose paper) is good for the environment and will give you a sense of pride that you're protecting Mother Earth.
- You can buy recycling bins from Target or from home improvement stores like Home Depot for your basement, mudroom, or garage, or you can simply place some appropriately labeled large cardboard boxes where everyone can find them.
- Remember, 65 percent of our lives is spent at home so make it a healthy place.
- Be sure to install battery-operated carbon monoxide, smoke detectors, and fire extinguishers on each floor of your home. Be sure to test the alarm; monitor and replace the batteries at least once a year.
- Be sure to make your home safe for your children by installing outlet covers over electrical outlets.

- Install safety gates at the top and bottom of each stairway.
- Avoid fire hazards by replacing furnace filters three to four times per year.
- Check and replace loose or frayed wires on electronics.
- Never run cords under rugs.
- Keep vitamins, medications, and chemicals locked up and out of the reach of children and animals. Make sure bottles have childproof caps.

Home Utility Bills

Home utility bills can creep up on you and become sky-high before you know it. It's important to keep an eye on your spending and use the following tips to manage your bills:

- Turn the lights off (and instruct your kids to do the same) whenever you leave a room.
- Maintain your air conditioning system to keep it operating at peak efficiency. Keep filters clean to increase efficiency.
- Schedule regular air conditioning system maintenance.
- Replace furnace filters at least once a year.
- Have an annual inspection to make sure the furnace is working properly and isn't emitting any dangerously noxious fumes.
- Close vents in rooms that aren't in regular use. There's no need to heat or cool a room that no one uses.
- Use ceiling fans to circulate warm interior air in the winter, and cool air in the summer, rather than running your heating and cooling equipment 24/7. This is an especially effective technique at night.
- Caulk and seal around windows and sliding doors to keep drafts out and seal cool or warm air in.
- Replace your windows, when the time comes, with energy-efficient models.
- Insulate your attic and around doors and windows.
- Keep your shades drawn in the warmer months to keep out sizzling summer heat; and open them wide in the winter to allow sunlight in.
- Replace old appliances with newer, energy efficient models when your budget allows.
- Install a programmable thermostat, and set it to dial down the

temperature for those times when you and the rest of your family are away during the day and while you're sleeping at night.

- If you don't have a programmable thermostat, get into the habit of dialing it up and down manually every day to save on energy costs.
- Unplug any electric device or appliance that you don't use regularly (such as recharging stations, curling irons, and other small appliances), since they continue to draw a little power even when they're turned off.
- Alternatively, plug small appliances into power strips that can be turned off when the appliance is not in use.
- Warning: Don't plug major appliances that draw a lot of power like a vacuum cleaner or a space heater into shared power strips. They can overheat and possibly start a fire. For the same reason, never leave a space heater running when you leave a room. A child or pet could tip it over and start a fire.
- Avoid cell phone plans with unlimited talk and text, especially if you don't use your phone much, because these plans cost the most (often more than a hundred dollars a month). Instead, sign up for a plan that gives you a set number of minutes a month, as well as free evening and weekend minutes. Cell phone companies don't advertise these plans much anymore because they want you to sign up for the pricier unlimited plans, so always ask about them.
- You can also switch to a no-contract company like Consumer Cellular, which charges as little as ten dollars per line (plus taxes) each month, offers a free phone, and will port over (transfer) your old cell phone number at no cost.
- If you absolutely must have texting as part of your cellular package, go for a shared family plan, then establish limits for each person so usage is divided fairly.
- Watch for cellular data charges, in particular. Hackers have figured out how to highjack phones and use thousands of data minutes, which can cost a small fortune.
- Finally, always check the charges on each of your monthly bills carefully. While computers do the work when it comes to logging charges and sending statements, a human being still has to make the computer run, so there's always the possibility that a mistake has been made.

Caring for the Outside of Your Home

A well-cared for yard outside your home is a source of pride and reflects well on your family, too.

- Plants and trees, bushes and fences add a lot to the curb appeal and the value of your home, but only if they're well-tended. Establish a regular schedule for mowing, trimming, edging, and weeding every week, or pay someone to do it for you.
- Also, water your lawn, plants, and garden regularly to help them flourish. Just be aware that some communities have water restrictions that prevent you from watering except on certain days or at certain times. Check with your municipality to learn the rules.
- If you need to add some curb appeal to a too-drab yard, head for the local nursery and check out the offerings. Try to add flowers and bushes that bloom at different times of the spring and summer so you always have a pop of color to accent your yard and home. A good time to buy plant material is in the fall, when nurseries clear out their inventories.
- If you live further north, be sure to purchase only plant materials that are hardy enough to survive the winter. A nursery employee can give you some advice on what to buy.
- Don't forget to tend to the landscaping in your yard as well. Landscaping comprises lawns, plants, flowers, brick pavers, flagstones, brick borders, retaining walls, and so on. One way to install new landscaping on a budget is to prowl through home and demolition sites for discarded bricks, stones, and other materials you can have for free (but always ask first, of course.)
- Reclaimed brick and other recycled materials for landscaping borders and pathways can give your yard a unique and distinctive look. Look for free landscaping plans on the Internet or check with your local nursery.

Marriage

Commitment provides stability. In order to cultivate a spirit of commitment, you will need to think about marriage rationally rather than idealistically.

Marriage is a most common cause of personal failure. The relationship of marriage brings people into intimate contact. Unless this relationship is harmonious, failure is likely to follow. Moreover, it will be a form of failure that is marked by misery and unhappiness, destroying all signs of ambition.

Here are some important questions to answer when considering getting married:

- What are the benefits of marriage?
- What are the challenges you can expect from marriage?
- What do you expect your future spouse to be?

Be realistic—no matter how compatible you and your future spouse may be, you should expect to witness changes in future goals and expectations based on family growth, finances, and unforeseen conditions. But the problems you encounter will not make or break your marriage; that depends on how you deal with them.

- You will not always agree on everything.
- You will not always have the same priorities.
- You will not always enjoy the same activities.
- You will not always feel euphorically in love.

Atta's Advice on Communicating Well

An inability to communicate well is the single most important weakness I have witnessed amongst newcomers (refugees and immigrant communities) over the last four decades, in family life and in social, work, and professional environments. It is a weakness that causes major breakdowns, misunderstandings, and overall estrangement. I have personally learned to talk and communicate, no matter where. It is a personal attribute that I consider as the most significant and helpful one I have in building my personal and professional life. Healthy communication in my mind begins in the heart, with a wish to connect and a desire to let others know that I care. We should say, show, and feel that care, and let people know that we want to help them because we care. But it is also about going beyond conversation. Do your words, expressions, and attitude mean that you care? Your words will have to follow your actions or they are just that, "words."

PARENTING

PROTECTING OUR CHILDREN

Children of immigrants make up a substantial and growing proportion of most Western countries. As a result, governments should focus on studying and identifying the demographic characteristics of this population, the strengths they possess, and the barriers they face. On the other hand, immigrant parents bear real responsibility to do their part and provide the best opportunities in raising and protecting their children. The best way to do this is to pay attention to language abilities, educational attainment, and overall activities.

Parents are fully responsible for learning and informing themselves about school and college campus resources, services, and policies. Partner with your children in order to create a supportive environment while they learn. It is equally important for your children to be capable, to advocate and speak up for themselves, and to access campus resources.

It's also important to partner with the schools on your children's journey, being mindful that, due to legal constraints, schools may not be able to share information about your student that you feel you may want or need.

PARENTING'S MOST IMPORTANT ROLES

I believe these are parenting's most important roles: to love and nurture your child; to build self-esteem and self-confidence.

Are you sure you have done what it takes for your children to take on the world? Have you fulfilled your obligations fully?

PARENTING AND ITS UNIVERSAL RESPONSIBILITIES

Becoming a parent is humanity's absolute best privilege but one will not become or be called a parent without having a child, so it is always appropriate to discuss parenting in the same breath as discussing our responsibilities of raising our children. We want them to be safe and sound, fed and watered, attending the right schools, getting the right grades, taking part in the right activities, and gaining awards. Expect them to perform at a level of perfection and never argue with their teacher

Parenting can be exhausting, but it comes with expectations of a future we can brag about.

Parenting Challenges

Here are some of the obvious parenting challenges that parents and society face these days:

- a parenting style that impedes kids and gets in their way
- a lack of understanding of the definition of success for our children
- confusing love in exchange for proper care and values and attributes
- little interest in establishing real foundations such as true love, motivation, and professional success in life
- a lack of the impulse to roll up one's sleeves
- a lack of focus on real-life responsibilities and the effort it takes to improve life in general
- not understanding that happiness comes from true love and what really works for humans
- an inability to love themselves and others
- an inability to discover the humanity in everyone
- an overemphasis on building a big ego

How to Protect Our Children from Human Trafficking

The single most important responsibility for family members, especially parents, is to create an environment where children can comfortably and openly talk about potential dangers. This is critical, as each member of the family will then become educated on the dangers of human trafficking, while being alert to potential threats. This will also provide opportunities to learn about the environment you are creating for their growth:

- Know exactly when and where your children spend their time.
- Watch your children's interactions and see who they trust.
- Get to know their friends and their friends' parents and where they live.
- Learn if there are guns in their friends' houses and whether they are secured away from children. Ask!
- Know all children will be properly supervised by families and parents.

- Avoid child victimization by unfamiliar adults who pretend to be a friend or the parent of a friend.

Children Are Not Our Property

Even though we parents tend to think our children belong to us, they do not. Our children are not our property.

- They are gifts, just like you were.
- Enjoy them like precious gifts forever, even if they are not with you.
- Treat them as though you are raising a rare plant. You are!

Settling for Mediocrity

Why should there be hope for the person who is indifferent and maybe used to average or below-average standards? Way too many parents on our beautiful earth settle for mediocrity in their children. They are either used to or resort to mediocrity as a norm and refuse to pay a price for rising above average.

A Lack of Education

The majority of incompetent politicians and leader pretenders and parents have failed to educate themselves and to utilize education properly. This is a major handicap that can be easily remedied with courage and commitment in this day and age. There are plenty of role models who have proven that the best-educated people are often those who are known as "self-educated" or "self-made." The ones with dedication and commitment to education have learned to get whatever they want in life without violating the rights of others. They realize that education is really not about knowledge, but about applying knowledge and experience through consistency and persistence for a successful life.

A Lack of Self-Discipline

A lack of self-discipline is simply an inability to control both positive and negative emotions and qualities in life. Self-discipline is life's BEST quality and probably the most satisfying of all. How can you win anything in life without conquering yourself?

No one should expect to be successful and make progress without having good health, period. A staggering number of human beings, particularly in the West, have become too weak to control their diet.

Unfavorable Influences and Environments during Childhood

Too many parents and extended families are failing their children and future generations by caving in and allowing children to grow and acquire unhealthy and criminal tendencies through association and engagement with improper conditions.

Procrastination in Decision-Making

Procrastinating on making a decision is one of the most severe and widespread causes of failure in our world. This weakness clearly stands in the way of every human being, just waiting to spoil anyone's chances of success. The majority of us accept the failures in our lives, because we are waiting for "the right time," which never arrives. There is never any such thing except for the logical conditions of growth and proper stages. It is a good idea to work with whatever tools you may have at your disposal now, and know that better tools will come along as you make your decisions.

A Lack of Persistence

Most of us are good starters but poor finishers of everything we begin. Moreover, people are prone to give up at the first signs of defeat. There is no substitute for PERSISTENCE. The person who makes PERSISTENCE his watchword, discovers that "Old Man Failure" finally becomes tired, and makes his departure. Failure cannot cope in the presence of persistence.

Negativity

Human beings are far more negative now than ever before, despite amazing conveniences and possibilities. Older generations succeeded through will and personal power, obtained through their own hard work with the cooperation and efforts of others. A negative personality will keep others away forever.

Prejudice and Superstition

These two are really forms of fear and ignorance. Successful people move on fearlessly with open minds, while the ignorant burn and itch in their own living hell.

Intolerance

People with closed minds are actually a burden on others. These are people who fail to acquire knowledge about the realities of our world. The most damaging forms of these intolerances are connected with religious, political, and racial differences of opinion.

Failure to Cooperate with Others

More people lose their positions and their big opportunities in life because of their failure to cooperate with others than for all their other faults combined.

Dynamics between Parents and Children

One challenge for families is a lack of healthy dynamics between parents and children. Key to success of a healthy parent-child dynamic is ongoing communication and interaction. Responsible parents find ways to make sure they are fully aware of their children's needs and potential challenges.

- Parents often feel disappointed to see their children struggle to keep up in class.
- Many parents complain about their children suffering from bullying and discrimination as a result of cultural differences.
- Children are often placed in a class according to their age rather than by their ability. For those who are unable to speak the language in the classroom, it's realistically impossible to keep up.
- Adding further insult to injury is the fact that some parents may not have the education or language skills to help their children; they may not be able to communicate with school authorities.

Saving Children from Extremism

It is our responsibility to save our children from all forms of extremism. The world has unfortunately witnessed mass victimization of vulnerable youth in the hands of extremist groups during recent years. If you left your homeland for the variety of reasons discussed earlier, you are now in your new home and it's certainly a much more important one than your original home. Here is what I mean by its being more important.

- You are now living a completely different and very challenging path in a new home filled with mass uncertainty.
- It is really important to pay close attention and be on the alert in avoiding the lure of extremism for your children. Remind yourself and your family of our true human responsibilities and commitment to build a new life with new wholesome conditions for our families and ourselves.
- It is extremely important to understand that our actions and the direction we take from here on set the tone for establishing a life full of great human values. Key to your success is gaining the hearts and minds of your host and new environment inhabitants.
- Be always conscious and aware of the image you wish to portray.
- Life is about the future and not just today.
- Familiarize yourself with all laws and outstanding human principles in leading your life.

Child Trafficking

Over half of the world's refugees today are children. Some of these children may spend the majority of their childhoods away from their homes and separated from their families. Children are uniquely vulnerable to the worst parts of the forced-movement crisis, including trafficking, from the beginning of their journey until they reach their destination. There are many reasons for this.

- Children are often traveling alone or with limited resources.
- Being young, weak, and inexperienced, they are at a heightened risk of exploitation, including trafficking, sexual exploitation, and enslaved labor.
- Refugee children are five times more likely to be out of school, and they

often face discrimination, threats, and exclusion in their new country.

- Refugee children are also more likely to be deported because of a lack of legal aid and sponsorship. They may be sent back to countries where they will face worse dangers.
- Even those who aren't deported may be detained or incarcerated at their destination country over their migration status.

Family and Friendship

Nothing is more effective than positive family and social engagement, which leads to generating and enhancing positive emotions and pleasure. In my experience, nothing helps to reenergize me more than connecting and spending time with my family and friends. I find friendship is key to an energized and motivated lifestyle and the feeling that I am never alone. We all come apart at times in life and there will always be a need for renewal. When there is, therefore, I always recommend that we find time to connect with our family and friends, no matter when, where, how, what, and why.

Avoid Alcohol

Alcoholic beverages are designed to disrupt the balance of your brain. They increase aggression and anger, making stress harder to deal with. Avoid alcohol.

Spending Money

It may feel good to shop and spend money to reduce stress but in reality it adds to more pressure while jeopardizing your financial stability.

The Human Mind

"Garbage in, garbage out." I remember hearing this from two professors of sociology and psychology during a National Public Radio conversation many years back. This is honestly the BEST reminder and a matter of fact: garbage in, garbage out! I am now a firm believer in this slogan, which applies to pretty much everything from the human mind to food.

Atta's Recommendations for a Better Life

Having lived a fulfilling and rewarding life with enormous opportunities to witness and learn from many, I consider myself a very lucky human being. I highly advise following the few simple tips below:

- Stop focusing on the petty and on negativity.
- It may not always be your fault, but your response is within your control.
- Drama will always be there, coming from all over, whether from friends, family, politicians, or colleagues.
- You have a choice to take part and focus on the drama or simply let go and not hold a grudge against anyone.
- Learn to accept ambiguity and change.
- The end of one stage is only the beginning of the next stage. Be ready to change and be open to new ideas.

Chapter Four: Being Organized and Prepared

Atta's Lesson on Time Management

Almost everyone procrastinates once in a while, but rarely does procrastination become a life-threatening situation, as it was for me. In the mid-1970s, I had an amazing opportunity to travel to Bangkok for an excellent hotel management training program. But I was happy with my job managing a soccer club at the time, so I procrastinated about making a decision and eventually wasted a great opportunity.

Big political changes took place in Afghanistan shortly after that, which altered the course of life for millions of people, including myself. I faced numerous life-threatening challenges before I left the country and became a refugee, first in Germany, and ultimately, in the United States.

The experience taught me a huge lesson: Don't think of time as money only. You can earn money and buy all the amenities in life, then replace them if they are taken from you. But when time is wasted, it is gone forever. I have since become a firm believer that human beings need no more than seven to eight hours of sleep a day, and that the rest of the time should be dedicated to constant, productive work, and service in which you reach out to others and make a difference in their lives. Too many people waste precious time every day, either by procrastinating or sitting idle. Our global population would be much healthier if we all got off our couches and got engaged.

There are so many opportunities lying ahead of us. But procrastination steals those opportunities from us and must be avoided. Working harder does not necessarily bring better results; in reality unproductive activities may have exactly the opposite effect.

How do you manage time? The fact is that we simply cannot.

Time goes on. If we want to make the best use of our time and manage ourselves well, the real solution is to prioritize what is most important in our lives. As you can see, opening up to this reality and managing time properly touches many parts of our lives. I love the idea of writing a to-do list at all times. To tell you the truth, on a scale of one through ten where ten is doing a great job with my time management and organization list, I'd give myself a seven. But everyone has to start somewhere.

The question is, Are you ready to stop the glorification of being busy and start redefining success? The happiest and most productive people are the ones who manage the clock, who work it, not just watch it. They know how to prioritize and not let time manage them.

Time Management and Organization

"Time" is one of the most talked-about words—everyone around the globe talks about time and wishes they had more of it. If we just had a few more hours in the day, could we get everything done that we set out to do and be happy? That is of course a dream! The fact remains that most of us fail to take full advantage of this most precious resource and commodity.

Here are some facts about time. Everyone has the same twenty-four hours a day to get the things done that are necessary to keep one's home life, work, and personal time on track and organized.

With multiple clocks in our homes, watches on our wrist, and timers on our phones to track time, keep us on schedule, and determine when enough is enough, we're constantly aware of time. But even when we manage our time carefully, it's not uncommon to feel overwhelmed or stressed out. In reality what we're really doing is dealing with time *mis*management issues that come from trying to stuff too many activities into a day that's already stretched to the limit.

But there are simple ways to manage your daily life successfully without feeling exhausted, tired, and frustrated; the process starts with good organization. American statesman Benjamin Franklin said "Do you love life? Then do not squander time, for that's the stuff that life is made of." On that note, here are a few proven ideas and tips to help you improve your time management skills and your ability to increase personal productivity.

You Are in Charge of Managing Your Time

The first question should be "Are you managing time or is it the other way around?" This question should be on everyone's mind. It's fair to say the majority of human beings are unfortunately failing to manage their time properly.

You may have a great memory, but unless it's photographic (and few are), then you need to get into the habit of writing down and tracking your activities rather than relying solely on your memory. If you're like most people, you have a lot to think about in a typical day, and keeping mental track of your schedule isn't the best use of your brainpower. Here some proven suggestions to start:

- Get yourself an organizer or an app for your smartphone to help you stay organized and punctual. It's a really good idea to learn how to use the calendar tool on your smartphone, home computer, and other electronic devices. That way you can take it with you and make notes on things you need to get done, and pay attention when you receive an alert.
- Once you have that organizer in hand (or in the cloud), fill it with your activities. Be sure to note every activity in your life, from appointments to deadlines.
- Set priorities for yourself for the day, week, and month.
- Note memorable occasions (birthdays, anniversaries, and so on), business meetings, and recurring activities like your children's extracurricular events. That way, you won't miss an important deadline, family function, or any of the important things on your schedule.
- Take a few moments every morning to plan out the day's activities. It's easier to stick to a schedule when you have a general idea of what you need to accomplish that day.
- Use a digital recording device to record your ideas on the go. (This is a better idea than trying to recall a great idea later from memory.) Such recorders are inexpensive and can hold a lot of data. Just remember, though, that you will have to listen to the recording later and either transcribe the information verbatim or jot down the most pertinent points. This takes time out of a busy day that you may not have.
- Alternatively, you can use your smartphone as a digital recorder, but

doing so will decrease battery life. Plus cell phones emit pulsing signals when they communicate with local cell towers, which can be picked up by the digital recorders others in the room are using around you. In effect, your smartphone will ruin those recordings. So if you do use your cell phone as a recorder, place it as far away from any digital recorders as possible, to keep the peace with your coworkers.

- Yet another alternative is to get into the habit of carrying a small notebook or scratch pad with you, or use your smartphone's note-taking function to jot down important ideas, action items, and appointments that you don't want to forget. Be sure to transfer these notes to your master schedule so you don't miss a deadline or event.
- Be a clock-watcher but in a good way. Be aware of the time as you work so you know whether you have to speed things up or if you can do them in a more leisurely fashion, while still meeting your personal deadlines.
- By segmenting your time this way, you can keep your activities under control and prevent them from taking longer than they should. Of course, you don't have to be totally regimented about this, but having a general idea will help you accomplish what you set out to do.
- Create a to-do list on paper or electronically, then check off the completed items as you finish them. This will give you a sense of accomplishment and energize you for the next task.
- Be sure to take time to pray or meditate and focus on all that you are grateful for.

Important versus Urgent

Quite a few people confuse the important things with the urgent ones. Important tasks do not necessarily require deadlines whereas urgent tasks do; on the other hand, important tasks are far more important than urgent tasks. Understanding the difference between the two has huge impact on the quality and productivity of your personal and professional lives. Having all these strategies in place and working for you is one thing; not overextending or overcommitting yourself is another.

- Determine what's important and what's urgent.
- Prioritizing tasks this way will help you stay in control and not feel as though you're overtaxed.

- In addition, avoid activities that don't match or help you achieve your goals. Everyone gets tasked with busy work (nonessential activities) from time to time, but if you schedule too many of them, the important things on your list will go begging.
- Learn to say no. Sometimes, you just can't take on one more thing, and sometimes you're asked to do something that is so outside your realm of expertise that it would be difficult or impossible to do it well.
- You know your capabilities, so don't accept a job or task just to avoid disappointing someone. That person will be far more disappointed if you can't deliver what you've promised.
- Finally, work some time for yourself into your schedule. You probably won't have to go so far as to actually schedule the time, but do leave some time here and there to take a break, read a book or a newspaper, and otherwise take care of yourself. A daily walk in the woods or with nature soothes not just the body but the soul.

The Busy Nonsense

"Busy" is a misleading word that is really not a glorifying word and not something we should desire to use too often or even to be proud of. With money and power as two main metrics for success within many societies, we are forced to work longer hours and rest less; we are attached to phones, tablets, and laptops even while missing important moments with our loved ones. This busyness impacts our physical and mental health. The word "busy" becomes dominant, a huge buzzword. Why not replace "I'm busy" with "I'm being productive"; "I'm prioritizing"; "I'm finding a way"? This type of phrase will help us with our health and our sleep and not require us to work 24/7 just to live!

To determine the real impact of busyness on our lives, let's draw two columns and jot down the habits we engage in that result in improving our life versus the bad habits that keep us from becoming more productive.

Habits that Improve My Life	Bad Habits I Can Do Away With

Time Management and Your Health

Managing time properly has a clear impact on our health in how we manage our lives and the actions we take. Here is the big question. What are you doing to take care of yourself better before serving and reaching out to your children and other family members? Write a short list of items and activities you are engaged with to take care of yourself better, for example the following.

Take Time Off from Your Digital Devices

Too many people are attached to their digital devices these days. It is a weakness that we often talk about but we fail to take action. Are you one of those people who spends your time focused on a screen instead of the faces in front of you? When's the last time you turned off your cell phone and focused one hundred percent on the people you're with? Challenge yourself and your loved ones to take time off from digital interruptions. Trust that your emails and messages will be there when you turn your phone back on.

Minimize Your Social Media Addiction

Many recent studies point to the fact that many people, especially the younger generation, are failing to achieve a balance between digital and real life. Too many devote numerous hours to their social media consumption—it can become an addiction. It is unfortunately normal to find some people glued to their Internet devices waiting for the arrival of the next trouble signal or good news. In reality, these conditions make life more distractible; they take us away from being productive members of society.

Here are some tips to break this vicious cycle and still remain informed.

- Make it harder to access social media by deleting the unnecessary and less important applications.
- There's nothing wrong with logging out and giving yourself time to be away. Life will go on and your device will be there when you return.
- Ask yourself the question, "What is the worst-case scenario if I'm not logged in?"
- Why not limit yourself by designating time and space to access? Remember your parents set limits on how much television you could watch and how much time you could play? How about setting time

limits for yourself, such as no television after 10 p.m.; no social media before 11 a.m. or after 6 p.m. Set specific limits for weekdays and weekends.

- Gather all phones and devices and put them in a basket during social and family gatherings, especially during meal times. Also set limits on distributing them earlier than half an hour before departure.
- Know that your screens are not healthy for your eyesight, so try to get away from them as much as you can. Take a walk outside and leave your phone behind.
- Remember "garbage in, garbage out."
- Care for yourself first; paying too much attention to social media and your devices takes away from paying attention to your health, your time, and your responsibilities.
- Don't let social media manage your valuable time.

Learn More

We learn many of our life lessons from our parents, our spouse, and our children. We may not have appreciated or understood all the lessons our parents shared, but remembering their advice can shed light on a difficult challenge we're facing. Learning should never stop even when you're out of school—indeed, that's when learning may truly begin.

Listen Intently to Your Inner Voice

Have you ever had a feeling about something, ignored it, and then were afraid that you should have followed it? Indeed, we all do. Next time, listen to your gut feelings, your instincts, and your own thoughts.

Find Solitude

Meditation helps relieve stress and helps us tap into our inner voice. If you don't like being with yourself, how can you expect others to like being with you? Many of my best ideas have come to me when I am driving alone. I've often thought that my creativity has declined because I do not take long drives as often!

Always Give Back to Your Community

There are simply not enough words to describe the significance of giving back to your community. Honestly, acts of kindness make a difference in the lives of others. Being a kind and compassionate person who helps others can lead to solutions for some of society's biggest challenges. I am sure you can find a way to share your talents or time at an elders' home, a shelter, or your children's schools.

Exercise

Exercising is the most significant and easy thing you can do to help you feel energized. With it comes the ability to accomplish much more. The question I always pose to anyone with an excuse about the lack of time to exercise is, "How and why is it that we find time for everything, I mean everything, in life, but not enough time for exercise?" We all have time for social media, spending significant time on our electronic devices, time to socialize and much more, but not even an hour for simply walking around the neighborhood or the park?

- Your body releases stress-fighting hormones called endorphins only when you are active.
- Exercise boosts your happiness levels.
- It increases your self-confidence.
- It increases your strength and flexibility.
- Physical activities can significantly improve your mood and health while relaxing your body.

Effective Organization of Paperwork

It may sound strange, but being organized on both a personal and professional level can really help you have a successful life. Just think about it. How much time do you waste looking for the things you need? This is just one sign of unstructured living that can torpedo your efforts and make you unproductive and unsuccessful. Being organized is not just about labeling, color-coding, or filling up file cabinets. It means creating systems that work well for you and allow you to access the items you need when you need them, efficiently and without wasting time.

Filing System

Every good organizational system starts with an efficient filing system. Start with a simple accordion file (A to Z; 1 to 31; or 1 to 13), which is available from any office supply store. Or use a file cabinet. Create a separate file for each of your household expenses. For instance, you'll need a file folder or a slot for each type of utility bill, including the ones for gas, electricity, water, phone, and cell phone. Next, create additional file folders for these items:

- health-care-related information, such as physician, dentist, prescription, hospital bills, and receipts
- credit card statements; make a separate file for each credit card company
- car-related information, such as repair bills and car titles
- insurance-related information, sorted among home, life, and auto-insurance policies, bills, and receipts
- mortgage paperwork, including deeds, payoff documents, and property tax bills
- income tax paperwork, including year-to-date earnings, receipts, past tax returns

Create Separate Files

Next, create separate files for personal documents including the following:

- family birth certificates
- naturalization papers or permanent residence cards
- Social Security cards (US)
- passports
- marriage certificate
- divorce papers
- adoption papers
- powers of attorney
- death certificates

Be sure to safeguard these items—if they fall into the wrong hands, you could have a serious problem with identity theft.

Further Organizational Steps

As part of the organization process, also do the following:

- Scan your personal information and print a couple of sets of backup copies, including one for your safe deposit box at the bank, and one for a locking, fireproof box that you keep in an inconspicuous place at home. This way, you're covered if anything happens to your master file.
- Organizational experts say that 90 percent of everything we file away is never accessed again. For that reason, invest in a document shredder so you can purge and shred your files with personal information on a regular basis, say, every three years.
- Three years is the length of time the Internal Revenue Service (IRS) in the US generally requires taxpayers to keep tax return materials like 1040 forms and receipts, so the same guideline works for most other paperwork. (See "How long should I keep records?" on www.irs.gov for exceptions to this rule.)
- Some advisors suggest keeping copies of tax returns indefinitely, even though the IRS advises differently.
- Scan them and file them electronically, then shred the originals to cut down on clutter.
- The Canadian government requires its residents to retain tax return files for six years; Australia requires five years; Germany requires up to ten years.

Documents to Keep Indefinitely

Keep these documents indefinitely:

- mortgage papers
- immigration papers
- naturalization paperwork
- personal residence cards
- estate-planning documents
- life insurance policies
- pension documents

Additional Tips

Be sure to inventory the items in your safe deposit box and keep a copy of the list and a spare in a secure location (not just in the box itself). Also be sure to note the location of your safe deposit box key, or you'll be at the bank paying a fee to have the box drilled when you can't find it.

Also, take advantage of online bill-paying tools from your bank or credit union. These make bill-paying go faster because you won't have to spend time writing checks. This also saves the cost of stamps and the time it takes to mail the bills.

Finally, sign up for free payment alerts that are emailed or texted to you by your bank and credit card companies. They remind you when payments are due, which in turn helps you avoid paying late fees.

To protect the integrity of your personal data, password-protect your computer and smartphone to prevent unauthorized users from accessing the information.

Effective Electronic Organization

Home Computer System

If you don't already have a computer and you don't know much about computer equipment, it can be overwhelming trying to choose from among the many products on the market. Here are some best practices:

- Consult a computer-savvy family member or friend to help you buy and install the right system. Barring that, you should ask a lot of questions at the computer or office-supply store to make sure you're getting the right equipment for your needs.
- Pay extra to have someone install the software you need.
- For a fee, some electronics stores like Best Buy will even send someone out to your home or office to set everything up.
- Alternatively, a computer consultant (whom you can find on yellowpages.com or in the phone book's Yellow Pages) can get your system up and running. Don't try to cut corners on this—it's worth the cost to have everything set up right—and you'll save yourself a lot of aggravation.
- Likewise, don't skimp on your computer system to save money. Computers are pretty inexpensive these days, and it's tempting to buy the cheapest one on the market. But there's a lot of difference between that bargain-basement computer and the one that costs just slightly more.

You might be able to live with that just fine, but the lower priced computer also doesn't come with a wireless Internet card, which will cost you—you guessed it—about a hundred dollars. So if you just bought the next model up, you'd have the card installed already and you could get on the Internet right away, instead of spending time trying to figure out how to make the computer work with the parts you bought separately.

- If you're buying your first computer, you need to figure out whether a desktop model or a laptop will suit you better. If you will be doing most of your computing in your home office or in the spare bedroom, for instance, then a desktop (a.k.a. a "tower") model is probably your best bet. And, by the way, a desktop computer doesn't have to be right on the desk. It can go wherever the wires reach to connect it.
- A laptop is a great choice if you think you'll be using the computer on the go, or if it will be moving from room to room in your home. This is an important consideration if you have several people who will be using the computer throughout the day.
- Laptops cost more than desktops—a lot more, if you decide to purchase a Mac Book, for example—but the mobility is a definite advantage.
- There's one more type of computer that bears mentioning: the iPad. You've probably seen the commercials about how great an iPad is and how much it can do. And they're right. But iPads and other tablets are used mainly for entertainment and accessing the Internet. They do come with a virtual keyboard, meaning you tap on an onscreen keyboard, but they're difficult to use if you have a lot of typing to do. You can buy an external keyboard, but that gets hard to carry around.
- If you really want a tablet because "they're cool," a Microsoft Surface might be a better choice because it has a Snap-On keyboard that is actually made for word processing.
- But let's say you want to use your computer to keep yourself organized rather than for entertainment (and yes, for the occasional computer game). Some basic features you should look for include at least a 500MB hard drive, built-in wireless networking, and a multi-format DVD/CD-RW drive. Add in a wide-screen monitor or purchase a tower-plus-monitor package, and you're almost good to go.
- Also make sure the computer has enough USB ports, which are the slots into which you will plug the peripherals like printers, a mouse, flash drives, and chargers. It's helpful to have the ports right on the front of the computer for easy access.

- You can also buy a USB hub, which plugs into one of the USB ports and gives you up to ten additional ports.
- You'll also need a printer, and it's generally best to go with a wireless printer so you don't have a lot of dangling wires connecting your printer to your tower. A wireless printer gives you the ability to send documents from your laptop to your printer, no matter where it is in the house.
- Wireless printers generally are more expensive than wired models, but the convenience makes it worth it. Other than that, there is very little difference in quality between average home printers these days; the price is more about the number of features it has, the number of pages you print every day (usually not a consideration for a home user), and how fast the pages print. Other features include duplex printing (which allows printing on both sides of the sheet).
- A standalone scanner is another great tool for home organization. With a scanner, you can take pictures of (or scan) different size documents up to 8.5-by-11 inches, to save for long-term storage by date or name. This significantly cuts down on paper documents in your home, which translates into less clutter.
- One really useful type of scanner is the sheet-fed document scanner. This type of equipment has a hopper a.k.a. a sheet feeder on the top, so all you have to do is load the documents, and click or press a button, and they feed through automatically. A sheet-fed scanner allows you to scan documents of all sizes, including business cards, receipts, and letters, all at the same time (although it's usually best to scan them in same-size batches to avoid jamming). The documents are saved to a file on your computer, where they can be retrieved easily.
- If you're on a budget, a flatbed scanner works just as well. It does take longer to scan documents and they have to be loaded manually, one at a time. But the result is the same: less paper to manage, less clutter in your office, and more satisfaction with your workspace. It's important to note that most printers are equipped with scanning and faxing capabilities.
- Anti-virus software is right at the top of the list of must-haves for your computer. Most new computers come with a trial version that is good for about ninety days. But you absolutely must buy the full program once the trial expires so your computer is protected when

you're online or if you transfer files from other computers via a flash drive or CD-ROM.

- Once you get your computer up and running, you'll be in business, so to speak. Just remember to save your work frequently as you're word processing or scanning so you don't lose anything important if the power suddenly goes out (it happens). Also, back up your computer files regularly—say, daily or weekly or once a month—on external media like a flash drive or CD, or pay a company to do the job for you. (You simply email your files and they'll provide you with a backup.) This is important because if your computer crashes (stops working) or it's damaged in any way, you'll have separate copies of your files and you won't lose any valuable information.

Recordkeeping Guidelines

Use these lists to determine how long you should keep important papers. Rely on secure online and secure offline recordkeeping whenever possible to limit the possibility of identity theft through the physical retrieval of papers, as well as to cut down on the amount of paper in your home and home office.

Retention Time	Type of Record	Online Access (Y/N)
One to three months	Grocery Receipts Receipts for Cash Purchases	N N
One year	ATM Receipts Bank Statements Brokerage Statements Cable TV Checks Cancelled Checks Cellular Phone Bills Credit Card Bills Electric Bills Gas Bills Major Purchases	Y Y Y Y Y Y Y Y Y Y

	Phone Bills (Landline) Social Security Statements Trash Collection Bills Water/Hydro Bills	Y Y Y Y
Up to seven years	Tax Returns Retirement Portfolio Statements	N N
Forever (preferably stored in a safe deposit box)	Adoption Papers Antique Item Records (while owned) Birth Certificate Citizenship Papers Custody Agreements Deeds Divorce Papers Home Appraisal (for as long as property is owned) Jewelry Certificates (while owned) Life Insurance Policies Living Trusts Marriage Certificate(s) Military Records Power(s) of Attorney Warranty Papers (while owned) Will(s) (store at home safely rather than in the safe depoit box at the bank)	None of these is likely to be available online

Identity Theft

Take the time now to read the material on protecting your data against theft, provided in chapter two. Identity theft can occur when we're traveling and when we're settled in our home. Further precautions are listed below.

- Limit the number of credit cards you apply for. Accumulating lots of cards is not a contest; it's a way to increase the odds of being ripped off, as someone could take the cards out of your mailbox, steal your wallet or purse, or otherwise relieve you of your charge cards.
- Never give out personal information to anyone who phones you, sends you a letter through the mail, or emails you, no matter how convincing the person is or how much he or she offers you. Check the person's credentials

or call back the company he or she represents to make sure the request is legitimate.

- Never open email attachments from someone you don't know. The link could load a virus onto your computer, or take you to a website that looks legitimate but is a front for criminal activity.
- In fact, in general, you might not want to open attachments at all, to avoid unleashing a virus on your poor, unsuspecting computer when you click the link.
- Never click links you receive in unsolicited emails, even from people you know since hackers know how to highjack the address books of unsuspecting people, then send emails to everyone in that address book. A person's email account could have been hacked, and those links could lead to a computer virus that can damage or destroy your computer and the data you've saved.
- This is especially important when it comes to emails from banks and other financial institutions. If you wish to visit a site for which you've received a link, go directly to the website instead.
- Watch out for phishing attempts, which is when someone fraudulently poses as a real financial institution (typically) for the purpose of stealing money or identities from unsuspecting people. Phishing is a big problem, so you'll probably get plenty of these emails. (One "famous" one is the Nigerian prince phishing email, in which a person claiming to be a prince wants to give you a huge amount of money if you send him a few thousand dollars in advance. Don't do it.)
- Never, ever provide your password, personal information like your birth date, Social Security Number, or account numbers to someone who requests them by email. Your bank or credit union will never ask for information this way. Criminals are so clever that when you click the link in such an email, you'll be taken to a website that looks just like your bank or credit union's website, and if you log in, you open the door for crooks to steal your information, then drain the cash from your accounts or open new credit cards or other accounts. If you're in doubt about whether an email is real, call the financial institution directly.
- Another way to check whether an email is a phishing attempt is to go to Snopes.com, which usually can give you the background on any suspicious email you receive.
- A PIN code or password login on your phone or laptop is all that

stands between passing strangers and your online accounts, so make sure there's one in place.

- Whether your devices offer password protection, fingerprint ID sensing, facial recognition, or iris scanning, make sure there's something there that stops other people from logging in.
- Never carry your Social Security or Social Identification card with you, but do memorize the number in case you need it. When you're asked for your number when making a transaction, ask if you can provide a different form of identification, like your driver's license. The answer will probably be no, but it's worth asking to keep your number private.
- Remove yourself from the mailing lists of companies that send pre-approved credit card offers so they don't fall into the wrong hands (that is, anyone's but yours). Look for opt-out options.
- Put all your phones on the National Do Not Call Registry to reduce unwanted telemarketing calls. In the United States, you can sign up at fcc.gov; in Canada, go www.lnnte-dncl.gc.ca.

For additional information about identity theft in the US, see the Federal Trade Commission Identity Theft Center at www.ftc.gov. Canadians should view the Royal Canadian Mounted Police's Identity Theft resources at rcmp-grc.gc.ca. In the European Union, search for "identity theft" at europa.eu/european-union/index_en.

Online Safeguards using Passwords

No doubt one of the reasons you plan to buy a new computer or you use the one you have is so you can surf the Internet. Then, it doesn't take long before our existence is scattered across the Internet and each and every one of those accounts is a potential avenue into our private life for a hacker. So we must secure them. Here are some of the best practices to keep your accounts safe and secure and, importantly, not ignored. Old and unused accounts are easy targets for hackers so it is really important to keep the number of accounts you are using to a minimum; just use the ones you really care about.

Here are some important safeguards you should take to keep your personal and private online information safe from prying eyes.

- Use different passwords for different uses, even though it's much easier to remember and record fewer usernames and passwords.
- Set up a password manager or a separate password-protected passwords

file. Update it regularly with new information and change your passwords often.

- Password manager programs can also generate ultra-secure passwords, saving you from having to create and remember lots of different ones or resort to using the same one for everything.
- Again, change your passwords on a regular basis—all of them. You've then got much less to worry about should a big batch of them become available to hackers, because you'll likely have changed yours.
- Avoid using obvious passwords, such as your birth date or your children's names, for any password-protected account. Naturally, this includes your credit card and bank accounts, but also should include simple things like your library pass.
- The best passwords are words that don't exist in the dictionary (including words in your native language) or are a combination of letters (both upper and lower case), numbers, and some symbols. For example, a password like "happy camper" can be strengthened by typing it this way: haPpYCamPEr. Add in a number or two and an underline (haPpY6_7CamPEr), and you'll make it virtually hacker-proof.

Software Updating

Software updating is a common operation that's necessary to safeguard most digital electronics these days. Updates may include ongoing improvements, detected problems as result of consumer feedback, or simply the addition of features for smooth operations of the device. Unless you install something really sketchy and terrible, anti-virus programs and other bits of security software can't do any harm and may well do a lot of good—like guarding against phishing attacks.

Use a Secret Email Address

If someone knows your email address, they're halfway to knowing how to log into your accounts—and these days it's not that difficult to find out someone's email address. Setting up a private email address (that doesn't relate to your name) solely for logging into your social media accounts is another way of keeping them more secure.

Keep Your Accounts to Yourself

On a related note, it's well worth setting up your own account on a shared computer or your browser or your tablet to keep other people away from your important accounts. We're not saying your toddler or your housemate is actively trying to hack into your Facebook account, but from a security perspective it's always best to limit access as much as possible.

Watch What You Share Online

Your accounts are only as secure as the weakest links protecting them—and those links often involve someone impersonating you. Make sure personal details that can be used to verify your identity, like your home address, your birthday, or even what soccer team you support (is that your "secret security question"?) aren't all over your social media profiles.

Effective Professional Organization

No matter what type of work you do, staying organized is key to getting things done correctly and on time. So no matter whether you work in an office building or at a discount department store, here are some suggestions for keeping your work life on track:

- Designate a place where you can routinely put the things you need for your job so you can grab them quickly on the way out the door. Maybe it's a portfolio for a client meeting, the apron you wear while serving at a restaurant, or your reading glasses.
- If you put these things in the same place every time you come home from work, you'll find them again easily the next time you leave.
- Important note: If leaving things around in the open is too unsightly, drop everything into a basket, then tuck the basket away in a closet or the mud room where it will be easily accessible.
- Plan your wardrobe in advance. This may sound crazy, especially to men, but if you know what you're going to wear the next day, you can be assured that you'll look your best. That's because you'll know before you put a shirt on that a button is missing, or that a stain didn't come out of the fabric when you washed it. You don't want any surprises when you get to work or school.

- Planning your wardrobe in advance also keeps you from wasting time in the morning searching for a particular garment, socks, shoes, or other apparel.
- Leave early enough to get to work on time—or better still, leave a little earlier. That way, if traffic is slow, you'll still be on time, you'll have time to pick up your favorite cup of coffee at the drive-through window if you're driving, or you'll have a few free moments to look at the newspaper before work.
- Make a list of everything you have to accomplish that day, and then prioritize the list according to the importance and deadline of each project. It's easiest to do this on a computer because you can move things around, but a simple list numbered by hand also works. It helps to look at the big picture and make a weekly and monthly list.
- Set up a filing system in the office similar to the one you have at home. Being organized on the job will make it easier to accomplish tasks, because whatever information you need will be right at hand.
- Use the calendar function on your smartphone or a planner to note business appointments, and set a timer to remind you when it's time to go. Make sure you build some free time into your schedule as well, because unexpected things can crop up; plus you need a break from time to time.
- Try to complete one task before going on to the next. It's true that sometimes you have to multitask to take care of things that crop up, but whenever possible, finish what you start. You'll have a feeling of accomplishment as you check another project off your list.
- Stay off social media sites like Facebook or Twitter during business hours, and don't send personal texts. Work is just that—work. Social media and texting distract you from that work and turn you into an underachiever—something the boss will notice.
- Finally, take a break between projects. You deserve it.

Emergency Preparedness

Key to successful emergency preparedness is considering the length of time and how well you prepare before an emergency occurs. Too many people have lost many of their valuables as a result of fires and other disasters because of a lack of preparation.

Get Started

Get started for emergency preparedness by taking these steps.

- Review suggestions in the Emergency Preparedness Guidelines published in your community.
- Check your house for supplies that you already have on hand.
- Decide where to store supplies (food may be packed together in a single container or kept on shelves for easy rotation).
- Supplies may be stored all together in a large plastic garbage can with wheels, putting the heavy items at the bottom.

Meet with Your Family to Plan

The best way to prepare an emergency plan is to meet with your entire family to build awareness and gather their input.

- Discuss the types of disasters that could occur.
- Discuss how to prepare and how to respond.
- Discuss what to do if you need to evacuate.
- Practice your plan.
- At the end of six months, review what you have done, starting with month one of the calendar.
- Evaluate, rotate supplies, and replace as appropriate based on expiration dates and other instructions.

Emergency Preparedness Tasks

Awareness by and participation of the entire family are key to the successful implementation and timely execution of all emergency preparedness tasks. It is easy to lose track of all the potential life-threatening situations without planning properly, assigning tasks, and being fully aware.

- Make sure to establish out-of-area and out-of-state contacts to call in case of an emergency.
- Prepare a list of all important phone numbers, contacts, physicians, family, banks, creditors, and insurance companies.
- Remember that during an emergency there might be no electricity and you will be unable to recharge cellphones. Only corded landlines will work without power, as long as the phone systems still function.

- Gather brochures and handouts from your local Red Cross or other organizations.
- Gather enough information about hazards and other critical conditions.
- Locate and educate the entire family on gas meters and water shutoffs while attaching proper tools near them.
- Be sure to videotape or photograph all the contents of your home for insurance purposes.
- It is a good idea is to back up your electronics and even store certain important items with relatives and family outside your home.
- Review and understand your home insurance and/or rental insurance policies for details of emergency coverages.
- It's important to note that you should store one to two gallons of water per person for each day. This water is for consumption and sanitation.
- When medical supplies, flashlights, and emergency items are placed near the top, they can be located quickly for inspecting and restocking. Remember to rotate your perishable supplies and change the water every six months.
- Make sure to follow instructions on your home water heater diagrams to reduce hazards.
- Contact your child's day care or school to make sure to learn about their safety and emergency plans and communication processes.
- It's a very good idea to learn and attend First Aid classes.

Storage Tips

- Keep food in a dry, cool spot—a dark area if possible.
- Keep food covered at all times.
- Wrap cookies or crackers in a plastic bag and place them inside a tight container.
- Empty opened packages of sugar, dried fruits and nuts into screw-top jars or air tight cans to protect them from pests.
- Inspect all food for signs of spoilage before use.
- Mark and date all food items properly for use before their expiration dates.
- Use foods before they go bad and replace them with fresh supplies.
- Place new items at the back or bottom of the container in the storage area, and older ones in front.

Suggested Foods

Select foods according to your family's needs and preferences. Store low-salt, water-packed varieties where possible. Here are some suggestions:

- canned meat: tuna, chicken, raviolis, chili, beef stew, spam, corned beef
- canned vegetables: green beans, kernel corn, peas, beets, kidney beans, carrots
- canned fruit: pears, peaches, mandarin oranges, applesauce, fruit juices
- cereal: Cheerios, Chex, Kix, Shredded Wheat
- quick energy snacks: granola bars, raisins
- peanut butter
- instant coffee and tea bags
- powdered soft drinks

What You Need to Store

It is important to note that you may not be able to purchase or get hold of some important items due to a power outage. It is therefore important to store some items for immediate and short-term use and prepare according to your family size.

1 gallon of water for each person
a bungee cord
a camp stove and fuel
a crescent wrench
a hand-operated can opener
a permanent marking pen to mark date on cans and bottled water
a sewing kit
a tarpaulin
a thermometer
a waterproof plastic container for first aid and other supplies
antiseptic liquid and pads
disposable wipes
duct tape
heavy rope
scissors
sleeping bags for all
tweezers
two flashlights with batteries
waterproof matches

Atta's Lesson on Home Management

One of my greatest frustrations during my early years in America was a lack of information about some of the most ordinary day-to-day things. I had so many questions, such as what should I do in the case of an emergency or the death of someone else? Who should I call? It was truly shocking to realize that I didn't know what to do in my new land. The situation was even worse after my big family arrived. Escaping my homeland Afghanistan by myself and making my way ultimately to my new home in the US seemed easy compared with sponsoring my mother, my older brother and his wife, plus my other eight siblings. They also had to escape Afghanistan and make it to the US. I sponsored them all with help from the Lutheran Social Services of San Francisco. Life was no longer just about me, but about being responsible for a big family.

Eventually I created a family planner, kind of like an operations manual. It covered everything the family needed to know, from how to react in a life-threatening situation (like a natural disaster or a health crisis), to where to go for medical help, and even where to go to have fun. I shared my "manual" with the whole family.

Next, I organized our personal documents. I had them translated and figured out where to store them to keep them safe. That way, if we ever needed them, everything would be accessible and ready to use. This made me feel a lot more confident that I was in control of my life.

You should do the same thing. You'll be amazed how much better you'll feel knowing you have a plan for every situation.

Home Life Checklists, Worksheets, and Records

Here are some samples checklists and worksheets. For easy access to various forms to help maintain and keep your household information up to date, please refer to my website at www.attamoves.com.

Family Information

	Name	Work phone
Mother		
Father		
Child		
Child		
Home phone		
Other designated relative you authorize to pick up and drop off a child		

Family Emergency and Contact Information

Agency	Number to dial
Emergency	911
Local Police	
Fire Department	
Pest and Poison control	
Other	

Children's Information

Items	Information
Name	
Birthplace	
Date of Birth	
Day care name	
Day care address	
School	

School address	
Phone number	
Class room information	
After-school activity	
Name of person in charge	
Phone number of person in charge	
Address of activity	
Second after-school activity	
Name of person in charge	
Phone number of person in charge	
Address of activity	
Third after-school activity	
Name of person in charge	
Phone number of person in charge	
Address of activity	
Medical Alerts	
Medical note	
Allergy	
Allergy	
Medication	
Medication	
Primary doctor's name	
Primary doctor's phone number	
Primary doctor's office address	
Hospital name	
Hospital address	
Health insurance company	
Health insurance phone number	
Health insurance policy number	

Schools

Child's Name	School's Name	Address	Phone	Email

Citizenship Certificates

Name	Number	Date of issue	Place Issued

Green Card or Other Work Permit

Name	Number	Date of issue	Date of Expiry

Passports

Name	Number	Date of issue	Issuing Authority	Date of Expiry

Embassies and Consulates

Item	Information
Name of Embassy or Consulate	
Address	
Phone number	
Name of contact	
Name of another contact	
Other contact phone number	
Fax number	
Website	

Item	Information
Name of Embassy or Consulate	
Address	
Phone number	
Name of contact	
Name of another contact	
Other contact phone number	
Fax number	
Website	

Item	Information
Name of Embassy or Consulate	
Address	
Phone number	
Name of contact	
Name of another contact	
Other contact phone number	
Fax number	
Website	

Family Physicians

Item	Information
Primary Doctor	
Street address	
Mailing address	
Phone number	
Fax number	

Health Insurance Company

Item	Information
Name	
Address	
Phone	
Email	

Hospitals

Item	Information
Name	
Address	
Phone	
Email	

Primary Physicians

Item	Information
Name	
Address	
Phone	
Email	

Pediatrician

Item	Information
Doctor	
Phone number	

Other Medical Specialists

Item	Information
Name	
Address	
Phone	
Email	
Specialty	

Item	Information
Name	
Address	
Phone	
Email	
Specialty	

Family Dentists

Item	Information
Name	
Address	
Phone	
Email	

Pharmacies

Item	Information
Name	
Address	
Phone	
Email	

Monthly Housing Income

Item	Credit	Debit
Salary 1		
Salary 2		
Salary 3		
Overtime		
Tips		
Bonuses		
Child support		
Pension		
Social Security		
Other income		
Investment dividend		
Savings account expense		
Mortgage payment		
Mortgage insurance		

Car payment 1		
Car payment 2		
Car payment 3		
Car Insurance		
Health insurance		
Gas		
Electricity		
Water		
Phone		
Mobile phones		
Homeowner insurance		
Homeowner association		
Transportation (bus, subway, train, light rail)		
Gasoline		
Tolls		
Car maintenance		
Groceries		
Entertainment		
Child care		
Clothing, uniforms, and shoes		
Child support alimony		
Credit Card 1		
Credit Card 2		
Credit Card 3		
Total		

Charities and Nonprofit Organizations

Item	Information
Name of Charity	
Address	
Phone number	
Fax number	

Post Office

Name	Address	Phone	Email

Banks

Name	Address	Phone	Email

Cars

	Model and Year	VIN	License Plate	Expiration Dates
Car 1				
Car 2				
Car 3				
Car 4				

Auto Insurance Companies

Name	Address	Phone	Email

Home Insurance Companies

Name	Address	Phone	Email

Immigrant Legal Resource Center in Community

Organization	Information
Name of organization	
Address	
Phone	
Cell phone	
Other phone number	

Attorney

Item	Information
Name of law firm	
Name of attorney	
Name of attorney	
Phone	
Reception contact	
Fax Number	
Website	
Mailing address	
Street address	

Chapter Five: Your New Home—Getting Out and About

Accessing Services

It is important to research, become aware of, and access the services within your community. While also avoiding seeing a doctor or getting legal guidance, newcomers usually fail to take advantage of many services that are available to them for various reasons.

- Difficulty with speaking English, trouble taking time off work, and having limited transportation are some of the real issues.
- Accessing mental health assistance is a real challenge in some countries like America. Many refugees and immigrants have been subject to violence, rape, and even torture, but they may not know help is available or how to seek it.
- Mental health issues continue to be taboo in many cultures, creating an additional barrier for those in need.
- Even though refugees may manage to obtain the services they need, their experience can be quite negative due to law enforcement professionals misunderstanding a victim's statement due to language barriers, and doctors misdiagnosing sick patients for the same reason.
- It is important to realize there are existing services for refugee families within your own neighborhoods.
- Law enforcement and fire department officials are also excellent sources of information within your community.

Look for These Amenities

Key to establishing and settling successfully within a community is awareness. Learning about various services and amenities can be motivating and serve as an opportunity for networking. It is also best to leverage low-cost or free services that some may be unaware of. Look for these amenities:

- advocacy and protection agencies
- banks
- business development providers
- educational facilities
- emergency services
- employment services
- government services
- hospitals that are near
- job-placement centers
- language schools
- legal service providers that are free
- service providers
- skill-training centers
- vocational training schools

Assess What's Happening in Your Community

Social engagement and community awareness are everyone's responsibility—assess what's happening in your community. This is particularly important for families with children for gaining a sense of responsibility and belonging within a new environment. Learn about these aspects:

- social awareness
- security issues and concerns
- threats (safety, security, risks)
- political events

Immerse yourself in your community.

- Be sure to maintain a productive and creative lifestyle while taking advantage of your skills and talents.
- It's extremely important to keep your children engaged. Encourage them to participate in lively and healthy activities. They certainly have the right to be heard and properly taken care of when it comes to the matters that affect their future. Keep them engaged as part of your discussions, assessments as well as input. Encourage their ability to initiate positive change and development.
- Become a volunteer to demonstrate responsibility within your community and become an active participant in local committees and other consultative mechanisms like municipal and district development committees.
- As a professional, become an advocate for progressive legislation at all levels of government and within local institutions to encourage work

permits, vocational training skills, training skill centers, health, education, and employment for refugees and immigrants.

Transportation Options

Transportation is a big issue that affects almost all aspects of life for everyone. As a newcomer, understand your transportation options and learn how to navigate the roadways. This will protect not only you, but also your family and others around you.

Despite the fact that so many people drive their own vehicles, if you're an inexperienced driver, it's usually best if you start out using public transportation before driving a car. Granted, there are certain urban areas where it can be very challenging to find reliable public transportation, but if there's a way to get around town by having someone else drive, it's highly recommended.

While many refugees and immigrants do rely on public transportation to get around, it can be incredibly frightening for some. It is simply not easy to maneuver one's way because of unfamiliarity with roads, traffic signs, and different transit options.

Information to do with driving your own vehicle is in chapter two, where "Driver's License" is listed in "Important Personal Documents"; it's also in chapter eleven, "The Big Purchases—A Home and a Car," which includes "Obtaining a Driver's License"; and it's in chapter thirteen on insurance, which includes auto insurance. Here, other transportation options are discussed.

Inner City Transport

Most large cities in Europe and North America have inner city transport, which includes a local bus, light rail, and subway system to take you everywhere from shopping centers to churches.

- Buses stop frequently—possibly as often as every few blocks—to get you as close to your destination as possible.
- City transport tends to offer extended hours daily, with shortened schedules on weekends and holidays. The best thing about local bus services is that it's fairly inexpensive. The bad thing is that in some major cities where crime is a problem, the buses may not be as safe as you would like and the frequent stops can make your commute slow.

- Avoid wearing flashy jewelry or clothing, or using expensive electronic devices (including iPhones) while waiting for or when on board a bus. If you are aware of your surroundings at all times, you should be fine.
- Research and find free transportation options for children and the elderly in your community.
- You'll need exact change, a bus token, or a bus pass to ride on a bus. You can buy tokens (which are usually discounted) and bus passes at bus transit centers, automated vending machines, online, and other designated locations like libraries and grocery stores. If you need to transfer from one bus to another to reach your destination, you'll need to purchase a transfer when you board the first bus.
- Fares are usually based on the distance traveled across different zones. As with buses and subways, you can purchase discounted frequent traveler fares online or at the rail station.
- Buses often have designated seating at the front of the vehicle for senior citizens and people with disabilities. Please be courteous and give up your seat if a senior or disabled person comes aboard.
- Trains that travel along city streets on fixed tracks are known as light rail. Light rail trains are also variously called streetcars, cable cars, or trams.

Commuter Bus System

Commuter buses carry business people and other workers who live in the suburbs to their big-city jobs quickly and affordably. They usually travel longer distances without stopping, so you get to your destination faster.

- These buses usually run Monday through Saturday during peak rush hour times (typically 5 a.m. to 10 a.m. and 3 p.m. to 8 p.m.), although some cities have extended service from 5 a.m. to midnight.
- Riders usually leave their personal vehicle at a Park and Ride location, then catch the bus for the trip to the city.
- Commuter buses usually accept cash and bus passes. You can get a good discount if you buy a monthly pass, although you'll also get a discount on a daily or weekly bus pass.
- As with local bus systems, you can buy passes at the bus station, online, or at other designated ticket sellers.

Subways

Subways (a.k.a. "metro systems") aren't as prevalent in North America as they are in Europe and on other continents, but if you have a subway nearby, it's a great way to get around. Major cities in North America like Mexico City, New York, Chicago, Washington, Los Angeles, and Toronto have their own rapid transit systems, and the trains run frequently every day of the year. As with local buses, it's important to be vigilant when you're riding them to avoid trouble. You can purchase subway fares and passes right at the subway station.

Intercity Bus Companies

There are bus services within North America such as Greyhound that transport people from one town to next.

Rail

North Americans don't travel by rail as much as people in the rest of the world, but the rail system is there if you need it.

- The US passenger rail line is called Amtrak; in Canada, it's VIA Rail. Both offer high-speed intercity rail service and cross-country travel and, especially in Canada, they service remote areas.
- Europe has outstanding rail and train systems throughout.
- Rail trips are a great way to see North America, and both Amtrak and VIA Rail offer vacation packages.

Carpooling

A great way to get around cost effectively while doing something to save the planet is by carpooling. Also known as ride sharing, carpooling is a way for two or more people to travel together to work or other destinations. This saves gas, parking costs, tolls, and wear and tear on personal vehicles—and your nerves. Carpooling is also environmentally friendly; carbon emissions that can harm Mother Earth are reduced when the number of vehicles on the road goes down.

Carpooling works best when the participants live close to each other or can get to a central meeting place, and if they all work at the same place or close by. If each person in the pool takes his or her turn driving, then that person handles the expenses. If one person prefers to do all the driving, the other carpoolers should contribute an agreed-upon amount of money to offset the cost of gas and other expenses.

Taxicab

If you need a lift unexpectedly or other transportation isn't available, try a taxicab. In cities with dense populations like New York and Toronto, you'll find cabs trolling the streets, looking for fares. Otherwise, you'll have to call for a ride. Cab companies are easy to find using your smartphone or the Yellow Pages.

Alternatives to Taxis

The entire world is witnessing a huge revolution in taxi services through new brands that provide on-demand rides. You can now download applications for these brands and order the service from the comfort of your hand-held device. Learn more about some of these major services: Uber, Lyft, Curb.

Special Needs

The availability of transportation other than a car for those with special needs is one of the most important priorities of European countries and governments. Various options allow their citizens to travel with ease, safety, and more importantly choice. This provides opportunities for more spontaneous travel and choice flexibility in order to enable users to reach their desired destinations.

- A family of services enables travelers to select the one that best suits their requirements.
- Conventional public transport services are sometimes accessible to passengers in wheelchairs.
- Some buses have mechanisms and spaces to enable you to carry your bicycle with you.
- Some bus service routes use small vehicles that pick up and discharge passengers close to their origin and destination. This service is

particularly appropriate for areas where demand is low (for example, in rural areas).

- Conventional taxis often offer user-side subsidies in order to reduce the fare for senior citizens or the disabled.
- Dial-a-Ride service exists for door-to-door travel for passengers who require assistance or who use a wheelchair that cannot be accommodated by a taxi or a bus.
- Accessible pedestrian infrastructure allows access to all transport services and to make journeys wholly on foot or by (powered) wheelchair or scooter.

Other Ways to Get Around

Bicycling

Depending on where you live, you may find that your city has bike paths you can use to get around town safely. A word of caution: buy a bicycle lock and chain to deter theft when you leave your bike unattended, or take it inside your building.

Walking

Though not strictly a form of transportation, walking is a viable way to get around. It's true that because America and Canada are both so large, and the US is so car crazy, not a lot of people choose this healthy and cost-effective way to get where they're going. But major urban centers—New York, Chicago, Seattle, Boston, and Toronto, for instance—are laid out to walk around comfortably. Just be sure to have the price of a bus ticket or a taxicab in your pocket in case the going gets tough due to weather or fatigue.

Shopping

No matter whether you just shop for the necessities you need from day-to-day, or you love to "shop 'til you drop," you'll find the variety of merchandise and stores where you can buy things is breathtaking virtually everywhere you go in the Western world. Even places with sparse populations—like Wyoming or Nunavut—have an impressive selection of whatever you need.

Read here about the various places you can spend your hard-earned dollars, from brick-and-mortar stores to online storefronts, as well as the various ways you can pay for those purchases.

This guidebook uses North America as an example of shopping heaven! Other Western world countries also are known as perfect destination for shopping from design shops, second hand shopping, outlets and malls.

If you've lived in North America for any length of time, you probably are well aware that bigger is better here. We have big cars, bigger houses, enormous parks, and humungous packages of cereal purchased from huge grocery stores. So you might find it hard to believe that North Americans also like smaller shopping venues that probably resemble the types of small businesses you shopped in back in your home country. Here's a look at the various types of stores from which you can choose.

Mom-and-Pop Corner Stores

This type of business is very small and is usually run by the owner and possibly a helper or two. A mom-and-pop shop can be as small as an outdoor roadside stand that sells vegetables in the summer to a small store that shares space with other small businesses in a brick-and-mortar building. Because they're so small, they usually don't have their own building. Also, they're not just run by moms and pops; that's just a colorful name for them. Mom-and-pop stores can sell anything from produce to jewelry. They're fun to shop in because the owner, who may be willing to negotiate a better price, runs them. It never hurts to ask.

Boutiques

This type of store is also usually quite small and specializes in fashionable, one-of-a-kind, and often expensive items like wedding gowns, designer clothing, and jewelry. There are even food boutiques that sell upscale items like caviar and fine wine. You may find a boutique inside a high-end store (like Nordstrom or Saks Fifth Avenue) or sharing space with other pricey boutiques in a resort town. And those stores you find at the airport, like the duty-free shop? They're a type of boutique, too.

Of course, not all boutiques are high-end. Rather, what makes a boutique unique and fun to explore is its specialty merchandise, which may include everything from handmade beaded jewelry to trendy or funky clothing, shoes, handbags, and even bed linens.

Small businesses like the mom-and-pop stores and boutiques have their own promotional days.

Chain Stores

A store that can be found in numerous cities and sells the same type of merchandise in each location is known as a chain store. Dollar stores are chain stores and can be found everywhere from Walla Walla, Washington, in the Pacific Northwest, to Orlando, Florida, in the southeast. This is handy when you move from city to city—you always know what the store will carry, no matter where you are. Chain stores usually have their own building and are located in a retail area next to other stores. Target, Kohl's, and Macy's are all chain stores.

Chain stores tend to be department stores—that is, they have numerous departments selling a wide variety of merchandise, all under the same roof. For example, at Target, you can shop for clothing, handbags, sporting goods, electrical items, furnishings, prescriptions, and food all in the same store.

Big Box Stores

This type of store is usually a chain store, too. But it differs from department stores in that big box stores normally are *huge*. They often specialize in a certain type of merchandise, like electronics (Best Buy) or building supplies (The Home Depot). The name "big box" refers to the interior of the building—it's usually wide open with no frills, just like a big box. For this reason, you'll usually need a shopping cart to carry your purchases from one end of the building to the other.

Supermarkets

Basically, a supermarket is a big box store for food and household products, organized into product aisles.

- Most products are self-serve, meaning you pick them off the shelves yourself and take them to the checkout counter.
- Exceptions to the self-serve rule include (1) the meat counter, where

a clerk will package the fresh, prime cut of meat or fish you choose, or will slice and package luncheon meat and cheese; and (2) the bakery department, which generally stores the fresh cakes, bagels, and other products in a display counter.

- Of course, you can also choose prepackaged meat, fish, cheese, and other products right out of the refrigerated cases so you don't have to wait in line.
- Usually, unprocessed fresh products such as vegetable, fruit, dairy products, and meats fill the perimeter of the store; processed products fill the central aisles.
- In addition, supermarkets often have nonfood departments, like a pharmacy and a florist, and some even have bank branches, post office locations, and coffee shops, as well as a gas station in the parking lot.
- Not all supermarkets are big box stores—smaller supermarkets abound, too. These stores have a smaller selection of merchandise, which is handy if you only need a few things or you don't like shopping in a huge store.

Membership Warehouse and Wholesale Clubs

Speaking of big stores, the largest retail stores around are known as membership warehouse and wholesale clubs.

- This type of big box store usually looks just like a warehouse, with shelves of merchandise stacked as high as the very high ceiling, and giant bins of fresh produce, meat, fish, and whatever else you need.
- These types of stores are no-frills, meaning they're very basic. Although warehouse stores do tend to sell more than just food, you won't find specialty shops like a florist inside—although you might find bunches of flowers in a bucket on the floor.
- Also, you have to buy a *lot* of whatever you're shopping for. Everything is sold in multiples—for example, you might have to buy ten boxes of macaroni and cheese in a single package, five jars of spaghetti sauce, or twenty-five rolls of paper towels. Items are sold this way to keep the prices down, since purchasing a higher quantity leads to bigger savings.
- If the packages are too large for your family—or your pantry—consider splitting the package and the cost with other family members and friends.

- Warehouse clubs you may have heard of include Sam's Club, Costco, and BJ's Wholesale Club.
- You have to be a member to shop in one of these stores. Besides paying an annual membership fee, you'll pay an extra percentage on the total bill when you check out. Even so, you can save a lot of money shopping at warehouse clubs.
- Just be sure you have enough room to store all your discounted treasures.

Convenience Stores

At the other end of the shopping spectrum—that is, the small end—is the convenience store. Like the name says, they're a convenient place to shop when you just need a few things.

Stores like 7-Eleven and Circle K, and drug stores like CVS and Shoppers Drug Mart are convenience stores. In some cases, you can do a lot of your grocery shopping at a convenience store, since they generally have everything a grocery store carries except the fresh items like meat, fish, fruit, and vegetables. But beware: You'll pay extra—and sometimes a *lot* extra—for that convenience. But if you're in a hurry, convenience stores are a great place to shop.

Strip Malls

Speaking of convenience, if you're looking for a smaller shopping venue where you can buy a variety of items, then a strip mall may be the place for you. Strip malls are usually in well-populated areas, and consist of a bunch of stores connected to each other in a line or a strip. The stores tend to be one-of-a-kind shops or smaller chain stores, although it's possible to find a strip mall that is anchored by a larger retailer, like Sears or J.C. Penney. Typical strip malls include businesses like clothing stores, a hair and nail salon, a cellular service company, a package delivery company (like UPS, FedEx), and possibly a restaurant.

Because strip mall stores are smaller, they tend to charge higher prices. But like convenience stores, they allow you to find your item, make your purchase, and get out fast, which can make the extra cost worth it.

Malls

Another variation on the many-stores-in-one-place theme is the shopping mall. While some malls have outdoor access to their various tenants, most malls are enclosed.

- Inside, all of the stores open into a main arcade, which makes shopping and browsing easier, and protecting you from really cold and overly hot weather conditions outside.
- Malls generally are anchored by large department stores, such as J.C. Penney, Macy's, and Dillard's in the United States; and The Bay, Marks & Spencer (or as the locals call it, "Marks & Sparks"), and Zellers in Canada.
- Malls will also have a variety of other stores and amenities under their roof, including shoe stores, music stores, bookstores, and more.
- Many malls have tenants with reasonably priced or discounted goods. But some malls, especially in cities like Houston, Los Angeles, Scottsdale, and Miami, to name just a few, have tenants with extremely expensive merchandise.
- You can get a reasonable idea about how expensive the retailers are by the mix of stores. If the mall is anchored by either Eaton's, J.C. Penney, or TJ Maxx, the prices will be appealing to the average person. But a mall that features Neiman Marcus, Saks Fifth Avenue, and Bloomingdale's will be much more upscale and expensive.

Off-Price Stores

So what do you do if you're on a budget or you're a bargain hunter? You certainly can get deals in traditional stores by shopping sales and clearance events. But for everyday off-price shopping, you might want to try the following shopping venues:

Farmers Markets

Generally run by the people who grow the vegetables or raise the animals whose meat they sell, farmers markets offer fresh food at reasonable prices. They can do this because they don't have the overhead of the big grocery stores. Depending on the climate, many farmers markets are open air, or they might have a canopy or roof over them.

Orchards, Berry Farms, and Vegetable Patches

If you're willing to pick your own apples off a tree or harvest ears of corn right from the field, then these pick-your-own-produce farms are a great source of extremely fresh and reasonably priced food.

Roadside Stands

Wherever you see fruit and vegetables growing, you're likely to see a roadside stand, which is usually just a table or a small covered stand at the side of the road. Bring your own bag and cash if you shop there. Purchasing is often based on a system of trust—you take what you want and drop your money in a box—the grower is off looking after the crops.

Outlet Malls

If you're looking for good quality, brand-name merchandise, chances are there's an outlet mall in your area that sells it at discounted prices.

- The merchandise in an outlet mall often consists of past-season items, products that are flawed in some way, factory overruns (caused when a factory makes more items than can be sold), and so on.
- Many outlet malls sell low- to mid-priced items, but some sell designer clothing and upscale products. For example, the stores at Birch Run Premium Outlets (one of the largest outlet malls in the US) in Birch Run, Michigan include Coach, BCBGMAXAZRIA, Tommy Hilfiger, Longaberger, Lancôme, and Bose, to name just a few of its nearly one hundred and fifty stores.
- It's a good idea to take your iPhone or other Wi-Fi device with you when you shop the outlet stores. Sometimes, the prices aren't much better than what you'd pay in a regular retail store, and you might be getting a factory second (imperfect) item rather than something of the highest quality. If you have your phone handy, you can do some price checking while you shop. And you can also locate the person you came with, in case they have wandered off in a new direction.

Pawnshops

This type of business offers secured short-term cash loans to people who wish to pawn or sell an item temporarily. Often, people pawn "big-ticket items," or merchandise that originally cost a lot of money, such as diamond jewelry, big screen televisions, fur coats, and even luxury automobiles.

- The pawnshop holds the item for a certain length of time, like ninety days, and the seller can return during that period to "buy back" his or her item by paying back the loan plus interest.
- If an item isn't picked up, then it goes on the shelf in the pawnshop for anyone to purchase.
- You often can get very good bargains on expensive items, so it's worth taking a look.

Thrift Stores

If you're in the mood for some outrageously discounted retail therapy, head for a thrift store. They are often run by charitable organizations like the Salvation Army or Purple Heart, and they sell new and used merchandise that has been donated by caring individuals. Thrift stores have clothing, shoes, knick-knacks, books, furnishings, and tons of other stuff. Going to a thrift store is like going on a treasure hunt—you never know what you'll find, and what you do find is usually priced way below retail.

Flea Markets and Swap Meets

You won't find any fleas at a flea market—hopefully—but what you will find is a crazy mix of new and used stuff in every product category. Looking for a steel coil box for the 1913 Ford Model T you're restoring? You'll probably find one there. Or how about a steamer trunk you can use as a coffee table? Start looking. In fact, you usually have to do a *lot* of looking to find what you want or need. But for people who love flea markets, that's part of the fun. Here's something else you might like about flea markets: it's usually possible to negotiate a better price with the seller, much like you might do in your home country. People in Western countries call this "haggling," and not everyone will do it. But it never hurts to ask.

Garage Sales

These are like flea markets on a tiny scale. A person cleans out his or her garage, house, car, and so on, puts a sign in the yard or an ad on Craigslist (discussed a little later), sets up a table, and starts selling. Garage sale items sell for just a fraction of their original cost, and you often can find brand-new and perfectly good used items. You'll need cash to shop a garage sale. No credit cards accepted.

Cable TV Shopping

A revolution in shopping via cable TV began with the debut of QVC in 1986. The network adopted its current 24/7 broadcasting schedule in 1987, and other shopping networks have followed suit. These shopping networks sell a little of everything: clothing, jewelry, upscale handbags and shoes, beauty items, kitchen and food items, electronics, and much more. Purchases are paid for with credit cards or by using the company's payment plan on certain items.

Online Shopping

Of course, these days you don't have to turn on cable TV or show up in person at a brick-and-mortar store or other physical site to buy whatever you need. You can shop online twenty-four hours a day, seven days a week on the Internet. Online shopping is also known as electronic commerce (or e-commerce), and stores that exist on the Internet are called online or virtual stores or webstores. Following is a sampling of your online shopping choices.

- Most of the stores you like are probably on the web, from Nordstrom and Target, to Pizza Hut and Dollar Tree, Coach and Payless ShoeSource. (The cable television shopping networks also have online stores.)
- One of the largest Internet stores is Amazon.com, where you can buy pretty much anything you need. But it's not just companies that are selling—it's also average people like you, who sell both new and used merchandise.
- One of the good things about Amazon is that if you buy twenty-five dollars' worth of qualifying merchandise, the order will ship free to your home or office.

- Free shipping might encourage you to spend more than you should, which is why you might want to use Amazon's online shopping cart system, where you can virtually "park" items you want until you're ready to buy them. Just wait until you have twenty-five dollars' worth of qualifying merchandise before you place an order to save the shipping costs.
- Other huge online marketplaces include Overstock.com, Walmart.com, Costco.com, and Samsclub.com (although as noted earlier in this chapter, you have to be a member of these warehouse clubs).
- EBay.com is probably the world's most famous online marketplace, where anyone can sell virtually anything, just like on Amazon.com. EBay is an auction site, meaning you have to bid on what you want and hope no one bids higher than you before the clocks runs down.
- You'll also find many "Buy It Now" auctions on eBay so you can lock in your price immediately instead of waiting for an auction to close. Whatever you win or buy outright is mailed or shipped directly to your door, but you have to pay the cost of getting it there.
- It's actually a lot of fun to look at the offerings on eBay, even if you're not buying.
- Craigslist.com is an online classified ads website. Classified ads are brief notices describing both job seekers and items for sale by their owner. Most items on Craigslist are used, which means you can get some great bargains. At Craigslist.com, type in the name of the largest city near you. That's important because the private sellers on Craigslist generally won't mail items to buyers. You have to make arrangements to pick up your new treasures.

Shopping Tips

Whether you love it or hate it, shopping is one of life's necessary chores. You need to buy food for the family, pick up new clothes for school or work, and buy other daily necessities. But while most people shop only for life's necessities, others see shopping as a fun recreational activity that in some cases can become an addiction. There's even an English word for people who shop for fun, "shopaholic."

The companies that sell us everything from toothpaste to luxury automobiles are very smart marketers. They know what to say and how to show it off to tempt us into buying things we may not need or can't afford. This can be a special problem for people who are not native English speakers, since they may not always understand exactly what they're getting into. So here are some tips to help you avoid costly shopping mistakes and make the best use of your money and time:

- Establish a budget before you shop, and make sure you don't exceed that amount.
- Be disciplined and pay off whatever you buy on credit within the credit card's thirty-day grace period.
- Buy only what you really need; don't just stroll around a store to kill time. You'll be tempted to buy things you don't need or haven't budgeted for.
- Compare prices carefully. Just because something is on sale doesn't mean it's cheaper at that store—it just means the retailer has discounted the item. You might find the same item cheaper elsewhere.
- Go for the best quality you can afford. Paying a little more for an item that will last longer is the wisest choice. This is particularly important when it comes to big-ticket items like appliances and furniture.
- Watch out for "bait-and-switch" techniques, in which a retailer lures you into the store with an advertised "low" price, then tries to sell you a higher priced product instead.
- Avoid paying with a credit card. A Dun & Bradstreet study showed that people spend up to 18 percent more when using a credit card instead of cash.
- Carry just one credit card with you when you shop. You won't be tempted to buy more stuff because you can spread the total cost over more than one card.
- Don't shop when you're in a bad mood, or if you're hungry or tired. You may be tempted to buy something to make yourself feel better.
- Bring a family member or a trusted friend along when you're purchasing a big-ticket item, like a wide-screen television or a car. A companion can help you avoid making a bad purchase and remind you to stick to your budget.
- Ignore a "limited time" deal, which is often just a trick to get you into a store and isn't really limited. Worse yet, the "deal" may actually cost more.
- Shop at the end of each season, when retailers clear out items to make

room for new merchandise. You can often get a great deal during clearance sales.
- Want a bargain? Some of the best bargains are found at garage sales, pawnshops, flea markets, auctions, liquidation centers, off-price stores, book fairs, art shows, Christmas markets, and thrift shops, as well as in the classified section of the newspaper or on Craigslist.
- Use coupons and read grocery store circulars to find weekly specials that can save you lots of money.

Your New Country's National Particulars

Familiarize Yourself with Your New World's Realities

Each country of origin (even regions within the same country) has its own customs, practices, food preferences. It is rewarding to learn these attributes while you add your own values to your new locale.

National Anthem

You are now in a new home and a country that could well be your permanent place of living, so listen and learn the national anthem of your new host country. One of my favorite moments while enjoying the Olympics and other sporting events is listening to the national anthems of countries. I get goose bumps when I listen, no matter which country! It is a matter of having respect for others. The world is not only about you or me!

National Symbols

It's important to learn about some of the national symbols of your new host country. Here are a few samples of the United States of America's symbols:

- Mount Rushmore National Memorial
- The Bald Eagle
- The Great Seal of the United States
- The Liberty Bell
- The Lincoln Memorial

- The Statue of Liberty
- The US Capitol
- The US flag (fifty stars on a field of blue; thirteen stripes)
- The White House

National Holidays

Know exactly when and what is the purpose for the national holidays of your new host country. Here are some main holidays observed worldwide:

- New Year's Day: January 1
- Labor Day: first Monday of September in the US; International Workers' Day: May 1 in European countries
- Columbus Day: second Monday in October
- Veterans Day: November 11 in North America; Anzac Day; April 25 in Australia and New Zealand
- Thanksgiving Day: in the fall (for example, the fourth Thursday in November in the US; second Monday of October in Canada; near the harvest moon in the United Kingdom
- Christmas Day: December 25

Other Celebrations and Observances

While these are not federal holidays, the following observances are celebrated unofficially in most Western countries:

- Valentine's Day: February 14
- Earth Day: April 22
- Mother's Day: second Sunday of May
- Father's Day: third Sunday of June
- Patriot Day: September 11
- Halloween: October 31
- Pearl Harbor Day: December 7

To learn the meaning behind these holidays and observances, peruse your host country's national website.

Ethnic and Religious Holidays

Various ethnic and religious groups celebrate various dates with special meaning, even though these are not national holidays. For example, Christians celebrate the resurrection of Jesus Christ at Easter; Jews observe their high holy days in September or October; Muslims celebrate Ramadan; Africans and African Americans celebrate Kwanzaa.

Chapter Six: Education

A Good Education Is Precious

Education is one of the most precious things you can earn, and it remains part of who you are for a lifetime. It opens the doors to greater job opportunities, which can increase income. It boosts economic growth and business opportunities, which can improve the standard of living for the populace and reduce poverty. It can even foster peace, since education helps one develop a broader worldview, introspection, and more tolerance, characteristics that are necessary to develop peaceful relations among people.

This chapter covers the educational systems in general around the world. The systems in general actually share a number of similarities. I reference the most universal systems.

In my lifelong experience in dealing with thousands who are trying to advance, find solutions, and manage, my main question has always been, "How confident do you feel that your skills will take you through to the end of your career?" My next question is "How confident do you feel about advising your children on the education that will prepare them for their own futures?"

As we all know, globalization and technology are both destroying jobs and creating them. It really depends on where you are and the pace of growth within your social and business sectors. It is fair to say that all occupations will go through amazing changes.

Some Facts About Education

Here are some facts about education in our twenty-first century.

- Education and training systems are not keeping pace with the rapid changes and the escalating destruction of jobs.
- Studies indicate that 66 percent of children entering primary school will take jobs that do not yet exist and for which their education will fail to prepare them.
- This clearly creates massive skill gaps and future unemployment globally.

- It is also a fact that major training and skill-building programs continue to be underdeveloped and unable to support learning for the currently active workforce of nearly 7.5 billion people around the world.
- Outdated cultural norms and current institutional standards create roadblocks for the majority of the world's talent.
- On the other hand, despite the inspiring women's movement around the world, the rise in education levels, and the focus on worldwide issues in this twenty-first century, the participation of women in general in paid workforce remains unacceptably low globally. This is particularly true in underdeveloped countries.

More Facts About Education

Experience has proven that the best-educated people are often those who are known as "self-made," or self-educated. It takes more than a college degree to make one a person of education.

- Any person who is educated is one who has learned to get whatever he wants in life without violating the rights of others.
- Education consists, not so much of knowledge, but of knowledge effectively and persistently applied. **People are paid, not merely for what they know, but more particularly for what they do with what they know.**
- While education is vital for all children, it's especially crucial to help equip refugee children to succeed in work and life.
- Education is also a key contribution to keeping alive the hope of refugees, and in situations in which despair is so prevalent, going to school, learning, acquiring knowledge and skills are fundamental.

Atta's Take on Education

Education is rewarding. I love the word "rewarding"; it fits education properly. Something that I am personally very proud of as I think of the life I have lived is the fulfillment of learning from others, which in turn allowed me the ability to pour my education into other people's lives. That quality tops it all for me! So pour your education into others' lives by teaching and helping them. Nothing is more rewarding than giving and adding value in any way you can. It is the best thing you can do for people.

It is a fact that educational systems are behind the mark on keeping up with the pace of change today; in most cases, they are disconnected from real labor markets. The real key areas in my mind that require attention are early childhood education; aggressive professional, technical, and vocational training; better exposure to digital fluency; openness to education innovation; and, critically, a new approach to lifelong learning.

In my view, education must be compulsory and FREE for all children around the world. Realistically, the age at which students can end their studies by choice varies by country, but it is usually sixteen or seventeen years old. Early departure must be completely discontinued as part of humanity's expectation, because it can greatly impact a child's social development, overall contribution, and future earnings potential.

Bottom line, the short- and long-term challenges along with unprecedented geopolitical issues, mass migration, economic and demographic factors, and promising new technologies are enormous. Skill gaps in the workforce are more difficult than ever for both workers and organizations. All this paves the way for new occupations and skill-building opportunities for our growing world population. There will certainly not be any shortage of jobs but appropriate skills education will be key. You need to become a continual learning machine in order to be successful.

Public School System

The public school system in most countries is tax-subsidized, meaning it's provided at no charge to schools funded by property and school taxes, levied regionally. The public education, known as the K-12 system in North America because it teaches students from kindergarten up to grade twelve—consists of the following levels:

Preschool

Preschool (a.k.a. "nursery school") is for children as young as six weeks old. Often, parents elect to enroll their child in nursery school because both are employed, so the school acts as a type of day care. The overriding goal of nursery schools is to socialize their small charges. Naturally, at the earliest ages, infants and babies benefit more from cuddling and early developmental activities, but as soon as they are ready, play-based education helps them develop mentally, emotionally, and physically. Nursery school is not usually considered to be part of the K-12 educational systems, and so parents must pay for their children to attend.

Kindergarten

Kindergarten is for children aged four to five. The focus is still on play-based activities, as well as on arts and crafts, singing, and other activities that develop intellectual, creative, and social skills. Focus is also on developing the children's self-esteem, cultural identity, independence, and individual strengths. Children's time in kindergarten also will include outside activities (weather permitting), story time, snacks (no doubt the reason why adults universally look forward to lunch while on the job), and nap time to recharge for the next task. Children will learn their letters and numbers, start learning how to read and use a computer (if they haven't used one at home already), and learn how to speak better.

Elementary School

Elementary school (also known as primary school) is for children ages six to twelve. Elementary school runs from first through fifth or sixth grade and focuses on subjects such as math, reading, language arts (writing), science, history, and social studies. Students are often introduced to foreign languages like Spanish in elementary school (particularly in the Southwestern United States), and art and music may also be part of the curriculum. The educational mix varies from one school district to the next. Students usually earn a diploma upon successful completion of their studies.

Junior High School

Also known as middle school and secondary school, junior high school educates students aged twelve to fourteen as they work their way up from either grade six or seven to grade eight. Students continue the studies begun in elementary school but at a more advanced level. They're also likely to take computer, art, drama, and physical education classes. Students who graduate earn a diploma.

High School

Students at this level are aged fourteen to eighteen and they progress from grades nine through twelve. The high school curriculum is the most rigorous in the public school system and is often seen as preparation for college. Honors classes or college prep classes are offered specifically for this purpose. Most subjects are taken for the entire four years of high school and they include the following:

- language arts including literature, linguistics, and specific languages
- math (usually a sequence that includes algebra, geometry, trigonometry, calculus, and statistics)
- sciences (biology, chemistry, physics, and earth-space sciences)
- social studies (local and world history and government, economics, geography)

Many of these classes are available as advanced placement classes meant to help students excel on college application tests. In addition, many high schools in the United States require students to take at least one year of foreign language instruction (most often Spanish, French, or German), as well as a year of computer applications. Other countries will provide different language options such as Chinese, Latin, and Welsh. Physical education and the arts generally round out the curriculum.

Gifted students typically take advanced placement courses and may actually graduate in three years rather than four. All students earn a diploma at the end of their high school studies. Students who enter high school but drop out before completing their four years of schooling can earn a General Equivalency Diploma (GED), which is a high school equivalency credential. They must take a test to demonstrate their proficiency in reading, writing, math, science, and social studies. These students may also have to take high-school-level classes to prepare for passing the exam.

Receiving Grades in Public Education

The grading scale differs depending on the educational level. Children in kindergarten usually aren't graded, per se, while children in grades one and two typically receive grades of S ("satisfactory"), meaning the student meets the grade level requirement; P ("progressing"), meaning the student is making progress that doesn't quite meet grade level standards; or U ("unsatisfactory") meaning the student is not making progress nor meeting grade level standards. From grade three and beyond, the academic grading scale usually is A (excellent), B (above average), C (satisfactory), D (below average), and F (unsatisfactory or failing). Some school districts use a plus-minus system to make grades even more representative of achievement. For example, an excellent grade might be expressed as A+, A, or A-. An unsatisfactory grade of F is always expressed simply as F (no F+ or F-).

Some schools, including the Montessori schools mentioned below, don't award letter grades at all, preferring instead to provide written and oral narratives documenting a child's success, supported with a portfolio of their work. Whether or not grades are awarded depends on the schools' educational philosophy.

Alternatives to Public K-12 Education

There are many alternatives to public education, because not everyone chooses the traditional public school route. Following are some other options.

Charter Schools

Charter schools are public schools (for ages fourteen to eighteen) that are similar to a private school. Incoming students are selected by lottery, because there are only so many available spots each year; they pay tuition if they're fortunate enough to be selected. Charter schools tend to have more rigorous standards and use more innovative teaching methods than public schools.

International Baccalaureate Schools

For children aged three to nineteen, International Baccalaureate (IB) schools "help develop the intellectual, personal, emotional, and social skills to live, learn, and work in a rapidly globalizing world," according to the IB website (ibo.org). Classes are student-led, with teachers acting more like mentors than educators. The theory is that students learn more when they're immersed in the learning process. IB programs also emphasize critical thinking, writing, and group activities, and require students to participate in various community service activities. There are currently more than 4,600 IB schools in the world, plus some public schools have their own IB program as part of their standard curriculum.

Parochial Schools

Parochial schools are private primary and secondary schools (no kindergarten) that are supported by religious organizations. Most of the parochial schools in the United States are affiliated with Roman Catholic parishes, but other religions—including Evangelical Protestant, Lutheran, Muslim, Orthodox Jew, and Seventh-day Adventist—also offer parochial schools. Parochial schools charge students tuition to attend.

Private Schools

These grade-one-to-twelve schools are independent of state and local jurisdictions and are funded by tuition rather than public taxation. As a result, enrollment is selective and based on entrance examinations. Day schools and boarding schools are examples of private schools.

Montessori Method Schools

Public schools that teach the Montessori Method operate independently of local and state jurisdiction and they charge tuition. The Montessori Method calls for students to work in mixed-age classrooms in three- to six-year age-range groups (for example, ages zero to three; three to six; and so on), through age eighteen. They work and learn in uninterrupted three-hour blocks of time. In addition to academic pursuits, Montessori schools focus on character education to encourage students to become self-sufficient, polite, considerate, and helpful.

Home Schooling

Home schooling can be a great way to educate your kids, especially if you have any concerns about the curriculum or the safety of the local school district. Keep in mind, though, that home schooling can be as much or more work for you as it is for your kids. It will depend on your approach as to how you devise and select from the curriculum, researching and buying educational materials, organizing educational field trips, and keeping your already rambunctious kids in line and motivated. For these reasons, some parents choose to employ a tutor instead to do the deed. Home schooling is legal in most Western countries, though it is illegal in some, such as Germany. Research and read about the education laws in your country.

Higher Education

Beyond grade twelve, students have the option to either go directly into the job market or to continue with their schooling and get a vocational certificate, a diploma, or a college degree. Higher education (a.k.a. "post-secondary education") is also known as tertiary education.

Post-Secondary Preparation Guide

Following is a guide for successful college preparation, along with the recommended timing.

During Junior High School

College preparation can begin as early as age eleven and twelve when students are in grade six.

- It is best to take the most challenging classes.
- Make a list of the classes you plan to take.
- Develop goals, actions, and practice sessions with the help of parents and teachers.
- Volunteer in your community.
- Determine your areas of interest.
- Try various skill assessment tests in those areas.
- Engage with counselors and parents about careers that interest you.
- Sign up for summer school enrichment programs.

During Freshman and Sophomore Years in High School

The freshman and sophomore years in high school are the first and second, grades eight and nine, when students are aged fourteen and older. Plans for the future can start to solidify.

- Retake various skill-assessment tests to establish potential career options.
- Discuss options and the education required for your desired careers with school counselors.
- Review college expense options and plans with your parents.
- Research and find out your school's requirement and program preparation for taking the SAT and the ACT college tests.
- Participate in extracurricular activities.
- Sign up for the challenging classes to improve your knowledge and skills.
- Sign up for college credit classes.

During Junior Year

Junior year in high school is grade eleven when students are aged sixteen and older. College preparation starts to get really serious.

- Attend college and financial aid events and programs.
- Seek help from mentors.
- Mentor others.
- Take the Preliminary SAT (PSAT) during early fall in preparation for taking the SAT.
- Explore future career options; investigate the type of education needed.
- Research university and college websites; request materials and information.
- Visit schools that interest you.
- Participate in as many extracurricular activities as possible.
- Ask for financial aid and admissions forms.
- Sign up for classes that provide college credits.
- Take the ACT, which is available on several dates from the fall to the following summer, or the SAT, which is only available in the fall and winter.
- Enroll in available enrichment programs.
- Save money for college by working a part-time job.
- Look for paid internship programs.

- Continue to research and learn about various private scholarship options.

During Senior Year: Fall

The last year of high school requires the most intense preparation for college, beginning in the first term.

- Take the most difficult and challenging classes.
- Narrow down your potential career choices by taking career-interest assessment tests.
- Participate in extracurricular activities.
- Volunteer in various community activities.
- Create a résumé of your academic and athletic activities and achievements.
- Visit campuses of schools you're interested in.
- Narrow down the list of potential colleges.
- Explore various facilities to get a good feel for what college life will be like.
- Check out school facilities, transportation options, community and sporting venues
- Sit in on a class or two.
- Talk to students and a couple of instructors.
- Meet with an admissions counselor and a financial aid counselor.

During Senior Year: December to February

College preparation activities ramp up.

- Apply to the colleges that interest you. Be sure to retain copies of your applications.
- Review your college payment plan and financial aid options.
- Apply for scholarships offered by the colleges that you apply to.
- Apply for financial aid right after January. Be sure to make the previous year's income tax information available.

During Senior Year: March to May

Your high school graduation is looming; it's time to make decisions.

- Follow up on your applications and review your offers of admission.

- Choose from among your offers.
- Make sure your school has sent your transcript to the college that has accepted you based on your final marks.
- Notify the college of your choice that you will be attending.
- Notify any colleges that have accepted you that you will be going elsewhere.
- Send required fees to the college of your choice.

During the Summer Following Your Senior Year

Congratulations. You have graduated from school. Life is about to change in a big way.

- Get a job; save as much money as possible.
- Review all college-orientation material thoroughly.
- Find somewhere to live during the upcoming college terms.
- Familiarize yourself with your college living conditions.
- Find a roommate (if one is not assigned).
- Establish communications with your future roommate. Meet in person to get to know each other.

Help from the Community

Migrant communities and parents often have high aspirations for their children, and can provide support that will help students in school matters and general life issues.

- Community members can motivate children along their educational path and further their involvement in society.
- Conversely, a lack of community involvement in formal educational matters and mismanagement of education policies may negatively affect the integration of immigrants and their children, with significant social and economic costs.
- In light of the mass migration of refugees during the last few years, the majority of Western countries may need to evaluate and structure their educational initiatives better and help improve integration and social cohesion.
- Canada, with its approach to welcoming refugees (through language classes and free college education), is an excellent example of a country that is successfully integrating migrants.

Post-Secondary Student Life

Your First Semester

Study hard and make your parents proud! There is nothing more rewarding and proud-making for parents than watching their children growing and following the right path in life. The students themselves have many new experiences to take into account within their new communities.

Roommate Relationships

Living with someone they didn't know before, learning to negotiate new freedoms, and finding their own voices are all valuable learning processes. Whereas living with someone unknown can be new and exciting, it is not necessarily devoid of challenges.

Beyond the Campus

Whether living on campus or in the local neighborhood, students technically are representatives of the university to the community-at-large. Educational institutions expect students to adhere to the same high standards of conduct and behavior that are consistent with the students' developing role as responsible and accountable citizens.

Alcohol, Drugs, and Biases

While community colleges, colleges, and universities have set guidelines around the use of alcohol, marijuana, and other drugs, students will go to schools with varying experiences and biases.

- Therefore, as a component of their orientation, all new students participate in programs that address the use of alcohol, marijuana, and other drugs; sexual violence; and biased behaviors and attitudes.
- These programs are designed to facilitate safe and inclusive living and learning environments.
- I encourage you students to use these programs as opportunities to engage in conversation with your university administration and fully understand the rationale and the approach.

- Universities support students who assume personal responsibility and accountability for their actions as they learn to establish their independence.
- Colleges also recognize that the process of establishing personal independence requires support and, at times, assistance or intervention.
- On the occasion of repetitive infractions from the guidelines, as a means of support, college administrations may notify parents or legal guardians of students as they transition from high school to college. Whenever possible, the student will be involved in a discussion about their choices before a decision to notify parents or guardians takes place.

Community Values

Regardless of location or conditions, it is important and incumbent upon all students as members of the community to promote values consistent with academic and personal excellence.

Post-Secondary Institutions

Community College

A two-year post-secondary institution that offers an associate degree to people in a particular geographic location (often a city or county), as well as to those who live outside the immediate area, is known as a community college.

- Also known as a junior college, these institutions offer curricula that focus on the liberal arts and the sciences, as well as on vocational training (such as law enforcement) and technical education that allows graduates to enter the workforce right after passing their exams.
- Some people attend community college, where the tuition is less expensive, for the first two years of post-secondary education and then transfer their credits to a four-year institution, where they can earn a bachelor's degree.
- Community colleges also generally offer noncredit courses for adults through continuing education programs, and industry-specific training that doesn't lead to a degree.

- A high school diploma or General Equivalency Diploma (GED) is necessary to attend.

Degree-Granting Facilities

Degree-granting facilities are institutions of higher learning that—at the least—offer four-year, undergraduate Bachelor of Arts and Bachelor of Science degrees. These bachelor degrees may also lead the way for someone to gain a master's degree and a doctorate.

These facilities are called by a variety of terms. Many people assume that the term "college" refers to a private institution and "university" refers to a state-funded school, or some may think a university provides better education than a college. Colleges are smaller institutions that typically offer undergraduate degrees. (As previously mentioned, junior colleges and community colleges offer only two-year degrees.) In fact, the difference between a university and a college and a school (a term that's also used at the degree-granting level of education) can be quite confusing. Generally speaking, universities are able to provide more diverse programs and classes than colleges, due to their larger enrolment numbers. For that reason, "university" is the term that will stand in this book for all these degree-granting facilities.

Admission to most universities is very competitive. Applicants must have a certain high school grade-point average (GPA) upon application, meet expectations on a standardized college admission test (such as the SAT or the ACT), and submit letters of recommendation and an admission essay. Students can also transfer to a university after they have successfully completed their two years at a community college. Those who qualify and are admitted may come from any locale but students from outside the immediate market area usually pay higher tuition. Because many people come from outside the area, universities usually offer on-campus, dormitory-style housing. They may have a high percentage of students who commute as well.

Universities may also offer medical and law degrees. Some may offer other special programs to students who can earn both an undergraduate degree and a graduate degree in a short amount of time. Many universities offer graduate-level (post-bachelor) degrees, including Masters of Arts, Masters of Science, and doctorate degrees (including Doctor of Philosophy (PhD) and Doctor of Education (EdD). It can take an additional two to three years of full-time study to earn a master's degree after earning a bachelor's degree;

and three to five years full time, depending on the field of study, to earn a doctorate.

Medical degrees (Medical Doctor (MD), Doctor of Osteopathic Medicine (DO), Doctor of Dental Surgery (DDS), and others), which are equivalent to doctorates, take four years or more of full-time post-bachelor education working at a hospital, whereas a law degree (Doctor of Jurisprudence (JD)) generally requires three years of post-bachelor education.

Online and Distance Education

Many colleges and universities, including some of the nation's most prestigious, offer online courses that allow students to complete many or all of their degree requirements in a virtual environment rather than in person, and with the same course load and schedule as in a face-to-face class. This is a great time-saver for students, especially those who are pros at using technology to manage their time. But working from the comfort of home robs students of the college experience—absorbing course material in real time in the classroom, interacting and bantering with other students and professors, and soaking up the rarified feel of higher education. Still, it's a viable option for those who are motivated to complete the coursework as assigned.

Trade and Vocational Schools

Vocational schools offer coursework that is specific to the trades and vocations covered. They never or only rarely provide instruction in liberal arts and other core fields found in colleges. Trade school courses prepare students for careers as computer-aided designers and drafters, automotive technicians, electricians, machinists, commercial truck drivers, and other callings. They also generally assist graduates with finding employment. It takes as little as a few months to earn a diploma, and students pay tuition to attend. Whereas a full week at a degree-granting facility might actually fill only ten to twenty hours in an arts program and twenty to thirty hours in a science, a full week at a trade school fills thirty-five hours a week with heavy homework expectations.

Atta's Lesson on Upgrading One's Education

I feel extremely lucky that I had a very disciplined and diverse education in my early years. But when I came to the United States, I found myself completely overwhelmed by the system, and at first couldn't figure out how to use my skills and education. To combat this, I enrolled in various classes and training courses to improve my skills.

I believe this happens to most immigrants who enter North America. They are overwhelmed by the job market and are upset to find that the education and credentials acquired in their homeland may not be recognized here. So instead of trying to fix that, they sit back and go through their lives without trying.

This is a sad and costly fact within many immigrant communities. But this doesn't have to happen to you. Look for ways to broaden your knowledge and expand your expertise. There are many online courses and other education programs to upgrade and enhance your education and skills.

Adult Education

Many school districts offer reasonably priced, introductory-level classes to motivated adults through their community adult education programs. Classes run the gamut from business pursuits (accounting, marketing, and so on) to leisure-time activities such as watercolor painting and low-impact aerobics. Adult education classes are a great place to learn computer and Internet skills.

The Internet has made adult education outside the classroom both easy and rewarding. The majority of universities, colleges, and schools in virtually many Western countries now offer noncredit distance-learning opportunities, which are great for people who work nontraditional hours, who are too far away from a brick-and-mortar classroom, who cannot leave home, or who prefer to work at their own pace.

Literacy Classes

Be sure to ask about literacy classes that may be available in your community.

These classes focus on improving students' language skills in reading, speaking, and writing. There's usually no charge for these classes but be sure to research that first.

Alternatively, you may be able to take a low-cost class through the continuing education department of your local community college. And don't forget to look for the English as a Second Language (ESL) websites on the Internet, which have exercises, reading materials, and quizzes to help you improve your skills.

Never Stop Learning

Your local library is a great place to continue your own education, even if you've been out of school for years. This free resource is packed with printed books, books on tape, newspapers, and magazines. If the library is large enough, it may even have books in your native language. But now that you're a resident of the Western world, it's a good idea to work on the language skills of your country. Pick up materials written at a level just slightly more difficult than you can read now. That will challenge you to work harder. Or try reading books written for middle school or high school students. The writing style will be less complicated and the vocabulary will be easier.

Paying for It All

Financial Assistance

Between tuition and fees, books and living expenses, attending a community college, a trade school, or a university is a very expensive proposition. But the good news is financial assistance may be available to help put your child through college.

- Gifted children may be eligible for scholarships, while others may be able to secure low-interest government loans that come due after a grace period at the end of the loan (typically six to nine months).
- Other forms of financial aid, like grants, may also be available, but you have to go looking for them early enough to secure them when you need them. Banks and lending companies are the top places to go for financial aid loans, but other reliable sources include private

organizations such as clubs and religious groups, regional governments, and the colleges and universities themselves.
- Start the search for financial aid by filling out the appropriate form. It must be filled out before the deadline imposed by the school you're applying for, so be sure to fill it out and submit it early.
- Research and learn about student loan programs within your host countries and communities.
- A number of grants that do not have to be paid back are also available.
- Most European countries provide free higher education programs but it's a good idea to research and learn about them in your host country. For general information and updates about various student programs refer to www.attamoves.com.

Savings Plans

Loans and scholarships aside, you'll still need to set aside funds if you wish to make college a reality for yourself or your child. Optimally, as a parent living in the Western world, you should start saving for college as soon as you bring your little one home from the hospital. Many regions have college funds that grow as your child grows and, with a little planning, will yield enough cash for him or her to enjoy the college experience without the threat of tens of thousands of dollars in debt hanging over his head.

The United States has a tax-advantaged savings plan just for saving money for college. Called the 529 plans, or qualified tuition plan, this savings vehicle gives you a safe and reliable way to save.

Yet another vehicle for saving for college is the prepaid tuition plan. Usually sponsored by state governments, this type of plan allows you to purchase "credits" toward future tuition costs, and possibly room and board expenses. It's also possible that the educational institution you're interested in may offer a prepaid plan. Similar programs exist in other Western countries. The Canadian government for example offers Canada Student Loans.

Personal Guidance

All the activities necessary to get into college can be a lot to take in, especially when you or your child is just embarking on the college application process or your English-speaking skills are still basic. So it may make sense to hire a college consultant to steer you in the right direction and help you make the right course corrections along the way. These specialists are well-versed in both the application process and the financial side of college, and can help you and your student figure out what needs to be done and when. Typically, a college consultant starts working with a client and his or her parents around the ninth grade. That gives the family and the student plenty of time to identify promising colleges and steer the student in writing the college essay and looking at course choices. In grade nine, high school and extracurricular activities like volunteering can help your student look motivated, mature, and civic-minded.

College consultants don't come cheaply. Generally speaking, you can expect to pay a minimum of $3,000 for a consulting package, which includes consultations on the college essay, high school activities, applications, and so forth. But the amount charged will vary by geographical region. This might seem like a lot of money when you're also trying to save for college tuition. But college consultants—the good ones, anyway—have a knack for matching students up with the college where they'll thrive and excel, and that can make the expense worthwhile.

To find a college consultant in the US, go to the Independent Educational Consultants Association website at www.iecaonline.com. Alternatively, you can ask friends—parents of college-aged children—if they can recommend a reputable consultant.

Student Loan

While some of the Western world's countries provide free or minimum-fee education, student loan business and debt is considered a huge burden and a credit crisis and frankly a truly ethical dilemma in the United States of America.

Here are the facts:

- The majority of students at the top-tier schools are being taken care of, but those at the lower end (in community colleges and other less-competitive institutions) are lured and forced into various forms of lending games.
- The formula is simple: the higher ranking the school, the more money one will be charged and the more likely the student will be to reap the benefits through a solid return on the loan.

- This is of course an ethical question as to whether the lenders discriminate against the much larger yet less well-educated economic chunk of the population.
- Tuition in general is on the rise in the United States more than in any other Western country. This causes a rather radical shift in student financial aid—from a system relying primarily on need-based grants to one dominated by loans.

Best Education Practices for Students

Your level of education is relative and important to the level of success you wish to achieve. So it is extremely important to commit to learning and then applying information, theories, and ideas in order to achieve personal and professional goals. Here are some best education practices for students:

- Don't procrastinate. Finishing your homework should be your number-one priority. Television and electronic devices should be accessed only after all homework assignments are completed.
- Organize your school gear. The number-one problem for failing students is a lack of organization (forgetting homework, leaving books and notes at home, and so on). Always pack your school bag in advance so you can grab it and go in the morning.
- Ask for help when you need it. It's okay if you don't understand an assignment, need help getting it done, or don't know what to do about a personal situation. Your teachers are always willing to help with schoolwork; your parent, siblings, and other family members understand and will support you in other matters.
- Prepare for college. With the help of your counselor, create a four-year development plan for your years in high school. This will help you set short-term goals for future college success.
- Get involved in school clubs so you can learn how to lead, network, and interact with others.
- Start investigating colleges in your third year of high school (grade 11); take the SAT or the ACT (US) college tests to assess your readiness.
- Have fun!

Atta's Advice on Higher Education

It is really important for students to start thorough research well in advance, preferably in your early high school years, and to continue researching throughout high school to decide on the proper course of action in terms of choosing your optimal field as well as your best potential options.

It is particularly important to search and compare costs and future ramifications consistently. Quite a few people with student loans are faced with paying off their debt through installments and carrying that burden well into middle age and even toward their retirement. As a result, parents and students are forced to think and consider different options as they prepare for higher education, at times limiting their choices and aspirations to be educated in the field of their dreams. It is once again increasingly important to begin work well in advance while saving and planning for the future.

Upon the birth of my first child in 1989, one of my coworkers who was a professional financial planner named Mr. Oniel congratulated me and handed me a gift for my son—a check for two hundred dollars. Then he told me to sign it and give it right back to him. I was surprised.

While laughing, he said, "This is not for you; it's for your son," and he asked me to write my son's name on the check. I gave it back to him. He then proceeded to open a Child Education Fund for my son Edreece. He also made me sign a form that deducted money every month from my paycheck and deposited it into the fund.

Over the years, I increased my monthly contributions, and eventually, upon Edreece's graduation from high school, my son's account had a balance of $85,000 thanks to Mr. Oniel's generous and smart gesture and our monthly contributions. I was able to fund the majority of my son's four-year college education in one of the US's top schools with the tax-free education fund. Looking back we wished we had increased monthly contribution even more as the money was not sufficient to pay for his master's and advanced education.

That money would probably have never been there if it hadn't been for the great advice and actions of that professional financial advisor, Mr. Oniel. The point is, while it's important for you to become knowledgeable about finances so you can take control of your money, you also should resist the temptation to do all your financial planning alone. Instead, seek help from a professional advisor. Your bank branch is a great place to start finding help.

In light of rising education costs and mass student debts impacting millions of students and families, it is extremely important to start your child's education fund at the birth of every child and start depositing all gifts and contributions while setting up and maximizing payments to the best of your ability.

Chapter Seven: Health

Health is something we all think about; it is in reality human beings' number one priority, for peace of mind and quality of life. An adequate health service is also a subject that the majority of governments and leaders continue to struggle with, as very few countries are able or willing to provide it. Far too many people around the world are being denied proper health care and are subject to suffering from poor health and chronic diseases. A lack of access to even basic health care causes millions around the world to live in fear while ignoring or putting off going to a doctor unless they get hurt or suddenly have to deal with a major medical issue.

I will try to share some basic facts and best practices in this chapter, but the real responsibility lies with you on your ability to learn all you can in order to help yourself, your family, and your loved ones. I am also a firm believer that we as human beings can do a lot to take better personal care of our health. Here are my thoughts before jumping into health-care coverage and what it means to you.

- Your goal should be to remain healthy; you must take responsibility and do your part.
- No human being may enjoy success and longevity without good health.
- Many of the causes of ill health are subject to a lack of self-mastery and self-control. We live at a time when millions rely on medication but neglect to take care of their health through personal means.
- Having traveled the world and worked with thousands of people of different ethnicities, I am quite confident about the fact that many people could live a much healthier lifestyle, but they simply don't have the will and desire to do that.

Lifestyle

Poor Health

Let's focus first on a few facts about poor health. The following factors impact our health:

- living an unhealthy lifestyle
- weakness of mind
- falling victim to the influence of medications
- being lazy
- the too-busy nonsense
- overeating foods that are not conducive to health
- a lack of proper physical exercise
- an inadequate supply of fresh air
- worrying rather than doing something about yourself or your health
- a lack of true awareness about your own health

A Healthy Lifestyle

Here are some questions and a suggestion that are key to leading a healthy lifestyle.

- Do you consider yourself healthy?
- What are you doing to take better care of yourself before serving and reaching out to others?
- Write a short list of items and activities you are engaged in to take better care of yourself.

Sleep Patterns

What is your sleep pattern? Are you getting enough sleep?

- Getting insufficient sleep is clearly associated with health risks and higher stress levels.
- Sleeplessness is a major challenge for many people around the world and it has direct impact on their well-being.
- Getting enough sleep time is simply a matter of discipline and proper time management. Way too many deprive themselves of proper rest and sleep resulting in various illnesses, anxiety, depression, and various other challenges.
- If you aren't getting enough sleep, get more.

- Every element of your life can be improved by getting at least seven to eight hours of sleep nightly.

Other Unhealthy Practices

We may not have appreciated or understood all the lessons our parents shared but remembering their advice about other unhealthy practices can truly shed light on a challenge or difficulty we may be facing.

- Do you appreciate and think of the lessons you've learned from your parents, spouse, children, and siblings?
- Are you one of those who, during social times, spends their time focused on a screen instead of the faces in front of you?
- When's the last time you turned off your cell phone and focused one hundred percent on the people you're with?
- The messages, the emails, and the news will be there when you turn your phone back on.
- Learning shouldn't stop when you're out of school; in reality that's when learning starts for many.

Inner Voice

Do you listen to your inner voice?

- Can you think of times when you had a hunch about something, ignored it, even while knowing that you should have followed it?
- The next time this happens, please listen to your gut feelings while also staying in touch with the perspective of your own thoughts.
- Do you spend time alone?

Solitude

Finding solitude for prayer and meditation helps relieve stress by getting us in touch with our inner voice. In America, Canada, and Europe, mindfulness practices that began with Buddhism have been institutionalized into many organizations and are prevalent in schools, workplaces, and communities.

- How can we expect others to like being with us, if we don't like being with ourselves?

- Frankly, most of our best ideas come to us when we drive alone or stay alone.
- Our creativity declines if we do not take long walks and the time to be alone as often as we need.

Your Community Contribution

Are you giving back to your community?

- Being a compassionate person and helping others can truly help solve some of society's biggest problems.
- It's important to find a way to share your time and talent with your local shelter, an elderly home, or at your children's school.
- My take is that opening up to opportunities puts us in touch with reality and helps us thrive in life.
- Be upfront and honest with yourself; you have to start somewhere.

Here is the main question: Are you ready to add value and make a difference in the lives of others?

Post-Traumatic Stress Disorder

Post-Traumatic Stress Disorder (PTSD) is a trauma- and stress-related disorder that may develop after exposure to an event or an ordeal in which death, severe physical harm, or frightening violence occurred or was threatened. Traumatic events that may trigger PTSD include violent personal assaults, natural and unnatural disasters, accidents, and military combat. Many refugees and immigrants suffer from PTSD. If you suffer in this way, you may want to find a medical practitioner who specializes in this field. Also, take the time to read "Appendix A~ Stress Survival Skills for Refugees and Immigrants" by Judith Trustone and her advice on dealing with PTSD.

Experiencing a life-threatening event, re-experiencing chronic exposure to abuse, and the aftermath of a horrific event can lead to the development of PTSD. Survivors of accidents, rape, physical abuse, sexual abuse, and crime; immigrants fleeing violence in their countries; survivors of earthquakes, floods, and hurricanes; and those who witness traumatic events may all end up suffering with PTSD. Family members of victims can develop the disorder as well, through vicarious trauma.

Some symptoms are associated with reliving the traumatic event:

- having bad daydreams and night dreams and distressing memories about the event
- behaving or feeling as if the event were actually happening all over again (known as flashbacks)
- experiencing dissociative reactions or the loss of awareness of present surroundings
- having a lot of emotional feelings when reminded of the event
- having a lot of physical sensations when reminded of the event (heart pounding or missing a beat, sweating, difficulty breathing, feeling faint, feeling a loss of control)

Some symptoms are related to avoiding being reminded of the traumatic event:

- avoiding thoughts, conversations, or feelings about the event
- avoiding people, activities, or places associated with the event

Some symptoms are related to negative changes in thought or mood:

- having difficulty remembering an important part of the original trauma
- feeling numb or detached from things
- a lack of interest in social activities
- an inability to experience positive moods

Health-Care Best Practices

US health-care costs are high, just as they are in some other countries. Here are some easy ways to save on these costs without sacrificing the quality of your life.

- Use company-sponsored health-care resources like smoking-cessation programs, fitness memberships, and health assessments. Some companies even offer a cash incentive to employees who complete annual health screenings or can demonstrate that they're tobacco-free.
- Use an urgent care facility rather than the emergency department when you need after-hours medical care. Even if you have insurance that covers an emergency department visit, the cost will be up to ten times higher than you'd pay for urgent care.
- Do what your doctor tells you. Studies indicate that up to 20 percent of people don't follow their physician's orders or don't take the medications prescribed for them until the end of the prescription, and they

end up right back in the doctor's office. That wastes both money and time.

- Ask your physician to prescribe generic rather than brand-name drugs. Generic drugs have the same active ingredients as their higher-priced prescription counterparts, so they're safe and effective.
- Request ninety-day prescriptions from your physician rather than thirty-day supplies. Pharmacies often offer a small discount for ninety-day prescriptions, plus you'll save time because you won't have to go to the pharmacy as often.

Stay Healthy

It is always a good idea to set realistic goals for staying healthy. You never have to change your lifestyle overnight. Establish small goals and increase them over time. For example, exercising two or three days a week is all you need.

Walk, Walk, Walk

The simplest and easiest exercise in the world is walking. It is a natural and easy regimen. Everyone should be able to dedicate at least twenty to thirty minutes of brisk walking every day.

Drink enough water. One simple daily-recommended amount of water for adults is sometimes listed as sixty-four ounces (eight 8-ounce glasses). Other authorities recommend adult males should drink thirteen 8-ounce glasses of liquid daily, whereas women are recommended to drink nine. A greater intake of water cleanses most of the toxins from your body while keeping you hydrated and ready to take on increased physical, mental, and emotional activities.

Stop Eating Junk Food and Fast Foods

The majority of fast foods are simply junk; candies and snacks sold in packages are also primarily junk. While you may feel too tired to cook, it is never a good idea to opt for fast food as an alternative. Preparing your meals and proper snacks ahead of time based on a schedule is key to staying healthy, saving time, and saving money.

Stay Active by Moving

The majority of people within European countries take public transportation, walk, or bike to work, whereas in North America, the majority rely on driving their cars. While conditions vary within each country and region, forcing yourself into walking or biking is simply a matter of discipline and choice. You should target walking at least ten thousand steps daily plus exercising rigorously for a minimum of thirty minutes at least three times a week.

Taking Supplements

Supplements are everything we swallow in the line of vitamins, minerals, and homeopathics that is not prescribed by a medical doctor.

- The supplement industry is a forty billion dollar business.
- The majority of people believe that supplements are regulated under the same regulations as drugs; they are not.
- A drug manufacturer has to prove a drug is effective and is potent for it to be approved for use.
- Supplements do not have to prove anything, but their manufacturers are responsible for ensuring they are safe.
- You are on your own; you are not protected; period.
- Weight loss supplements and medically prescribed pills and liquids may damage bodily organs and impair driving or create other challenges.
- It's always a good idea to read the instructions and other details carefully before use.
- Meanwhile, quality supplements do have a place in good nutrition.
- Naturopathic doctors will recommend supplements.

For many of you coming from a different culture, healers, herbs, and ceremonies may be part of what you've known as healing. When you come to the West, you'll see that Western medicine is dominated by pills instead of prayers. Often this form of medicine conflicts with what you've always known. Europeans still support "alternative medicine." Britain's royal family uses homeopathy. In Germany and France, some physicians treat primarily with acupuncture and flower essences. You may find your cultural medicine under these categories, though medical insurance probably won't cover them so you'll pay out of pocket. To learn more, review such books as *Vibrational Medicine: The #1 Handbook of Subtle-Energy Therapies* by Richard Gerber.

Navigating North America's Health-Care Systems

Health-care systems around the world remain one of the most complex and difficult challenges for billions of people. Let us just navigate North America's health-care systems as we take a look at them as examples of Western world practices. Though the United States and Canada are similar when it comes to daily life, their health-care systems differ significantly.

The United States' health-care system is unique among industrialized nations in that it is entirely free-market based; that is, while government regulations require insurers to adhere to certain minimum standards, health-care insurers can set their own prices without government intervention.

In addition, it's a direct-pay system, meaning that either an insurance company (on behalf of its subscribers) or the health-care consumer pays for services. When the consumer pays, the cost usually comes directly out-of-pocket, although supplemental insurance and federally subsidized plans can help reduce the cost.

Canada and several European countries have state-funded, socialized forms of health-care programming that may be almost entirely paid for by tax dollars. All citizens and permanent residents of these countries have access to free, quality health care. This is an enormous saving, which, as a result, is considered to be one of the primary benefits of citizenship and residency. The few services that are not covered may be covered with supplemental insurance to reduce consumers' out-of-pocket expenses.

This overview of the North American and European health-care systems should answer some of your questions about access to health-care services for both you and your family. But it is extremely important for you to research your options thoroughly and learn about what is available for one of the most important necessities of life.

Here is a look at some of the world's biggest economies' health-care systems and options.

Health Care in the United States

The United States spends more on health care than any other nation and it has the greatest number of choices of plans. While it might sound great to have many choices, the reality is that health-care costs in the US are the highest in the world and the system is complicated and difficult to navigate. Ongoing changes cause ongoing challenges. Many experts point to the potential loss of health-care coverage and rising costs for millions as a result. Research thoroughly to learn about the best options, costs, and affordability for your personal situation.

Health-Care Insurance in the US

Large companies (with more than fifty employees) usually offer some kind of medical benefits package for its employees and possibly their dependents. Benefits usually include health, dental, and vision coverage. Companies with fewer than fifty employees are not required to offer insurance, which means employees will have to buy their own coverage.

Most companies pay only a percentage of the cost of their employees' medical insurance, which means you'll have to pay the rest. The cost of the monthly premium you're required to pay will be deducted from your paycheck, which is still likely to be much less than if you purchased your own insurance.

New employees usually have a month or so to sign up for these benefits. Make sure you don't miss the deadline, because that would mean you will have to wait until the next open enrollment period. That could be nearly a year away, depending on when you were hired.

Also, if your company covers spouses and dependents and your spouse is already covered, or if you're covered by your parents' insurance policy, it's possible that your employer will give you a small stipend, because it doesn't have to pay for your insurance. It usually doesn't amount to much, but it helps.

Where to Obtain Health Services

The United States has many clinics and other facilities where you can get medical treatment.

- The primary place is the office of a primary care physician (PCP). PCPs are generalists; they take care of a person's medical needs from infancy to old age. They also are diagnosticians; that is, they diagnose illnesses and injuries, treat those they are qualified to treat, and refer to specialists who have additional knowledge and training in a particular specialty. For example, a PCP can treat you for an upper respiratory infection or manage your diabetes care. But if your PCP diagnoses skin cancer that is too advanced to treat in the office, he or she will refer you to a cancer specialist.

- Specialists are on the next rung of the health-care ladder. Surgeons fall into this category, as do specialists like internal medicine practitioners, endocrinologists, podiatrists, psychiatrists, and any other physician whose practice focuses on a particular illness or condition. Like PCPs, specialists have their own offices where they see patients.
- It's also possible to obtain care at medical clinics, which are usually staffed by physicians who work on a rotating basis.
- There are clinics for general care, as well as for indigent care, which is care provided at no charge to people who for various reasons cannot afford to pay for their medical treatments. You can even find small clinics right inside drug stores.
- Nurse practitioners or physician assistants who can care for minor medical conditions like sinus infections usually operate medical clinics. They're also qualified to administer flu shots and give sports physicals, among other things. Finally, these practitioners can write prescriptions, which you can pick up right in the store.
- For more critical care, you may need to visit an urgent care facility. These medical offices are only open for certain hours of the day, generally after the regular office hours of a PCP. Common hours of operation are 7 p.m. to midnight or 7 p.m. to 7 a.m. Their main purpose is to provide care to people who can't wait for their regular medical office to open. For instance, if you had a severe sore throat, a urinary tract infection, or an eye irritation (including pink eye), you may wish to be treated at an urgent care facility so you'll start to recuperate faster.
- However, urgent care is not a substitute for emergency treatment. If you have severe chest pain, uncontrollable bleeding, trouble breathing, a gunshot wound, or pregnancy-related problems, among others, you should head for the emergency department at a hospital instead.
- Hospitals provide emergency care, as just discussed, as well as outpatient treatments and procedures (that is, treatments that allow you to go home the same day), and inpatient surgical care (which requires an overnight or longer stay). An example of an outpatient procedure is a colonoscopy, which is a test for colon cancer that requires sedation; an

example of an in-patient procedure is a coronary artery bypass grafting (CABG), which treats blocked coronary (heart) arteries.

- Hospitals also generally offer wellness services, health education classes, and seminars to help engender an improved quality of life.
- Mental health facilities are available for inpatient and outpatient use. They treat disorders of the mind. Psychiatrists are medical doctors who are skilled in the diagnosis and treatment of mental illnesses, including mood disorders like bipolar disorder, anxiety disorders like obsessive-compulsive disorder, and psychotic disorders like schizophrenia. They also treat eating disorders (anorexia and bulimia), as well as other mental illnesses.

Medical Treatment Outside of the US

The United States may have one of the best health-care systems in the world, but let's face it: it's expensive to obtain care here. For this reason, there may be times when US residents might like to seek medical care outside the country.

- For example, let's say you need surgery for a particular condition and your insurance company tells you the co-pay (your share) in your high-deductible insurance plan will be $30,000. You search the Internet and find you can have the same procedure done in Panama for $12,000. If you can verify the surgeon's skills and the safety of the hospital, it might be worth considering having the surgery there.
- There's even a term for going elsewhere to acquire medical care: medical tourism.
- Just be very, very careful that you'll receive quality care if you go outside the US. Certain countries are notorious for providing cheap care with questionable results. Your health and well-being are worth much more than saving a few bucks.
- In addition, some prescription medications are available at a lower cost from reputable Canadian companies.
- The US government prohibits cross-border mailing of prescription medications to US citizens because it claims there's no way to assure product purity and quality.
- However, Canadian citizens living in the United States may have their medications mailed, as long as a photocopy of the original prescription and proof of Canadian citizenship are affixed to the outside of the

package in a plastic pouch. That way, customs officers can inspect the documents. This applies to all medications, except controlled drugs and narcotics, which cannot be mailed under any circumstances.

- If you're an American citizen or resident living near a Canadian border and would like to buy your medication from a Canadian pharmacy, you can do so. Technically, US law prohibits it, but as long as you bring back no more than a ninety-day supply of a drug that is not a narcotic or other controlled substance and it's for personal use, border agents generally won't stop you.
- A final word of warning: it's usually best to avoid prescriptions obtained from any country other than Canada, especially drugs purchased over the Internet. You never know what substance you're actually getting in those capsule or tablets.

Health Care in Canada

Canada has a publicly funded health-care system informally known as Medicare in English and as *Régie de l'assurance maladie* du Québec in French. It is universal coverage, socialized care.

- Canadian citizens and permanent residents are entitled to insured services like preventative care and medical treatment from primary care physicians, as well as hospital care, dental surgery, and other necessary medical care.
- The system is almost entirely free, although technically, it isn't really free. Rather, it is a covered benefit paid for by the income taxes the Canadian government collects from everyone's paycheck. You just don't have to pay when you receive services.
- The exceptions are British Columbia, Alberta, and Ontario, which do require low health-care premiums for services. Check with the provincial health ministry for more information.
- In addition, with just a few exceptions, patients cannot be denied care, no matter what your previous medical history is, what pre-existing conditions you may have, or how much you earn.
- There isn't a single health-care system in Canada. Rather, health insurance is administered by each province or territory individually and differs from one location to another.
- When you immigrate to a Canadian province or territory, you must

apply to receive health coverage. The application form is available at doctors' offices, hospitals, pharmacies, and immigrant service organizations. The form is also available online through the provincial or territorial ministry of health. When you apply, you'll need to show personal identification like your passport, permanent resident card, or confirmation of permanent residence.

- All provinces and territories, except Manitoba, issue a health insurance card to each family member. (In Manitoba, only adults receive a health insurance card.) This card, known as the Care Card, has a personal identification number unique to the cardholder; the card can't be shared with another person. Always carry it with you because you must present the card when you go to a physician's office, clinic, or hospital for health services.
- There is a waiting period of up to ninety days in most provinces and territories before your public health insurance begins. Citizenship and Immigration Canada says you must apply for temporary private health-care coverage insurance within five days of arriving in your new province or territory, or insurers may not provide coverage for you. You'll find more information on private insurance later in this chapter.
- Canadian employers usually offer health insurance as part of their employment benefits package. The insurance usually covers medical, dental, and vision. If your company doesn't offer insurance, you can buy private insurance instead. You also can rely on Canada's publicly funded health-care system, but it covers only basic services. You'll have to pay out-of-pocket for things like corrective lenses, medications, and home care.

Insurance Portability

Another advantage of Canada's health-care system is that if you're already a citizen or a permanent resident and you want to move from one province or territory to another, your coverage will follow you. Under the *Canada Health Act*, insurance is portable, but only temporarily through the minimum waiting period (usually no more than ninety days). For this reason, it's very important to apply for health-care coverage immediately after moving.

In addition, because coverage varies from one province or territory to another, always check your coverage before you travel. If your coverage isn't compatible with that province or territory's coverage, you may need to purchase temporary private health insurance.

Supplemental Health Benefits

While the public health-care system covers most of the doctors' visits and medical services you need, not everything is covered. For this reason, you may need supplemental or private health insurance. Some non-covered health-care costs include private hospital rooms, prescription drugs, dental care, and prescription eyeglasses. Your employer may offer you the option of paying for any additional health insurance you may need through payroll deduction. If your employer doesn't offer this benefit or you're unemployed, you must cover these costs out-of-pocket instead.

Other Types of Insurance

Depending on your employer, you may be eligible for a variety of insurance plans other than medical, including insurance to cover accidental death and dismemberment; critical illnesses; short- and long-term disability; extended health care; and group life. What's available varies from one employer to the next, and larger companies are more likely to offer the additional coverage.

Atta's Lessons on Health

Shortly after my arrival in the United States in 1981, I met a close friend and coworker from Afghanistan who had gained weight since I had seen him a couple of years earlier in Germany. He immediately told me that I would gain weight, too, and be much heavier in a couple of years. I was determined not to allow that to happen so I vowed that I would never put on more than a couple of pounds for the rest of my life. To seal the deal, my friend brought a scale from the bathroom so I could weigh myself. At the time, I was 175 pounds. Today, I am 168 pounds, and I remind him about that all the time. I also happily inform him that I only have to visit my doctor's office once a year for an annual check-up. I walk ten to twelve miles a week and stick to a daily diet that consists of one banana, one apple, and various nuts and green vegetables. That's all I need—that, and the love of family members and friends and the thought of adding value to others.

Chapter Eight: Finding Employment

You have already accomplished a lot—running away from war and conflict zones, crossing the sea, separating from family, friends, and homeland, growing in limited-access refugee camps with few resources, traveling through country after country without being able to speak the host country language. And all the while, having the honor and bravery to give it all you have among people who don't have to deal with any of these challenges. Congratulations.

Immigrants are the backbone of economic progress around the world, especially in many Western countries and North America. Over 40 percent of the world's biggest top five hundred companies were started by immigrants and refugees or their children, creating millions of jobs and many successful brands and businesses.

While there are probably many reasons why you decided to emigrate—from political or religious freedom to freedom to work, speak, and feel safe—being able to earn a living and create a better future for your family was probably at or near the top of your list. It is important to note there are and will always be employment opportunities in different fields for people who are willing to work hard.

Atta's Advice on Finding Work

Upon my arrival in the United States in late December 1981, I set a goal to find a job within a month. I was determined to take advantage of my adequate English knowledge, and I remember wrapping up blisters and wiping blood off my feet for quite a few days as I walked the streets of San Francisco in search of a job.

I met my goal: I landed a bank teller job within two weeks, thanks in part to my personal role models. My parents and friends taught me that hard work and determination will take a person far. I parlayed that teller job into a successful banking career that lasted twenty-eight years, culminating in a position as a senior vice president regional manager.

During my career, I met many other successful immigrants who have made amazing strides and progress despite many challenges. For that reason, I am a firm believer in hard work, dedication, and the realization that the sky is indeed the limit.

What You Can Offer an Employer

While it's true that there could be fewer jobs available in certain economies for various reasons, and it can be harder to find a job as an immigrant, generally speaking there is always something you can do to "keep the home fires burning," as the saying goes, until something better comes along. It's also important to note that the new technologies and conditions around the globe continue to create expanding opportunities. There's no denying, though, there might be some disadvantages within the new environment.

- Many educated refugees and immigrants with strong job experiences from back home find it frustrating that they can't obtain the same jobs in their new environments.
- Employers everywhere typically give preference to those with work experience within the employer's country; outside certifications don't transfer well or at all. That's the main reason we find out our taxi driver formerly worked as an engineer, doctor, or educator.
- Also refugees and immigrants are easy victims for discrimination and exploitation in the workplace. Some employers recognize the sense of urgency and desperation among these groups to keep their jobs, so they will have them take the less desirable and even dangerous roles.

Challenges to Finding Work

Let's take a look at some of the obvious challenges:

- having to start from ground zero in a new environment
- a lack of proficiency in the country's language
- not having the proper skills
- having to support oneself as well as one's family in the motherland
- a lack of personal transportation and unfamiliarity with public transportation.

While these disadvantages will not keep you from finding a job, they will of course limit your potential from finding the perfect job right away.

Fortunately, most Western countries particularly in North America present great opportunities for employment and building a sustainable lifestyle.

Here, you'll find proven practices and strategies that you can use to become gainfully employed or move into a better job if you're already working. Here are the main facts before we dive deeper into this chapter:

- Employers need employees with really solid skills no matter what, where, and how they gained them.
- There are laws in most Western countries that protect people from discrimination on the basis of race, color, religion, gender, sexual orientation, and ethnic and national origin. But let's face it: if you don't have the basic host-nation language or English skills, it will be more difficult to find a job and harder to keep it.
- So the first rule of thumb for you and your family is to work on building your skills and improving your language at the same time.
- Sign up for language classes for students within your community. Start with conversational classes in your host country's language. Then move on to more advanced language classes that will teach you writing and public-speaking skills.
- Even after you find your first job, continue with your language classes.
- It is your responsibility to search and find language classes within the education programs at high schools, community colleges, community centers, and through some libraries and churches. Some communities even offer free literacy programs to help you hone your skills. Invest the time in yourself. You are worth it.

Reenergize

Let's reenergize through work and find ways to make a living. There is no such thing in life as being able to keep going and self-sustain without renewing. That is how and why we sometimes come apart. The question is how and what shall we do to reenergize! I firmly believe reenergizing can best happen through work in a new environment.

First and foremost, it is important to keep in mind that there have and will be employment opportunities in numerous industries for people who are honest and willing to work hard. Building a sustainable life without language skills is almost impossible. Language efficiency adds great value, regardless of location and industry.

Personal Evaluation and Inventory

Before you can find a job, you need to consider exactly what skills you can offer an employer. Maybe you have great organizational skills. Maybe you excel at strategic thinking. Or maybe you're good at plumbing, caregiving, selling, writing, or any one of a thousand other tasks.

Figure out exactly what it is you can and are trained to do as a way to narrow your job search and improve your odds of finding a job for which you're qualified.

- Your educational background will play a major role in your job search. Employers generally want a certain set of skills in job candidates, backed by a solid educational background.
- Job hunters commonly make the mistake of thinking that even though they're not one hundred percent qualified for a job they're interested in, an employer will recognize their potential and hire them anyway. Unfortunately, it doesn't work that way, especially in this age of computers and résumé databases.
- Employers typically scan or otherwise enter all the résumés they receive into a searchable database, and when they're looking for an employee for a particular job, they search that database for keywords that match the job description. So if your résumé doesn't have those desirable keywords that reflect your skills and capabilities and their needs, you'll never be called in for an interview.

The First Steps

Take these steps first.

- Create a personal inventory of your skills and strengths.
- Draw three columns on a sheet of paper or create a three-column table using a computer program like Microsoft Word. Label one column "Skills," the second "Interests," and the third "Goals."
- List everything you can think of that you've done that relates to each category. This type of self-evaluation will help you figure out exactly what you bring to the table and will help you decide what you'd like to do.

What Are Your Job Values?

No, this is not about money at this point! Now that you are ready to take on the responsibility to look for and secure a job, it is time to answer some questions enroute to building your résumé. Take a few minutes to think about your answers and get ready to highlight what you might value in a job as you build that awesome résumé.

- What could be your next ideal job? Describe your ideal position in terms of industry, location, compensation, role, title, culture and, most important "Must haves."
- What is your career path? Think of your desired goals within these time frames.
    - next year at this time
    - three years from today
    - five years from today
- What is unique about you? To be realistic, think of how the people around you would describe your unique qualities.
- List some of your best qualities such as the drive, competencies, knowledge, skills, and abilities you have developed during your life.
- What are the best adjectives that describe you?
- What adjectives would other people use to describe you?
- List your top three to five major accomplishments.
- How did you get to this stage?
- What are your overall accomplishments and highlights that will help distinguish you from others applying for the same job?
- Reflecting back on your career, what are you most proud of?
- What is your greatest concern that keeps you up at night?
- What other qualities and attributes you would like to share on your résumé?

Transferable Skills

We all have transferable skills but the majority of people simply do not know how to display their skills to a new potential employer. Mass movements, layoffs, and the creation of new businesses means that it is possible you will have to leave your industry or specific area of expertise for a different industry.

Here are some tips that may help you transfer your skills to win your next job.

- Begin jotting down your transferable skills.
- Never limit your identity to a title. You are much more than a job title.
- View your work experience as a set of competencies and roles that you have mastered and that can be useful from one occupation or industry to another. This is what "transferrable skills" means, where you show your versatility. Your adaptability may open up new possibilities.

Tie Benefits to Transferable Skills

Selling our skills alone is not enough. Try to sell benefits of those skills.

- Especially today, skills are just a commodity.
- Most employers buy results and are less impressed when a candidate promotes a laundry list of skills. So be sure to define how those transferable skills have been assets in your previous positions.
- Think beyond even your skill sets and job duties, and list every possible example of how you have helped save time for your employer (time equals money).
- In reality, by including several specific achievements, you separate yourself from your competitors and are much more likely to gain the attention of your next employer.
- Focus on the end result, the benefit to the client or employer as a result of something that you contributed.
- Your goal should be to list between five and seven great achievements that focus on the bottom line and can impact the company.
- Last but not least, ask yourself what you can do for this employer that your competitors can't.
- You have a unique set of skills, experiences, and talents. Now turn them into a "unique selling proposition" for the employer. That means turning those skills into achievements.

Your Application

Your Résumé

A résumé is a document used to relay your accomplishments and qualifications to a potential employer, preferably on a single page or two. Its ultimate goal is to get you an interview for a job. Assemble a résumé that showcases your talents and experiences.

Let's take a look at the purpose of a successful résumé.

- It is a promotional piece you design to showcase your achievements.
- It successfully explains that you are trying to get a job for the first time.
- Alternatively, it justifies why you are changing jobs.
- It should show, briefly and all in one place, everything you have done in your working life so that an employer can read through it quickly to see if you are a match for their position.
- In effect, it's about you marketing yourself, so you should use it to present yourself in the best possible light and prove that you can do the job.
- People think that the more they have in their résumé the better. Not so. "Less is more." Show only the last three or four jobs and stay focused on what you do best.

Types of Résumés

There are two types of résumés.

A chronological résumé should list your jobs in the order in which you worked them, although in reverse chronological order, meaning that the most current job appears at the top of the list, followed by any other jobs you've held, from most to least recent.

A standard résumé focuses on the tasks you have handled rather than when you did them and who your employer was and so it's also called a functional résumé. A functional résumé tends to be a little less detailed than a chronological résumé as a result and can be a good choice if you don't have much work experience or if you have gaps in your résumé due to job losses like a layoff or an illness. This is not to say that you're trying to hide anything from an employer; rather, you're simply trying to present yourself in the most positive light.

The Header

This is where you'll provide your contact information:

- full name
- home phone number
- cell phone number

- email address

Contact information should appear at the top of the résumé in a slightly larger font size than the body text for better legibility. Here's one place where bold type definitely can be used. Put your name in bold to distinguish it from the rest of the type below.

Your Objective

This is where you'll indicate the type of job you want. Focus on what you offer the employer, not what you want the employer to do for you. For example, your résumé will meet with a more positive reception if you use an employer-centered objective; avoid using a "me-centered" objective (even if it's true).

Your Professional Summary

Your professional summary is the most important and useful section for showcasing special talents and skills you have. In two or three lines, summarize your professional ambitions, background, and talents. Mention your accomplishments such as the special projects you've completed, sales goals you've achieved, and ways you've decreased costs or otherwise helped to build another company's bottom line. This is also a good place to list tasks you've done for more than one company. For example, if you have worked as a receptionist at several different companies, some of the responsibilities were probably the same. So you can mention them just once in the qualifications section rather than repeating yourself later when you list the name of each company you've worked for.

Your Experience

Your experience is compiled in reverse chronological order, as stated above, which means your job history starts with the most recent job at the top, and then goes backward to the oldest job. This is done because employers usually are more interested in knowing what you've done most recently. Be sure to include the following:

- the dates you were employed
- the full name of the company, its location, and your job title
- a few details about what you did on the job

Formatting

Here are some important formatting tips.

- Keep the résumé to a one- or two-page document. Even the world's most successful corporate executives have one-page résumés. Remove some text if yours is too long.
- Generally, a résumé should be printed on quality paper.
- The document should be formatted with 1-inch margins on all sides and should be written in a standard font like Times New Roman in 12 point.
- Don't use a smaller font size to squeeze more words on the page—it won't be as readable.
- Avoid using italic type or a lot of bold text. Both can be distracting, as well as difficult to read when used extensively.
- Spell out all month names, since you can't abbreviate the shorter names (May, June, and July, for example).
- Use periods at the end of all complete sentences when writing bulleted lists; leave the punctuation blank at the end of sentence fragments. It's important to be consistent with this formatting throughout.
- If you've never written a résumé before, you'll find it easier if you use a résumé template for formatting. A template is like a pattern that you fill with information. Microsoft Word has dozens of preloaded résumés from which to select. Pick the one that showcases your background best.
- You may find that some of the résumé templates are better for job seekers with less experience because they have fewer fields to fill in and more white space.
- Using a template also ensures that you include all the information a hiring manager is likely to need to make a decision on whether your qualifications match the job.

Résumé Tips

- When compiling a list of job tasks, showcase only the ones that are closest to the qualifications of the job you're seeking. For example, if you're looking for an entry-level managerial job, but your first job out of school was as the office gofer (that is, the person who "goes for" coffee and anything else the executives need), you definitely want to omit that from your list of duties.

- Do include quantifiable information related to achievements like sales goals, cost-cutting measures, and other functions. For instance, maybe you increased production by 15 percent in one quarter, or you saved your employer $25,000 by streamlining operations, or you won an award for outstanding sales. Always include verifiable facts and figures like these, since they demonstrate your competence in and enthusiasm for your field.
- If you have more than fifteen years of experience, you might want to consider leaving the older jobs off your résumé. While age discrimination is illegal, it does exist, so if you have enough recent work experience to look attractive to an employer, it might be a good idea to focus on that experience and simply omit the older jobs.
- Use action verbs when creating this section. Here's a list of verbs denoting strength and success: *achieved, added, analyzed, arranged, assisted, awarded, changed, completed, conducted, contributed, controlled, coordinated, created, decreased, delivered, designed, developed, directed, eliminated, established, exceeded, expanded, gained, generated, grew, implemented, improved, increased, introduced, led, maintained, managed, maximized, minimized, optimized, organized, originated, oversaw, participated, performed, produced, promoted, proposed, recommended, reduced, saved, set up, sold, solved, supervised, supported, wrote.*

Education

This generally is the most important section of a résumé. Here are some helpful tips.

- If you hold degrees from a college, university, or community college either in your new home or abroad, list them at the top of the section, and include the city and country where you earned the degree. Finally, if you attended more than one institution, list only the highest degree(s).
- If your highest level of education is a high school diploma or its equivalent in your home country, use that instead. But anything less than that is ancient history as far as employers are concerned and won't help in your job search, so leave it off. Likewise, if you have an

academic degree, leave off any mention of high school altogether, even if you were a scholar or you earned academic awards. What matters is your degree.

- If you attended and/or graduated from a trade school, this information also will be useful to a potential employer and should appear on your résumé. This information is more important than a high school diploma but less important than a college degree.
- To summarize, here's the order to present your educational information, from most significant to most basic. For each degree and qualification, name the institution, the dates you attended, plus your major and minor fields of study. For high school graduation or its foreign equivalent, list only the school's name and the city, plus the country's name if it is a different country from where you are applying.
    - university information with PhD first; MA or MSc second, BA or BSc third
    - college information
    - trade school
    - high school or foreign equivalent

Another important thing to note: If you have education that matches the job you're seeking, but your past experience is in other fields, you should move the education section above your experience section. This will help convince an employer that you could be right for the job even though you have done other types of work more recently.

Special Skills

This is where you'll mention special knowledge you have, like computer software you know well, technical skills, clerical skills such as your word processing speed, and languages you speak fluently.

Volunteering and Pro Bono Work

Donating your time for the good of others (known as "pro bono" or free work) is a noble pursuit that employers view favorably. It's a good idea to include a list of your volunteer activities at the bottom of your résumé. Read more about volunteer work under "The Job Hunt" below.

Keywords

Keywords are specific adjectives, short phrases, nouns, and verbs describing abilities, experiences, and unique skills. Employers use them to find the right candidate for a position. Industries have their own versions and sets of keywords. Earlier, you read that employers usually store résumés electronically in a database, or scan the paper copies they receive so the information can be added to the database. Since employers conduct candidate searches based on specific skills, you should include a list of keywords at the top of your résumé that reflects the scope of your abilities.

For example, here are some keyword lists for a finance manager who has a bachelor's degree and three years of experience (I apologize if you don't know what some of these financial terms mean): *finance, financial, analyst, general ledger, due diligence, GAAP, capital financing, capital gains, capital losses, cash flow, collections, EBITDA, Bachelor of Science, three years' experience.*

Here's a keyword list for a person with clerical skills: *administrative assistance, clerical, screen calls, answer phones, receptionist, communication skills, records management, problem solving, scheduling, Microsoft Office*

Résumés that have more of the keywords the employer is seeking will rank higher in the search results, so include as many keywords as you can, up to about twenty, to improve your odds of making the cut for an interview.

- It is best to look for the company's job postings where you will be able to spot the keywords and attributes they are looking for.
- Also it's a good idea to browse through various résumé-building websites that offer strong key phrases.
- It's a smart idea to become creative while applying for jobs.

The Correct Placement of Keywords

It is best to place bold keywords at the top portion of your résumé. This allows your résumé to be elevated and get the attention of hiring managers as a viable candidate.

Résumé Don'ts

This list of don'ts is almost as important as the list of do's.

- Don't include personal information like marital status, number of children, health status, age, or religious affiliation. It's illegal for an employer to ask for this information, so don't offer it.
- Don't put your photograph on your résumé. Your appearance isn't important unless you are seeking an acting role; yours skills and talents are.
- Don't list your references. Print them on a separate sheet you can hand to the employer during an interview.
- Don't mention hobbies. They almost never have a bearing on the job (although some might argue that a good golf handicap might be helpful in some professions).
- Don't include your Social Security number. It's never needed until you've been hired, and only then so you can fill out employment paperwork.
- Don't exaggerate or lie about your experience or other facts on your résumé. If you're hired and someone discovers you haven't been truthful, you could be fired on the spot.
- Don't divulge your current salary. Occasionally, a company will ask what your salary requirements are, but that information, if necessary, should be included in your cover letter (discussed below).
- Be careful to not post about your work, policies, or products on your Facebook and other social media accounts.

Examine for Accuracy

The final step in the process is to proofread the document carefully to identify typographical and grammatical errors. Employment experts say that a single typo can get a résumé excluded from consideration, so use your spell check and grammar check to identify errors, then proofread the résumé manually. You may also wish to ask someone else to proofread it for you.

Usage Issues

Check for correct grammar, spelling, and punctuation.

Capitalization

In titles and headings in formal writing (articles, books, journals), nouns, pronouns, verbs, adjectives, adverbs, and first and last words are also capitalized. In résumés, capitalize these:

- the word at the start of each sentence and the start of each bullet

- the name of universities, colleges, trade schools, and schools
- your degrees and diplomas
- company names and department names
- your job position's title
- days of the week and months
- names of cities, states, countries, and languages
- brand names

Punctuation

Refer to a book like *The Gregg Reference Manual* or a website like the Purdue Online Writing Lab for help with punctuation.

Articles

Nouns in English almost always take an article (*the, a, an*) in front of them (*the train, an apple, a quarter*).

Run-On Sentences

Run-on sentences are two separate sentences that are incorrectly stuck together without punctuation or conjunctions. For example: "I love traveling in California the weather is great there."

Consistency

Be sure to be consistent. Use a single space after a period; punctuate bulleted lists the same; indent new positions the same way.

Get Professional Help

Finally, if your grammar skills for the language in your new host country is still under construction or if your writing skills are lacking, consider hiring a professional résumé writer. Then you'll know it's letter-perfect and will represent you well in your job hunt.

Whether your like it or not, your application for your dream job doesn't go straight to the person hiring you for the role these days. Instead, it has to pass through a gatekeeper—typically someone in human resources who is responsible for vetting and evaluating your résumé before passing it along to the hiring manager. You have only a few seconds to make a good impression or risk getting your application tossed into the reject pile.

Summarizing Your Résumé's Goals

Your goal should be to make a good impression through your résumé first.

Hiring managers know exactly what they're looking for in a candidate, and a few misused words on your profile (or résumé) could cost you your chance at the position. Even though you liked the company enough to send the first message, you'll receive the customary "thanks, but no thanks" email in return that will have you wondering where you went wrong.

What do you need to do in order for your résumé to attract enough attention to get invited out on a first date, that is, an interview? Here are some tips that will make a big difference on your résumé.

- Always avoid clichés—fluffy, and generic statements such as "I have great communication skills" and "I love multitasking." Even if they are true, many words are so overused that the hiring manager won't consider them as selling points.
- Remove generic, broad, and old skills; for instance, "I am proficient in Office 2007 to 2012" when it is already 2017.
- It is important to be specific about your skill sets. It is a bad idea to simply copy from résumé samples of others.
- Your résumé should always highlight exactly what you are specifically good at and avoid generalities. Just list skills relevant to the position you're applying for, and leave the extras out. It is a good idea to be upfront but not too bold in your résumé.
- Stay away from highlighting, underlining keywords, and italicizing; stay organized and simple.
- Be careful about mentioning your location. Some organizations and hiring managers don't want to consider an out-of-area candidate for a job opening due to the cost of moving them in and their potential lack of familiarity with the area. It's a good idea to only put your name, phone number, and email in your résumé. If you are willing to relocate, then it is easier to explain your willingness through your cover letter.

An All-Star Reference List

References are people who are willing to speak on your behalf about your skills, qualifications, and personality.

- You need to compile a list of personal and professional references that you can share with interviewers. Keep in mind that interviewers *will* check your references, so make sure you name people who know you well.

- Also, be sure always to ask the person if he or she is willing to be a reference. Most people will say yes, but some won't, and you want to find that out before you pass along that person's name and contact information to a potential employer.
- Format your reference list on a sheet of paper separate from your résumé and cover letter. It's a good practice to include one to two personal references (anyone *except* family members—friends, neighbors, and classmates are good choices) plus two or three business references.
- If you have little or no job experience and, therefore, no references, you can ask the religious leader at your church, mosque, or synagogue to be a reference.

Cover Letter

The majority of recruiters consider cover letters to be an important factor when evaluating candidates so it's actually a good idea to cover your bases and include a cover letter with every job application.

Best Practices

Here are some best practices for writing excellent cover letters.

- A well-written, error-free cover letter personalized for the job you're seeking is essential in a job hunt. It might seem strange, but even companies that advertise online generally will require at least a brief cover letter to go with online applications.
- Employment experts say that the cover letter can make or break your chances at getting an interview. That's because a cover letter reveals how good your communication skills really are; if your letter contains typos and other errors, it reveals that you're not as careful about your image as you need to be.
- Format the letter the same way you formatted your résumé, with one-inch margins using 12-point Times New Roman type.
- Whenever possible, address the letter to a real person, not just to "Dear Sir" or "To whom it may concern." You may have to speak to the company's receptionist or go online to find the name of the right recipient.
- Think of your cover letter as your sales pitch to the hiring manager. Instead of spending the entire time talking about yourself and your

wants and needs, consider the needs of your prospective employer.

- Remember, the recruiter already has your résumé—there's no need to rehash your entire work history in your cover letter. In fact, I believe this is why so many employers disregard the cover letter; they've read so many bad ones—which merely summarize their candidates' résumés—that employers see no need to read them.
- One cover-letter best practice is to surprise the hiring manager by using your first paragraph to demonstrate your understanding of the company's position in the marketplace and their needs, and then to highlight your experiences and accomplishments that speak to these requirements.
- Always include your return address at the top of the letter, as well as a section at the bottom where you can sign the letter before sending it.
- Of course, if you're applying online, you won't be able to sign the letter physically. Instead, simply type your name after the complimentary closing.

Match Your Cover Letter to the Job Description

A job description is like a roadmap; it leads you to the job you're seeking. For this reason, your cover letter should be tailored to fit the job description.

- Pick out words and phrases from the job posting ad, and use them in your letter.
- Mention any skills you have that are a match for those in the job description.
- Also if you're proficient in or at least familiar with a particular software package or a particular program that would be required, mention that, too. Your goal here is to draw as many parallels between your experience and the job as you can.
- It is okay to talk about yourself. Some people find it uncomfortable writing about themselves. But to get a job you have to provide good evidence that you're the right person to fill it, and that means talking about yourself, your skills, and your accomplishments. After all, the reader doesn't know you, so this is the only way to give him or her insight into who you are and what you can do.
- If you find it too difficult to praise yourself this way, consider having

someone else draft the letter for you.
- Orient the reader to your reason for writing in the opening statement ("I am interested in the marketing position you have open at XYZ Corporation.").
- Use active verbs when describing your experience and capabilities (*directed*, *spearheaded*, *coordinated*, and others listed earlier in this chapter).
- Say more than just what's on your résumé (give more details or expand upon your experience without restating your résumé).
- Provide your contact information—again—for easy access.
- Ask directly for an interview.

Sending Your Résumé

There are various options for sending your résumé (email attachment, email as an inline, fax, and mail). It's important to follow your potential employer's instructions carefully. The vast majority of employers are however resorting to posting résumés and requiring applicants to create their profiles through their websites. Follow their instructions while making sure your entries match your résumé.

- If you'll be sending a résumé and cover in plain text in the body of an email without submitting your information into an online job search form, you should create what's known as an inline résumé. In this type of document, all the type is moved to the left margin (known as "flush left with ragged right").
- In addition, decorative devices like centering, bolding, and italic type are not used.
- You can, however, use a row of equal signs (======) or tildes (~~~~~) if you wish to separate the different sections of the résumé from each other.
- And here's an important tip: Always email a copy of your résumé and cover letter to yourself first before applying, to check that the email journey won't scramble the text. Sometimes email programs corrupt the format, making the margins all askew, adding weird line breaks, or double-spacing. Sending yourself a test document will help you identify any problems so you can correct them before you send a live copy to an employer who will have a critical or discerning eye.
- Alternatively, you may be able to attach PDF or Microsoft Word

documents to the email. As a courtesy, save your documents as PDF files, if possible, because it's harder to transmit a virus attached to this type of file. You don't want a prospective employer to be saying you sent a nasty virus to his or her mailbox.

The Job Hunt

The job hunt is a methodical process that is conducted one step at a time. So here are some steps you can take to make your job hunt more successful.

- If you commit to doing the right things to secure a job, you will find it, and you will probably never have to look for another job.
- The right job can make your life exciting whereas the wrong job can be draining and time consuming. Find the right fit.
- The right job exists but you have to go find it.
- Of course, money matters a lot. The best you can do is to come to terms as to how much money matters to you and live with it.

Where to Look

Start looking at the job market. You can approach this in various ways.

- The Internet is the most common place to look for a job.
- There are numerous job-hunting websites, including Monster.com, Careerbuilder.com, Geebo.com, and Indeed.com, to name just a few. But these sites are not, by any means, the only place to job hunt, and, in fact, they're pretty oversaturated with job seekers.
- So in addition to using a job search engine like monster.com, use the Internet to identify companies you might be interested in working for, then go directly to their website and apply there.
- Applying in person can be a brilliant search strategy, because most people take the easy way out and apply over the Internet. Stop by the human resources department of the companies you're interested in and ask to apply in person. It's possible that you'll be directed to a computer to enter your information, but you could have an edge simply by showing up in person. In fact, sometimes it's even possible to get an immediate interview right on the spot.
- Networking is another viable way to find a job. Think of everyone you know—friends and neighbors, people at church, your children's school,

community organizations you belong to, and so on—and mention that you're looking for work. People genuinely like to help other people, and if they happen to be an employer themselves, they like to hire people they know. So it's worth a try.

- Headhunters and placement agencies also can be sources of good jobs. A headhunter is someone who helps companies identify good candidates for openings. Normally, a headhunter looks for the candidates directly, but you also can send your résumé to a headhunter in the hope of being matched with a job.
- Placement agencies, on the other hand, wait for you to come to them. They'll compare your qualifications against job openings in their database and hopefully will set up employment interviews for you.
- With both headhunters and placement agencies, the company that's seeking employees pays for the placement fee; only occasionally is the job seeker responsible for the cost. Make sure you ask upfront if you use one of these employment professionals.
- Always search in your community as most will host a job fair where you can meet a lot of employers all in the same place on the same day.
- Employers who take the time out of their busy schedule to attend job fairs usually have jobs they need to fill immediately, or they may have openings coming up in the near future.
- The telephone still works well as a job search tool. Making phone contact without an appointment is known as cold calling, and some employers will respond well to your effort to find out what types of jobs might be available at a company you're interested in.
- Employers today really don't expect job seekers to prospect this way, so taking a proactive approach like this could result in an interview.
- If a company states that you don't have the right qualifications for their business even though you think you do, take some time to think about what you could have said instead about your experience, and be prepared to offer up that information the next time before someone raises the same objection.
- Another way to find work is to go through the "help wanted" listings in your local newspaper's classified section. Printed help-wanted ads are actually on the wane, as more people use the Internet to search for what they need. But there are still a surprising number of jobs that are placed in newspapers, especially entry level and blue-collar positions,

so be sure to look. If your reading skills aren't very strong yet, ask a more fluent friend or family member for help.

Target Small- to Medium-Sized Businesses

Other things to consider before applying for work are the hours you want to work, how far you are willing to drive to get to your job, and whether you prefer to work for a large or smaller company or department. Smaller businesses are most likely to take a chance on someone less experienced or who has little or no advanced education. At the same time, though, they're likely to have smaller budgets and may take longer to hire. But you'll probably have more chance to flex your creative muscles in a small- to medium-sized business while learning a lot.

Research the Company

You must research the target company first.

- Go through the company's website, annual reports, editorials, other posts, and other background information.
- Read what has been said about the company in the news.
- Learn about the industry it's in.
- Read up on its ongoing projects, future plans, and ultimate goals.
- Try to figure out the size of the company, how many they employ, and what kind of work environment they offer.
- You'll use this information to demonstrate your knowledge of the company during the interview.
- Research and learn as much as possible about a company's overall fringe benefits to you and your family before deciding to work for that company.

Research the Interviewer

It is a very good idea to research the interviewer's profile beforehand, in the news and in their social media profiles (LinkedIn, Facebook, and so on). Look for their title, experience, and overall personality. This should help you prepare questions and give you more confidence to face them in person.

Prepare the Questions You Want to Ask

Once you have researched the company, create a list of questions that you may want to ask an interviewer. Ask about the company culture, role expectations, and growth opportunities—anything that will give you a clearer picture of what it would be like to work for this organization. Asking questions shows you're not only engaged in the interview process, but interested and already thinking about your future with this company. You should ask questions toward the end of the interview, or when the interviewer invites you to ask questions.

Preparation

Make copies of your résumé, your cover letter, and your list of references in advance. You don't want to be scrambling to get your documents organized the day of the interview! Most recruiters will bring a copy of your submitted documents to the interview, but if they fail to, you'll be a step ahead.

Always go to a job interview prepared with plenty of background information about the company so you can talk about it with ease and confidence. This kind of preparation really impresses employers, because it shows that you have an interest in the company, not just in a paycheck.

Job Search Mistakes

As humans we all make mistakes. Job seekers are certainly not immune from making mistakes due to a lack of proper research, a sense of urgency to acquire a job, a lack of experience particularly for first time job seekers, and other pressing life conditions. Again, keys for success are preparation, research, and seeking support to avoid unnecessary anxieties and errors.

- It's always better to have a job already when you're looking for a new opportunity. So if you're unhappy with your job, you need a position that pays more, or you want to change career paths, sit tight in your current position until you actually land that new job.
- When you change jobs, you should do many of the same things you did before you landed your present job, from researching the market and the field the prospective employer is in, to investigating the companies that interest you.

- One thing *not* to do is to change jobs only to make more money. You could end up accepting a job you really hate and the money won't necessarily make it better. It's preferable to wait a little longer to find a job you will enjoy doing than to just jump for a bigger paycheck.
- By the same token, if you want to change careers, make sure you have adequate training and preparation for the new field. A person with a degree in history is not going to be successful as a financial analyst or logistics coordinator if he or she doesn't get the appropriate education first.
- Some companies do offer on-the-job training, but if the job you're seeking is too different from what you've done before, there's no incentive for the employer to even consider you.
- Finally, don't criticize your current or previous employer, either during a job interview or while you're at your new job. It's not professional to do so, plus you never know when you will encounter someone from your previous job, either in public or at another company where you wish to work. There's an expression in English that you shouldn't burn your bridges—this is a good example of when you should keep your lighter in your pocket.

Volunteer Work

Volunteering can help you can greatly in landing a job while in the meantime serving as a helpful contribution toward some of the most vulnerable in society. The most common suggestion from recruiters and hiring experts is to work part-time, to be a consultant, or to volunteer in a way that is relevant to your career and adds to your day-to-day business skills.

If you engage in an activity that fits your career path, there's no reason a consulting or volunteer position can't fill that space in your résumé.

- If you can't find work yet but you can get a high-enough volunteering position, then that's probably the best route to take.
- You're essentially doing a job and not just sitting around, wasting time, and feeling sorry for yourself.
- You are actually building some contacts and networking.
- You never know where volunteering will lead.
- There is no prohibition against listing consulting and volunteer positions alongside full-time work on a chronological résumé.

- Volunteer work depends on the individual role to a certain extent but language skills are always an advantage, although not necessary. Volunteer work can also help support someone who has been a victim of human trafficking through which they often lose everything in the process.
- An interest in other cultures, backgrounds, and beliefs is useful for volunteering, and a commitment to equality and diversity is essential.
- Most organizations that engage volunteers provide and reimburse all out-of-pocket expenses. This includes travel and meals.
- As a volunteer, you may be able to provide language and translation support to new arrivals with your particular ethnic background, helping them to fully engage with their new community through orientation events and classes.

Contract or Temporary Work

Performing contract or temporary work makes it easy to explain what the job seeker has been doing on the résumé, in the cover letter, as well as in the interview.

- Contract or temporary work can add the benefit of giving the job seeker some income.
- It puts the job seeker in a better position to find out about full-time job openings.
- If a full-time position becomes available in the company where the job seeker is doing contract work, it is more likely that the job seeker will be offered the position, since he or she is already a known entity to the company.

Stay Informed

Spend some time every day reading the local and national news in the paper and on the Internet to see which industries are hot at any given time. Jobs could open up when you least expect it, and if you're following particular industries or businesses, you'll be ready to apply when the opportunity arises.

Networking

Networking is a phenomenal way to make new business contacts that could turn out to be good sources of job leads.

- If you don't already belong to a professional association, you should sign up right away.
- You also should consider joining civic groups where you live.
- If you start a business, you definitely need to join the Chamber of Commerce, which exists in part to foster networking opportunities.
- Let friends, acquaintances, and people where you worship know you are looking for a job in your field.
- Go to an office supply store and have simple business cards printed up with your contact information so you can make it easier for people to contact you later or to pass along your information to someone who might be hiring. If you distribute enough cards, you're bound to get some leads eventually.

The Interview Process

Let's now look at the interview process. Once you get that call from someone to set up an interview, you have some important work to do. It helps to think of yourself as a salesperson going on a sales call. Think of going into every interview with one and only one goal in mind—simply to receive a job offer. Let the company see what a great fit you would be; that is by far your biggest energizer and motivator to give you genuine enthusiasm for the interview.

- You have already created your résumé. Now is the time to put it to work.
- Consider what you have to offer that particular employer, just like a salesperson would approach selling a product.
- Match your skills to the job description. If you don't know a lot about the job yet, peruse the company's website. A detailed job description might be posted there.
- Next, consider what you offer that makes you unique or different from the average job seeker. Maybe it's your foreign language skills or your technical skills.
- Make a list of your unique skills to crystallize them in your mind and help them spring out naturally when you're asked about them.

- Make sure you come up with examples to support your claims. For example, just saying you have strong organizational skills doesn't mean much until you back up that claim with evidence, such as describing a time when your organizational skills helped an employer (or your church or your family, if you have little job experience) carry out their business better.
- Practice making a "sales call." Practice introducing yourself and giving a rundown of your qualifications. Do this out loud, just as if you were talking to the employer. While it's true that you'll probably be asked a series of questions rather than just being given an opportunity to talk about yourself, practicing ahead of time will still help you deliver answers smoothly and confidently.
- You might find it helpful to conduct a mock interview with a family member or friend acting as the manager. Have that person ask you questions about yourself and the job so you can get practice thinking on the spot and responding promptly.

Sample Interview Questions

While it's impossible to know exactly what you might be asked during an interview, there are some common questions that you can expect and should prepare for in advance. They include these sample interview questions.

- "What are some of your major accomplishments?" This is an opportunity to highlight professional milestones throughout your life. A couple of precise examples will suffice when delivered confidently. If you have quantifiable data—sales figures, awards, and so on—this would be the time to bring them up.
- "What experience do you have in this field?" Speak about specifics that relate to the position you are applying for. If you do not have specific experience, get as close as you can.
- "Why did you leave your last job?" You need to respond positively, no matter what the conditions actually were. Never talk poorly about previous management, supervisors, or other employees. It will make *you* look bad.
- "Where do you see yourself in five years? Ten?" The interviewer wants to know whether you'll be committed to the company, not whether you want to be CEO someday. Prepare a reasonable answer like, "I see

myself with more responsibilities that will allow me to make a bigger contribution to the company's bottom line."

- "What salary are you looking for?" This is a tricky one. You don't want to ask for too much and put yourself out of contention for the job, or ask for too little and look as though you don't value your own abilities. It's usually best to say that the salary is negotiable (open for discussion) or to give a range. Better still, check a website like salary.com or payscale.com to find out what the average salary is for the job in your area so you know how much to ask. Then turn that figure into a range so there's room to negotiate.

Successful Interviews

In general, an interview can be a challenging process, but you can certainly find helpful tips online for successful interviews and landing the desired job. Here are some tips that should help. Certain tricks increase one's odds of getting the offer and making the hiring manager confident that you are the right applicant.

Energy

People in general are attracted to those who display positive energy, are upbeat, and are optimistic about their career outlook.

One of the biggest tricks to successful interviewing is sounding enthusiastic about the position and, by doing so, ensuring the interviewer that you are interested in the job and ready to contribute to the team effort.

Set Firm and Realistic Goals

The best companies set firm goals and do everything possible to attain them. As a job seeker, you should be no different—set firm and realistic goals for yourself.

- Prior to interviewing, take the time to write down where you want to be in one year, three years, and five years
- Be specific and map out a step-by-step plan to ensure that you get there. If we don't know where we are going, our overall achievements are going to end up being a fraction of what they could be.

- Be focused and tenacious in your goals and let the hiring company hear those ambitions.

What You Can Do for the Company

The best way to sell yourself is to talk in terms of what the other person wants—tell the prospective employer what you can do for company.

- Take the time to think about what benefits and skills you bring to the table. Read over the job description and envision the concerns and needs of that employer.
- By speaking about how you can deliver the desired results, you are more likely to get an offer and have more leverage negotiating the salary you want. In essence, give the employer what they want and you will get everything you need.
- Be approachable and likable. Employers look for real qualities in applicants, such as whether you will fit in with the culture of their company or how you will get along with the current employees and how you might enjoy the work. Likability is a huge factor in nailing down the interview.
- You have to remember you are going to talk about yourself and your skills. What is the point of being nervous, tense, or judgmental? The best dialogues and conversations take place when humans are genuinely engaged and focused on the task at hand.
- All the unrelated issues must be left outside the room. Most people simply find themselves distracted and nervous while lacking focus from the task on hand.
- There is no reason to fear anything but rather go in with enthusiasm and confidence. Being afraid of failure actually hurts, so be authentic and that will bring out the best you.
- Luck, most of the time, is on the side of those who are determined to reach a specific goal. Your focus and drive should be to nail down the interview and get the job and leave great impressions on your interviewers.
- Sound and appear like a winner.
- Focus on the positive aspects of the position.

Stay Upbeat

Naturally, you won't land every job for which you interview. So if you have to keep looking because the job you want doesn't pan out, make sure you keep your résumé up to date and stay confident. Even when the economy is depressed, there are far more people working than not, so something will come along for you, if not today, then eventually.

- Polish your skills.
- Never exaggerate your previous experiences. These are easily noticeable in an interview by a clever interviewer and you will be off your game immediately.
- In an interview, the recruiter wants to know you! The real you! Your character, your strong and weak points, your skills. In fact, the interview is to see if you will fit in with the company culture, handle the responsibilities of the position, and are capable of learning and improving your skills and knowledge.

Before the Interview

You have worked very hard to get to this point—sending résumés, networking with peers, attending job fairs, and taking classes to make yourself more valuable to employers. So the time before the interview puts you in a success-driven frame of mind.

I cannot stress enough the importance of interview preparation! You only get one chance to prove to a potential employer why you're the right candidate for the job. It's imperative you walk into each and every interview with a premeditated plan for selling yourself. Unfortunately, too many well-qualified candidates fail to spend enough time preparing for interviews and subsequently lose out on good offers. Interview prep not your forte? Try implementing this simple job-interview preparation plan to help you score your ideal career.

- Make sure you have done your work and familiarized yourself with the company and persons interviewing you. This will avoid any lull or challenges in the conversation.
- Be sure to prepare multiple copies of your résumé and also organize any other material you are taking with you.
- Be careful not to take unnecessary material.

- Plan to be there much earlier than the interview time by calculating and taking into account potential traffic, delays, and so on. Even practice travelling from your home to the interview location, just so you will be familiar with your route.
- Review your résumé one last time. Make sure you're one hundred percent comfortable with everything you've written.
- Plan how you'll answer those tricky questions mentioned earlier. "What are your strengths? What are your weaknesses?"
- Go online. Check to see if there has been any breaking news on the company since you did your initial research, and check for information about corporate officers. If the company has posted its annual report, look at that, too.
- Gather everything you'll need the next day. This should include additional copies of your résumé (four or five is a good number for reasons you'll learn later), a good quality pen (no plastic stick pens), a pad for taking notes, and a folder or briefcase to put them into. If you have business cards, be sure to tuck a few into your briefcase.
- Also check your interview clothing to make sure everything is neat, clean, and well pressed.
- Then get a good night's sleep. If you're tired, your energy level will be low and you won't be able to impress the employer with your energy and enthusiasm for the job.

On the Day of the Interview

It's show time—your opportunity to shine. You've prepared well already; now put that preparation into action. Here are some things to remember.

- Eat something beforehand. Too many candidates make the mistake of not eating before their interview and they then suffer from a lack of attention from low blood sugar. Before you go into your interview, eat a meal that contains vitamin E, omega 3, and antioxidants. This will improve brain functionality and help you stay alert.
- Be on time. If you arrive late for any reason—even a legitimate one like a traffic jam—you send a message to the interviewer that you aren't serious about the job. The interviewer may also see your tardiness as a

sign of disrespect, putting you at a disadvantage from the moment you arrive.

- Better still, arrive a little early—fifteen minutes to twenty-five minutes isn't too early—so you can observe people as they come and go. Watching the employees will give you some insight into the company culture.
- Arriving early sets the tone that you are a professional and will be reliable if offered the position.
- Don't use your phone or another mobile device to pass the time when waiting. Instead, you should spend this time practicing your prepared questions and responses in your head.
- It is all about first impressions. Be sure to walk, talk, and look great. It's important to stay confident but to not be cocky.
- Shake the hand of your interviewer firmly and confidently. If the interviewer is a woman, be careful not to crush her hand accidentally.
- Maintain eye contact, both while you're talking and listening. People in the Western world generally prefer direct eye contact, which can be difficult if it's not common in your culture to look at people steadily. Just remember that it's not impolite to have good eye contact, no matter what's considered normal in your own culture.

Answer the Questions Confidently

Speak clearly and with confidence when being interviewed. Play up your strengths and translatable skills to show how you could be a potential asset to the target company. Keep your answers short, simple, and honest. Don't try to be overly smart. Instead, present yourself as a confident and sensible professional. Never use slang words or clichés (for instance, "I'm a people person"), nor criticize a former employer.

Ask Your Questions

Prospective employers may ask questions throughout an interview; they are of course in control. But it is possible for interviewees to ask questions especially toward the end of the interview. This is the time to make use of the information you gathered through research before you went to the interview.

Here are some of the sample questions you should become familiar with. It is important to limit your questions to just a few and not ask too many, unless you see such an approach as being appropriate and timely.

- Do you promote from within the organization?
- What type of training programs do you offer?
- How would you describe your company culture?
- How often do you evaluate employees?
- May I ask why this position is available?
- What does the average work week look like in your company?
- What made *you* work for this company?
- Who will I be hearing from after this interview or should I contact you?
- What are some of the gaps you see in my qualifications that I need to work on?
- What do you believe I am missing in my qualifications. Might these stop me from getting this job?
- What have I accidentally said or done during today's interview that's inconsistent with your perfect candidate for this job?

Avoid Small Talk

Casual conversations and small talk at a party or over the fence with your next-door neighbor is one thing. But in an interview situation, always keep your conversation businesslike and on target. Small talk is best avoided.

- Even if you are asked a challenging negative question, you should portray yourself in a positive manner while avoiding any negative talk about your current or previous bosses or coworkers.
- It is extremely important to be prepared to answer the main question well—"Tell me about yourself." Focus on your skills that are relevant for the job. Keep your answer short and sweet.
- Focus on your skills that you can implement immediately. Every employer wants to hear how you can hit the ground running and help his or her company right away.
- Your story is important. Provide good examples and situations where you have developed, used, and enhanced specific skills.
- Wait and never raise the topic of money until the end of the interview. Allow the interviewer to bring it up and then ask about the job's financial details and particulars.

- Don't comment on the interviewer's appearance, the things on his or her desk, his or her family, the view outside the window, and so on. It might seem friendly to exchange pleasantries, but in most Western countries, it is preferable to stick to business. This might be totally different from the way you'd interview in your home country, so be careful not to overstep your bounds.

More Helpful Interview Tips

There are a few more things you can do to gain an edge over your competition both before and after the interview.

- First, try to schedule your interview early in the day. This will allow you to see the office and its employees when they're busiest, which will give you some insight into the corporate culture.
- Next, converse for a few minutes with the receptionist when you arrive. It's not uncommon for interviewers to ask the receptionist for his or her first and overall impression of a candidate. Also, if you're offered a tour of the facility, always accept politely. This will give you additional insight into how well the office runs and whether you think it might be a place you'd like to work.
- During the interview, stay focused. Turn off your technology so you won't be interrupted by a ringing phone (*very* bad form), and don't let your mind wander. Should this happen, take five slow breaths to reduce your tension, which should make you more alert. If you have to keep asking for questions to be repeated, it will be a signal that you're not paying close enough attention, and the interviewer will not be pleased.
- Focusing all your attention on the interviewer also will help if he or she says something you don't quite understand or don't quite catch. If this happens, politely ask the interviewer to repeat what was said. It's also okay to admit that you don't understand one of the words used and ask for an explanation. It could be an instance of company-specific lingo. A gracious interviewer will define the word and move on.
- After an interview, be sure to send a brief thank-you note to the interviewer. This can be sent by regular mail or email. Since email addresses can be difficult to obtain, ask the interviewer before you leave whether you can email if you have any questions, then write down the address you're given. Be sure to send the thank-you note no more than

a day or two after the interview, so you can be sure the interviewer still remembers you.

Panel Interviews

Most interviews are conducted one-on-one; that is, with just you and the interviewer in the room. But a trend has developed over the past decade toward panel or group interviews.

- This generally is done so the team you might work with, from decision-makers to coworkers, will have a chance to size you up at the same time. But it can be intimidating having questions tossed at you by several grim, unsmiling people all at once.
- In most cases, you won't even know you're going into a panel interview until you arrive, at which time your anxiety level is likely to climb. But if you've done your homework and have investigated the company and its executive team, you should be able to speak confidently and handle all their questions.
- If you are concerned that your stress level might get the better of you, jump forward in this book to "Appendix A: Stress Survival Skills for Refugees and Immigrants" by Judith Trustone. Do this prior to having your first interview. Then Judith's tips and techniques will have a chance to bring your stress levels down to a manageable level.
- Pay particular attention when the interviewers are introducing themselves. You'll want to send a thank-you note to each of these people after you leave, so you need to know who was present. You might seek the receptionist's help.
- If you miss a name, call the human resources department right after you leave and ask for the correct spellings of the names of the panel participants. In this case, you'll probably have to send a note by mail, since a human resources representative might be cagey about giving out email addresses.
- Bring four to five copies of your résumé. Here's when you'll use them. Before the interview starts, give a copy to every person at the table. Then when you're asked a question, speak to each member of the panel.
- Keep your eye contact steady, and slowly move your eyes from one person to the next. Avoid jerky, fast, or sidelong glances, because that will make you seem nervous.

- At the conclusion of the interview, ask for the job. This isn't being too pushy—it merely shows that you're excited about the opportunity and want to be part of the team. Then shake hands with each participant before you leave.
- It's acceptable to phone a few days after your interview to ask whether the interviewers have any additional questions and whether a hiring decision will be made soon.
- If the time drags on and you don't hear anything, you can feel free to call again a week or so later.

After the Interview

After the interview, take these steps.

- Always send a simple thank-you note after every interview.
- The format of the thank-you note depends on the type of job and company you interviewed with.
- Nothing is wrong with even a handwritten note when possible. It has more of an impact.
- It's okay to send a note through email as it is more efficient.
- Never tweet, regardless of how badly you wish to provide an update.
- It's never a good idea to share details of your interview on the Internet as your potential employer may be monitoring your posts online.

Unemployment

One day you could find yourself out of a job, unemployed. Even if you're doing a good job, you could lose it due to a downturn in the economy, the closure of a business, a lost client, or other factors. As you probably know, a lot of people get away with bad behavior without consequences. But you might not be so lucky.

- Unemployment can be devastating, especially if you're the sole support for your family. Unemployed people often feel hopeless, become depressed, and feel sorry for themselves in the aftermath of a firing or a layoff. This can crush their motivation to look for a new job. But sitting around and doing nothing is the worst thing to do. Instead, it's important to start looking for a new job right away using the same techniques described earlier.
- As soon as you find yourself separated from your job, you should apply for unemployment benefits. Such benefits are awarded at the state or federal

level in Western world countries; it's called employment insurance (EI). In the case of EI, you must have paid into the EI fund while employed to be able to collect benefits when you lose your job.

- While many people are eligible to receive benefits after losing a job, there are restrictions. Generally, you must be employed at the job for at least a year in most Western countries. You must not have been fired for misconduct, and if you quit your job, you're definitely not eligible for benefits.
- Check with your unemployment office to determine whether you're eligible and to ask for more details.
- While receiving benefits, you must be ready, willing, and able to work. Western world countries require you to be actively seeking work while collecting benefits, and you'll be asked to provide proof, usually by providing a list of the places where you've applied.
- It may be possible to work a certain number of hours every week and still receive EI benefits. For this reason, you may wish to find a temporary job to supplement your benefits. Try applying at an employment agency, which will have a list of available jobs. There's usually no charge for the job seeker; the employer pays the finder's fee.
- During your period of unemployment, review and revise your résumé and update your skills. There are many free resources available on the Internet, including tutorials, ebooks, and how-to videos. If you're financially able, this is also a good time to take courses to improve your business skills and make yourself more valuable to a future employer.
- Community colleges, high schools, adult education centers, and even libraries usually offer adult education courses at reasonable rates. Taking courses like this will demonstrate to a new employer that you're serious about your work and that the layoff or termination was only a minor setback on the road to success.
- By the way, if you're unemployed long enough, you'll end up with a gap in your job experience. These days, it's not uncommon for people to be unemployed for a while, but it's quite likely that a prospective employer will ask why you're not working. The best policy is honesty. If you were laid off, there's no stigma attached. But if you were fired, that sends up a red flag for an employer. Be honest, but in a way that doesn't put you in a really bad light. Say something like, "The corporate culture wasn't right for me," or "I had a disagreement over policy with my previous

employer." These replies are specific enough to reassure the employer without ruining your chances of getting a new job.

- It's really important to find a new job as soon as possible. Even though it's a discriminatory practice, the trend in business today is to not hire people who have been unemployed for a long time. Working hard to find a new job right away will help you avoid that problem.

Volunteer While You're Unemployed

Volunteerism is not just a noble act; it's one of the pillars that America was built on. But during a time of unemployment, volunteering also is a great way to keep busy, network, and fill any gaps on your résumé that might result from an extended period of unemployment.

Choose an organization that can benefit from your particular skills. For example, if you're an accountant or bookkeeper, find an organization that could use some pro bono (free) assistance filing its taxes. Or if you're a fundraiser, offer to help an organization promote its fundraising efforts. Volunteering also shows good character and integrity, two traits employers seek in their employees.

Public Assistance

In a tough job market, it can take a while to find a new job. If that job search lasts longer than a year or so and you have little or no savings, you may find yourself without any means to support yourself and your family. If that happens, you may be able to obtain public assistance from the government.

Known variously as general assistance (GA), public assistance, welfare, or social assistance, these programs are not meant to support a person for life. Rather, they offer a *hand up* in times of need, rather than just a *handout*.

GA recipients may also be eligible for food stamps, medical care, and other benefits. Contact your local human services department for information about whether you qualify and how to apply.

Early Retirement

Early retirement in reality is a personal choice depending on financial and other conditions. The actual retirement age varies in Western countries and is being extended due to longer life expectancies. Read chapter twelve "Preparing for Your Retirement" for more information on this stage of life.

Chapter Nine: Being Employed, Self-Employed, or an Entrepreneur

Atta's Lessons on Working Hard

Watching my father work to provide for our family of twelve in a third-world country like Afghanistan taught me excellent lessons about hard work. So when I arrived in Germany after leaving Afghanistan, it was heartbreaking to learn that refugees are not allowed to enter the workforce for a number of years. Worse yet, I discovered that there were no real job-preparation programs for most immigrants. Instead, they're confined to camps, which deprived them of the opportunity to become productive members of society.

But when I emigrated to the US, not only was I able to make a living, I was also able to lead the productive life I wanted. The bottom line is there are amazing opportunities in North America for immigrants to succeed as long as you embrace them.

One thing I have always been grateful for is the range of benefits offered by American employers. I will say, though, that they can be confusing for immigrants with limited language skills. In some respects, understanding benefits can be like navigating the ocean in a small sailboat. You know where you want to go, but it's hard to get there.

I learned about long-term disability the hard way, when I saw my young supervisor at the bank collapse right in front of my eyes just a few months after I started my job. He'd had a stroke and was never able to walk again. But he survived, thanks to excellent health-care coverage and long-term disability insurance benefits. Until then, I didn't know about the amazing short- and long-term benefits my employer offered, benefits I could get at a very low monthly cost.

As for payroll taxes, even as a banker, it took me a good ten years to figure out the various payroll tax benefits and advantages, during which time I literally lost thousands of dollars. Don't let this happen to you—seek professional advice so you understand your options, then share your knowledge with your entire family and your friends.

You Are Employed

Employee Orientation

Most companies, even small ones, will expect you to attend an employee orientation on your first day at work. The orientation may be very simple and brief—perhaps nothing more than a short meeting with your supervisor or someone from the human resources department who will welcome you to the company, tell you about office expectations like starting and quitting times, and explain the benefits the company offers.

Facility and Office Tour

If the building where you're working is very large, you may be taken on a tour to familiarize you with where everything is located, including important departments like human resources and occupational health (where you'll go if you're injured on the job), the company cafeteria, the restrooms, and other key sites.

Larger companies tend to make the orientation process more detailed. It's not uncommon for employees at these companies to spend a whole morning or even a full day in an orientation session. Furthermore, depending on the type of job you land, you may even find yourself sent out for training that can last a week or more. It all depends on the company culture and the nature of the work you're doing.

Employee Paperwork

It is common for all companies to require new employees to fill out various forms. The paperwork you'll be required to fill out as a new employee may require you have the following on hand: your identification card or driving license, passport, and social security card. You will be filling out income tax forms, benefit enrollment for insurance, retirement, and other forms. It is a good idea to be prepared and complete all required documents right away to avoid delays in your hiring process.

Review the Hiring Company Regulations

One real key to launching a successful career is learning everything about your hiring company's rules, regulations, and expectations. It is important to dedicate significant time to review and understand these rules and regulations, while also asking questions for clarification to avoid potential future challenges.

- You'll learn things like the company's starting and ending times, how to enter and leave the building and grounds, where to park, and so on.
- The typical workweek for full-time workers in most Western countries is thirty-five to forty hours, which generally includes unpaid time for lunch breaks.
- You're also entitled to two fifteen-minute breaks during the day in the United States; in Canada, breaks must be provided after every five hours of work and may be paid or unpaid at the discretion of the company.
- The business workday in North America typically runs from 8 a.m. to 4:30 p.m., or 9 a.m. to 5 p.m., but there are many variations depending on the company and the type of work it does. For example, hospitals, manufacturers, and law enforcement organizations work in shifts, meaning that employees cover all hours of the twenty-four-hour day in rotating groups. A typical twenty-four-hour day of shifts runs 7 a.m. to 3 p.m.; 3 p.m. to 11 p.m.; and 11 p.m. to 7 a.m. You could also have a job that has ten-hour days, so you'll work four days, then have one day off.
- You may also be asked—or possibly required—to work overtime hours, which is time worked beyond your basic workweek. Overtime is paid at the rate of one and a half times to twice your regular rate of pay if you are an hourly worker. Once you're a salaried worker, you're out of luck—there's no additional pay for overtime.
- Your new company may require you to have an identification badge, which probably will have a stripe on the back encoded with information personal to you and the access you have to various areas of the business's building(s). You'll use it to enter the building and secure areas inside, and possibly to enter and leave a secured parking area. You'll be photographed for this badge on your first day on the job. If

your religion requires you to wear a head or face covering, you'll be required to show your face when the photo is taken.

- Your company also may have a no-smoking policy in its building(s) and even its parking areas. Smoking regulations are very strictly observed and can be grounds for dismissal if you smoke anyway and are caught. Many—but not all—companies provide a sheltered place outside where smokers can take a break. Make sure you ask about this if you're a smoker so you don't break any rules.

Review of Employee Expectations

Most companies share their expectations of their employees through welcome packages, websites, and through official training programs. Department managers and supervisors may establish and share these expectations.

- Expectations may cover everything from behavior on the job (code of conduct), to onsite uses of technology like social media and smartphones, the company's sexual harassment policy, and annual performance evaluations.
- You'll probably receive an employee handbook or a link to an online version that details these expectations. You should read or skim through the handbook so you have a good idea of what is expected of you while on the job.
- It's quite common for employers to have a probationary period for new hires. This period can be as short as thirty days to as much as six months or even a year.
- During the probationary period, the intent isn't to get you to do something that can get you fired; rather, it's meant to be a time for you to learn and grow on the job.
- Occasionally, an employee will not make it through the probationary period and will be dismissed, but more often than not, you'll sail through without any problems.
- You won't get a certificate or other recognition at the end of the probationary period; more likely, you'll just continue to go about your job and no one will ever bring it up again.

Your First Paycheck

Getting that first paycheck at a new job can be an exciting experience, but one look at the many deductions against the gross (before taxes) amount can be a bit of a letdown. In addition to deductions taken to pay for the various benefits, you'll have inescapable tax deductions as well. Payroll taxes are deducted out of every paycheck and include federal and state-level taxes based on your income tax bracket. These taxes include the following.

Payroll Taxes

Employers are required to withhold a portion of each paycheck to pay state and federal income tax on your behalf. In the US for example, the federal taxes are paid to the IRS and are based on your income tax-bracket rate, which can be 10 percent, 15 percent, 25 percent, or more. The state taxes are sent to your state's treasury. On the federal side, you'll also pay FICA (*Federal Insurance Contributions Act*—a social security tax) and a Medicare tax.

Other Taxes

It is common for employers in most countries to collect taxes from employees for various reasons and amounts depending on city, state, and country laws. You will certainly need to start your research right away and learn about their impact on you and your family. It is important to research and find out the rules and requirements within your local and regional environment.

Understanding Your Benefits

Employee benefits also referred to as fringe benefits or perqs are about non-wage compensation. The main purpose behind employee benefits is the economic security of company staff retention, further motivation, and morale. The level and types of benefits vary from company to company worldwide. Certain successful organizations offer fringe benefits to members of family.

Behaviors to Avoid in the Workplace

Now that you've landed your new job, it's important to present a professional demeanor to those with whom you work. That means treating others with courtesy and respect, coming to work on time every day, remaining until the end of the day, and carrying out your duties competently and willingly. In addition, be sure to avoid the following habits, which can create bad feelings among your coworkers:

- Being unprepared for meetings and not meeting deadlines: this makes you look bad and shows a lack of respect for both your boss and your coworkers.
- Being "me-focused" instead of "you-focused": there's an expression in English that there's no "I" in "team." If you're not a team player, your value to the company is greatly diminished.
- Not being self-sufficient: you need to be able to solve problems on your own, rather than rely on your boss and your coworkers to do the work for you. When you have a problem you need to discuss with the boss, always go in with possible solutions. Don't just dump the problem on the boss and expect him or her to take the lead.
- Eating foods with strong odors, especially in crowded lunchrooms: ethnic foods like curry can be very pungent and may offend others who are trying to eat their own lunch in peace. Likewise, try to avoid eating such foods when you know you'll be in close contact with other people, particularly during meetings.
- Talking too loudly on the phone: many immigrants come from cultures where it's acceptable—and maybe even necessary—to speak loudly. But in North America, where people work in tight quarters, loud conversations are disruptive and annoying to others.
- Be careful in general about what you discuss on the phone in the office. Your private business should remain just that: private.
- Taking or making too many personal calls: you were hired to work when you're at work.
- It's okay to make the occasional personal call, but limit those calls to the essential ones. In general, you should turn your personal phone off while you're working.
- If you need to keep an eye on your kids, consider signing up for a home monitoring system like Comcast Home Control, which allows you to see what's going on at home right from your computer. It's an easy way to monitor your kids' or other family members' activities without being on the phone with them constantly.

- Going to work when you're sick: your dedication to your job is admirable, but if you're sick, you run the risk of making everyone around you sick, too. No one is so important that he or she can't stay home to rest and recover.

Things You Should Never Say to Your Boss

The following statements are some things you should *not* say to your boss, because they could cause trouble for you and disrupt the work environment.

- "I'm in this for the money." You can imagine how well that would go over. Even though it's probably true, don't say it out loud.
- "I need this job because I'm broke … I'm bankrupt … my spouse is taking all my money." That's no one's business but your own. Keep such information private.
- "I'm only here until I buy a house … a car … a motorcycle." This essentially gives your boss the go-ahead to find your replacement.
- "I'm so exhausted. I was up partying all night." Don't share this kind of information—you're supposed to be alert and ready to work. The boss might think you are trouble waiting to happen.
- "This job is so boring." To which the boss may respond, "Then go work somewhere else."
- "I can't get along with so and so." You can't pick the people you work with unless you're the boss. Get over it and do your job.
- "It's not my job." Yes, it is.
- "The old way works better than the way we're doing things now." Resisting change just makes things worse and makes you look like a complainer.
- Nonverbal language (like sighs, grimaces, eye rolls, or retching sounds when making any of these comments) makes your opinion very clear—and it's not worthy of a valuable employee. Such behavior is likely to offend or upset the boss and make him or her less confident in your abilities. If you want to keep your job, even if it's just until you find something better, avoid these behaviors.

Other Traits to Avoid or Reduce

- **Indecisiveness:** If you can't make a decision because you're afraid of making a mistake, you can't help the team. It's better to take a chance and make a mistake than never to try.
- **Distrustfulness:** Being suspicious of everyone and everything hurts your ability to contribute to the team in a meaningful way.
- **Undermining Others:** Acting as though you're cooperating but privately you're opposing people and undermining them causes trouble.
- **Arrogance:** Believing that you're better than everyone else causes resentment and anger among your coworkers.
- **Misbehaving:** Testing limits by "acting out" and deliberately pushing someone's buttons (irritating him or her) to cause trouble is both childish and immature.
- **Acting Flaky:** Exhibiting odd or unusual behavior (acting "flaky") makes others suspicious of you and is disruptive to the work environment.
- **Seeking Attention:** Being overly dramatic is a way to get attention in a bad way.
- **Toadying:** Trying to make everyone happy to avoid conflict while compromising your own values or the policies of the company is dishonest and never ends well.

Working from Home

Some employers will allow you to work offsite in your home office. This is known as telecommuting, and employers like it because it saves them money in their operating budget.

While working at home may sound like a dream job, there are drawbacks. First, you need to be much more disciplined, since you must stay at your desk during office hours. Second, you have to set ground rules for your family so they know you're not available to play catch, go to the grocery store, or fold the laundry. Finally, you'll need a physical space in which to work.

Still, if you have an updated computer system, a good phone, and some office furniture, this can be a good option. You'll save on the cost and time of commuting to the office, a business wardrobe, lunch money, and so on.

Not all jobs lend themselves to telecommuting, and new employees generally don't get this perq. But if you're interested, ask the human resources department about telecommuting after you've been on the job for a while.

Self-Employment

No matter whether you're one of those professionals who suddenly finds his or her credentials aren't strong enough for employers, you want to manufacture something, or you simply want to provide necessary services like tailoring or catering, you *can* be a "solopreneur" and grab your piece of the pie. If you just want to work for yourself, as a freelancer or on contract with another small company, you can be self-employed. Self-employment is a wonderful thing. You can pretty much do whatever you want, whenever you want to do it, all without a boss looking over your shoulder.

Here are some of the jobs you can do from and even in your home and make money doing them:

babysitting
general errands
housekeeping
mobile food truck
moving services
nanny, part time or full time
party and event organizer
pet care
senior care
shopping
special needs
tour guide
tutoring

Achieve your goals of self-employment by building self-awareness and community awareness while using today's technologies and social media to your advantage. Here are some keys to success while working from your home.

- Become an expert at what you do from the comfort of your home.
- Create your own brand.
- Embrace best strategies and practices in order for your service or product to stand out.
- Know your strengths.
- Think and let go of the fear of becoming self-employed.

Design a Brand

There will always be a demand for classic lines of good and affordable clothing. Your neighbors do not have time to design clothes, but are anxious to put their hands on new products. You can easily become a designer with an understanding of fabrics, color schemes, what to wear, and what goes with what. Here are some key tips.

- Know what to design.
- Be efficient.
- Think and set effective and reasonable costs.
- Set up your brand page on Facebook and other social media outlets such as Twitter, Pinterest, and Instagram.
- Create a small photo shoot at home to display your products.
- Set discount prices to start off in order to attract new customers.

Videography and Photography

If you are already a skilled photographer and/or you wish to follow this line of business, you have a very good chance of succeeding.

- Begin with a low-budget basic professional plan.
- Begin by volunteering at every family member's and friend's event that you attend to show your skills and full commitment.
- Always ask for permission first and then choose the best of your shots from all events and post them on your Facebook account appropriately without compromising anyone's identity.
- Create promotional deals for birthdays, weddings, and conferences within your community.

Food Supplier

If you have good cooking skills, especially if you and your family have enough preparation and storage space, then you can commit to developing a successful line of business by preparing authentic recipes for parties, events, school, universities, and canteens.

- Create your food page on Facebook and other social media outlets while displaying your great deals and meals to offer.
- Begin catering through online channels to all the upcoming events.
- A great idea is to offer a complementary side dish or a sweet dish for free.

Painting and Handicrafts

It is never too late for an artist to display their art through Facebook, other social media, and on their own website, and exhibit paintings and handicrafts online to those who are looking to decorate their rooms or workplaces.

Graphic Design

If you have experience or a background in visual arts and want to try your hand at graphic designing, then there are many firms looking for a freelance designer who is willing to understand their company website requirements and not only create their website but also manage it for them. You can create your personal graphic-design services page on Facebook and elsewhere, and channel it through small or medium businesses. Before you know it, you will have found work.

Online Tutoring

This is a global trend now; many families are looking for decent tutors who are willing to take responsibility for teaching their children. If you have what it takes to be an online tutor and are willing to take the challenge, then go for it; it's totally worth it. You can easily set up a Facebook Tutoring Service page and you are ready to teach.

Online Directory of Tradespeople

If you have a list of every visitor who comes to your house to fix this or that, people such as plumbers, electricians, painters, and cleaners who are reliable, then you are all set to create your tiny agency of people who are willing to work through you. You can offer these services online through a business name and send your tradespeople with a company receipt to the houses where they are urgently needed. And if it goes smoothly, your tiny agency will surely expand.

Become a Writer

If you believe in your writing skills, then you could create your online blog and share posts through social media. Many companies in the market are looking for responsible writers. This can then lead to a freelance position with several companies at once.

Entrepreneurship

If you have ever had a desire to start your own business, this could be the time to do it. Entrepreneurship is self-employment, but it also involves employing others and risking some capital.

North America in particular offers many types of employment opportunities to the people who step up to grab them—even those who are newly landed here or are immigrant residents. But among those people are individuals who dream big. They want to control their own destiny. They aspire to creating a livelihood that is fulfilling and satisfying. They do this by starting their own business. These people are "entrepreneurs," or what the *Merriam-Webster* dictionary defines as people who "start a business and [are] willing to risk loss in order to make money." Self-employed people mainly work for themselves, whereas entrepreneurs tend to manage their businesses by employing others.

Historically, many Western countries' migrants have been willing to take the risk and found great success. For example, Nikola Tesla, an inventor, engineer, and physicist who is greatly renowned today, was a Serbian immigrant. Sergey Brin, a native of Russia and cofounder of Google, the Internet search engine, was six when his family fled his homeland for America. Maxwell Kohl, the founder of Kohl's department stores, is from Poland. He grew his successful retailing chain out of a single grocery store in Milwaukee. Robert Herjavec, whom you might know from the television reality show *Shark Tank* , is a Croatian-born entrepreneur who founded two successful Internet security software companies. And the list goes on.

In fact, immigrants have had an impressive record of success in North America for decades. According to an article in *Forbes* magazine, immigrants and their children founded 40 percent of the Fortune 500 businesses, which are the largest companies in America based on revenue. That's an amazing statistic—and something that should inspire you.

The successes of the people just mentioned didn't happen overnight, of course. Every one of these people—and the tens of thousands of others who start small businesses—started out exactly like you can today—with a dream, a little cash, and a lot of determination. Keep in mind, though, that people who own their own small or large business tend to work harder and longer hours than they would if they were employed in a conventional nine-to-five job. But the satisfaction that comes with owning a business that you create out of your own hard work and innovation while providing the means to take care of your family well is indescribable.

There's another important reason besides personal satisfaction that drives immigrants to start their own business. It's a sad but well-known fact that even the most educated immigrants often find that their background and training are lacking in the eyes of Western world employers. This is not an insult; rather, the educational system in one country differs significantly from the system in another, and the two don't always mesh well. This is particularly a problem for highly educated professionals like physicians, lawyers, and even university professors. It's not uncommon to find an immigrant who has a doctorate degree in his homeland working in a minimum-wage job such as janitorial services after coming to North America, just so he can make a living. Owning your own small business will help you circumvent this type of distressing situation.

Self-employment does come with risks, many of them financial. But if you need to support yourself and your family right away (and who doesn't?), and you have a marketable skill, it makes sense to consider starting a business of your own.

Starting your own business has another benefit. If you ever decide to work again for someone else, you'll have that pesky hole in your résumé filled, plus most employers will applaud your effort to be proactive and productive.

Be aware that you may need some training in areas you're not proficient, if you're going to be your own boss. For example, if you have never created a marketing plan, or you are not proficient at recordkeeping, you will either need to take a class to get the knowledge you need or hire another professional to step in for you. For example, if you're not a computer wiz, hire a consultant who can come in and keep your equipment running well and virus-free.

When you're an entrepreneur, it's more important to spend your time on the things you do well rather than trying to figure out the activities that don't come naturally to you.

Entrepreneurial Challenges

One of the biggest challenges you will face as an entrepreneur will be structuring your time in order to fully experience the benefits of working for yourself while also being as creative and productive as possible. At first, the idea of systems and planning will make you cringe and hesitate. You will surely feel like they would hold you back from achieving your creative potential. It is however important to be open to new ideas and restructuring your business in this competitive environment.

- Map out your day, hour by hour, pushing for all the elements of what you consider to be an ideal day.
- Your problems will become much clearer and you'll know how to make sure you get things done, make time for yourself, and find time also for play, while actively pushing yourself outside your comfort zone.
- Sunday is a perfect day to sit down and map out your week by prioritizing what you wish to accomplish by the following Sunday.
- Outline the top three priorities you wish to accomplish by the end of the week.
- Organizing and batching specific items each day and allowing time for creativity are key to your success as an entrepreneur.
- Create a Monday-through-Friday schedule while inputting actions items, setting aside specific times on specific days for particular tasks and actions, so you never have to remember but know in advance how you will be spending your time.
- Assign a specific day and time for paying bills and clearing your email inbox.

Some Benefits of Entrepreneurship

There are many benefits to being an entrepreneur.

- You are in control of the entire operation.
- You can hire and work with the employees you choose.
- You control the level of rewards, from salaries and bonuses to time off.
- You control the financial risks, taking on only what you're comfortable with.
- You can follow your own instincts without fear of reprisal.
- You can establish a direct connection with your customers.

- You can reach out to serve your community.
- You can create a work-life balance that allows you to enjoy life while attending to the needs of your family.
- You'll have pride in your accomplishments while building a legacy for your children.

Laying the Groundwork

As with any other venture, it's important to make some plans before attempting to launch your own business.

- Start by making a personal inventory of your skills, strengths, and weaknesses, recognizing the areas that you need to strengthen and develop before you can confidently start a business.
- Your strengths may be your education, your previous record of success, or even just your confidence and enthusiasm. Your weaknesses might include low-to-no startup funds and sketchy English language skills.
- The best thing to do about the communication gap is to take conversational language classes. But it takes time to acquire fluency.
- Here's another option while you improve language skills for your new locale. Sell products and services from your old country to people in your new homeland. For example, you could specialize in selling products (either in a store or through a mail order company) that are used back home but are not readily available in your new environment.
- The Internet makes such products easier to obtain these days, of course, but not everyone is computer-savvy or has access to a computer. Just consider this: were there products that you really missed when you relocated to North America? Become a supplier of them.
- Are there services you could provide—say, financial, insurance-related, and so on—that other immigrants may not be able to accomplish for themselves because they don't understand English well enough to acquire them?
- This approach has two advantages. First, you'll forge a successful company that has the potential to provide you and your family with a good income. (It does take time though; be patient.) Second, you'll help other immigrants who may have struggled to find the products and services they need. It's a win-win situation, meaning both sides win.

The Finance Question

As for the financial side of the equation, not all businesses have huge startup costs. For example, let's say you want to be a hotel services consultant (like the guy on television who goes around showing how hotel owners can improve their operations) or a wedding planner or an undertaker (you need to be licensed). It's important to research and learn about potential costs before committing to a business.

- The most you'll need when you start out—besides clients and conversational English—will be a computer, a phone, some business cards, and a place to make the magic happen.
- That place can be right in your own home, which saves you the huge expense of leasing a commercial office space.
- If you plan to manufacture something—say, dog sweaters, or smartphone covers, or some innovative thing that everyone will want—you'll need more startup cash, which you may not have unless you can find investors or a silent partner (more about that later).
- And here's another suggestion: How about starting an eBay or Amazon business and selling items to people all around the world? Millions of people do just that. However, you will need startup funds for your inventory, plus it's advisable to have your ad copy written by someone fluent in English.
- To determine exactly what the possibilities are, do a financial inventory. Do you have enough money in the bank to purchase initial store inventory or establish an eBay storefront? Would you be able to survive for a while without earning much money in your new venture? (Not many people can.) Is there another person in the family who could cover the monthly expenses until you start making money? If so, you'd be freed up to pursue your new venture without fear of foreclosure or losing your lease.
- In addition, you'll need what is known as a "nest egg"—a certain amount of cash set aside that can be used to pay household and other living expenses, until the business actually starts making money. Optimally, that nest egg should be equal to a minimum of six months' worth of expenses. A full year of money for expenses is even better; three years is optimal.

More Business Options

Technology, population growth, and global interconnectivity continue to contribute more business options as new and expanded services around the world. This is particularly true in Western countries due to rising costs, transportation challenges, and worker flexibilities (the ability to work from home and other locations).

First—Part Time

Start your small business as a part-time or side venture and keep your day job so you can meet your monthly expenses while the business is growing. When the day comes that your small business is paying enough to cover those expenses, you'll be ready to quit your regular job. But make no mistake: it's difficult to juggle a job, a small business, and family obligations. But it can be done if you're determined.

Second—Find an Investor

Find someone who might be willing to invest in your small business and provide startup and ongoing funds. You could structure this as a loan or as an arrangement where the investor receives a percentage of business revenues once the company is profitable. Banks are notoriously reluctant to back new small business owners, so try approaching a successful entrepreneur in your community instead. Better still, identify and approach a successful person who comes from your homeland. That person, being an immigrant themself, is likely to be sympathetic to your cause.

Third—Find a Business Partner

This option of finding a business partner works only if you have some money in the bank and can share expenses. However, the business split doesn't have to be equal—if you can fund only 30 percent of the business, for example, your partner would be the majority shareholder by providing 70 percent of the funds. However, this means you will be giving up control of the company you've established and you and your business will be subject to the whims of your partner. If you choose to go this route and you eventually want to be the majority shareholder—or the only owner—be sure to work out a legal arrangement in advance in which you are able to buy out the other person's share. You'll learn more about partnerships and other types of business structures later in this chapter.

Set Up a Monthly Budget

When figuring out your financial needs, don't forget to include everything you currently pay in your household budget, from food and medical expenses, to utility payments, child care costs, home and auto insurance, car loans, and any other bills you receive on a monthly basis. If you don't have enough money to cover these expenses for six months to a year, you run the risk of having to close the business before it ever really gets started because you will run out of money to cover the day-to-day expenses.

Of course, if you're working a low-paid job now and you're sending money home to help the people you left behind in the "old country," you may have very little money left over to save for the future, let alone to build a nest egg for a business startup. But this doesn't mean that your dreams of self-employment must be abandoned. Rather, you'll need to keep your business expenses as low as possible every month, something that might actually cramp your business development if you need to travel for business, for example. If you don't have the funds, you'll simply have to postpone that particular plan or find another way to float it.

And incidentally, many small businesses are home-based, which saves a lot of money every month. If the space in your home is limited, try to find a quiet corner for a table, chair, computer, and phone, at the very least. But if at all possible, designate a room in your home—maybe what is now the den or a spare bedroom—and use it solely to run your business. Part of the reason is so you actually feel like you're going to work when you sit down at your desk for the day. The other reason is so others in the family respect that you are working. If you're sitting at the kitchen table trying to make deals while the family is preparing dinner around you or giving the dog a bath, you won't feel very professional—and worse yet, the client on the other end of the line won't think you are, either.

Business Ownership Structures

Once you've identified your skills and nailed down your finances, it's time to move on to creating the business structure. Forming a business in the United States and Canada is much simpler than it is in many other countries. You literally can decide to start a business today and begin operating immediately. But as discussed earlier, it's a better idea to put some thought into the process first. The type of business you form will dictate the type of business taxes you pay and the amount of risk you'll assume, so choose your business structure carefully. The legal forms of business available in the Western world are sole proprietorship, partnership, corporation, and a limited liability company.

Sole Proprietorship

This is the easiest, simplest, and least expensive business structure. The business is considered an extension of the owner—the sole proprietor—who usually operates it under his or her own name. Important to research and learn about specific rules for sole proprietorship within your host country.

Now for the downside: A sole proprietor is responsible for all business debt, and both personal and business assets may be seized to pay any outstanding debts.

Partnership

As discussed earlier, a partnership is a business alliance formed with another person or persons. This type of legal entity usually is formed to pool the funds, skills, and talents of two or more individuals, and ownership can be equal or unequal. Whoever has the majority share is the primary decision maker, so think carefully before giving away control of the company. Each partner also shares the risk inherent in the partnership, as well as the profits and expenses. Partnership income and expenses are reported on each partner's individual tax return, and business risk is shared. Because personality conflicts, workloads, and even honesty can be issues in a partnership, be sure to have a legal partnership agreement drawn up if you choose to take on a partner or two.

Corporation

Business liability is considered to be separate from the individual who forms a corporation, so this can be beneficial if your tolerance for risk is low. Forming a corporation is more expensive, and you must have articles of incorporation (a legal document), elected officers, and an annual meeting (even if you hold it in your living room).

In the US, there are two types of corporations: S corp and C corp. S corp is usually better for small business owners because it's taxed at the partnership rate, but profits and losses are reported on the owner's personal income tax form. However, you have to qualify for S corp status. C corps require more paperwork and are taxed at a higher rate because income is first taxed at the corporate level, then at the individual level, resulting in double taxation, which is *not* advantageous for a small business owner.

Make sure you research and inquire about the options available in your country.

A Limited Liability Company

There's one final type of legal structure of note—a limited liability company. This is termed an LLC in the US and a limited company in other countries. It can be owned by a single individual (similar to a sole proprietorship) or by multiple owners (similar to a partnership). As the name implies, the owner's liability is limited, and the owner receives the tax benefits of a sole proprietorship or partnership. A limited liability company is a great choice for someone who wants to reduce risk while maximizing profits.

Legal Entities

As you can see, selecting a legal entity can be a complex and confusing process. Most small business owners do well with a sole proprietorship when they start out, so you too might want to go that route. You can always convert to another legal business form as your company and your profits grow. When that time comes, you'll want to consult with an attorney who specializes in taxation to ensure you make the best choice for your situation.

Franchise Businesses

Before leaving this discussion of small business ownership, there's one more type of business opportunity you might want to consider. A franchise operates under a license granted by the franchise holder (the "franchisor") to market its products or services, but you actually own your location and make all the business decisions. With a franchise, you have what is known as a "turnkey operation"—a business based on a proven business model in which everything is provided to you to run it, from the building, to the inventory, and the promotional materials. You also get the benefit of the franchise's recognized brand name, which is extremely valuable for a new business startup. Examples of well-known American franchises are McDonald's, Hampton Hotels, and Supercuts. Some famous Canadian franchises include Shoppers Drug Mart, Second Cup, and Canadian Tire.

A franchise might sound like your business dreams come true, but there are some drawbacks. First, a franchise license for one of the best-known businesses can cost *big* bucks. For example, the cost to open a Subway fast food restaurant, which is one of the fastest-growing franchises in the world, ranges from $116,000 to $262,000 USD, while the initial investment for a Tim Hortons franchise in Canada is a staggering $430,000 to $480,000 CAD. Makes you wonder how people do it, doesn't it?

One way they do it is by pooling resources. For example, an entire family could sink their life savings into a franchise license, and as long as the franchise is successful, they could end up earning a good living for everyone. A business person could also take on a partner or two—or ten—to make the financials work.

Let's say you *can* make it work financially. There are some other things to think about before signing on the dotted line.

Overly Optimistic Franchise Financials

Remember that a franchisor is in the business of making the franchise look irresistible to aspiring franchise owners and may paint a much rosier picture of potential profits than is necessarily true. Also, historical data and sales do not always translate to future profits. So if you're interested in acquiring a franchise operation, make sure you analyze its financials and records of success very carefully. Naturally, a well-known operation like Burger King or

7-Eleven won't be as risky to buy into, which is why their initial investment cost is so high.

Out-of-Pocket Costs

Some franchises will let you buy in for a modest initial cost, then will sock you with additional fees after you've committed yourself. To forestall this, speak to current and former franchisees outside your target market area about their experience and ongoing costs. If they would buy another franchise location, it's a pretty good bet that the franchisor is treating them well.

Proven Business Model

Let's face it, while it might be exciting to sign on with a startup franchise because there's the potential to make a lot of money, it's a pretty risky venture that could cost you the business and your entire initial investment if it doesn't work out. Generally, it's best to go with a proven company with a history of success. Of course, you will pay more for that privilege, but it's the best way to make sure you'll come out ahead in the long run.

Lessons Learned

As an entrepreneur, it is really important to create the proper legal foundation for your business venture in order to avoid making mistakes that could derail your plans. While some entrepreneurs know this, quite a few still tend to avoid the legal stuff like the plague. Here are some of the reasons that you may have been procrastinating when it comes to handling the legal aspects of your business:

- because they're stressful and confusing
- because you have pretended you don't have to pay attention to legalities—because of that mistake, you decide you don't need to have contracts, register your intellectual property, or form a proper business entity
- because you're scared to find out that you've been doing it wrong all this time
- because you figure you can't afford to get legal help so you might as well ignore all the legalities while you can
- because you think your business is too small for anyone to steal it from you or sue you

Vet Your Business

To "vet" a business means carrying out a thorough search for other trademarks that exist before you invest large amounts of money in the name of your business or your product. Thoroughly research the name of your business, product, and service before you begin using or creating it. Not researching and vetting your business is a major mistake.

- It is devastating to later find that your trademark is infringing on someone else's trademark rights and, therefore, you have to change the name, lose your place in Google search results, rebuild your website, and destroy your products and marketing materials bearing the mark.
- So be sure to conduct a thorough trademark search before you commit to a new brand name for your business or one of your products.

Separate Your Finances

Not separating your business from your personal finances is a major no-no for managing business finances.

- How will you know how much profit you're generating if you're mixing and mingling your personal funds with your business funds? It is really hard for business owners to make smart decisions for their company without clear financial data.
- But from a legal perspective, commingling funds between a personal account and a business account has an even worse result—commingling is a surefire way to lose the liability protection from any business entity you have created.
- Set up financial accounts solely for business income and expenses—that means business bank accounts, business PayPal accounts, and business credit cards.
- No accounts should be shared between your business and personal finances.

Annual Corporate Records

Record everything that happens in your corporate business on an annual basis and take care of your annual filings each year. Have a corporate filing system with all of your insurance, contracts, leases, and other legal documents.

- Not maintaining annual corporate records for a corporation is when courts find that a business entity and its owner are not actually two separate entities, but one and the same because of the way the business is managed.
- This also means that business creditors can come after your personal assets, including your home, your car, your inheritance, your retirement accounts, and your future wages if you currently have a job or if you decide to get a job in the future.
- The way to avoid this is by updating your corporate records annually by drafting your annual minutes and submitting your corporate filings with the region your company is registered in every year.

Write a Contract for Your Business Relationships

The whole purpose of a contract is to prevent lawsuits by making sure that you and your clients, contractors, and business partners are on the same page about the terms of your arrangement. Not reducing your business relationships to writing is always a bad idea. Doing business without a contract is like not taking care of yourself and the people you work with.

Have proper contracts in place between your business and all of your clients, contractors, and business partners with terms covering what exactly is being exchanged, who or which company owns the resulting intellectual property, cancellation clauses, payment terms, and all that beautiful boilerplate that is sure to save you from any potential challenges.

Legal Notices on Your Website

Business owners' websites are their storefronts.

- If you collect information from those who visit your website, you will need a privacy policy.
- Post a privacy policy, terms and conditions, and appropriate disclaimers on all of your websites including your blog, landing pages, and sales pages.
- You should also have terms and conditions on your website to govern your relationship with your website visitors, subscribers, and clients, particularly if you sell products or services from your site.

- Disclaimers are a way to notify people of how to use the information on your website and put limitations on the inherent promises, advice, and guarantees that may be expressed in your website's content.

Protect Your Valuable Intellectual Property

This is about creations of the mind—inventions, literary and artistic works, symbols, names, and designs—used in commerce. The longer you are in business, the more intellectual property your business produces and the greater the value of that property. Things like logos, slogans, apps, ebooks, classes, written works, and visual designs are some of your businesses moneymakers and identifiers of your brand. It's really important to take steps to protect those company assets.

Atta's Advice on Entrepreneurship

While working as a senior regional manager in a branch of American Bank, I decided to pursue my dream of business ownership. That was in 2006, when I invested in a partnership restaurant operation. Not only did the resulting business venture get off to a poor start, but it also nearly cost me my twenty-eight-year banking career because of a lack of experience, improper planning and forethought, and inadequate research about drive-by traffic. I was at the peak of my banking career and I had no intention to leave my stable job in order to attend to this business full-time. I was simply naïve and did not think seriously enough about the potential risks and the level of customer support the business needed. I ultimately lost my entire investment in the partnership, as well as thousands of dollars in out-of-pocket costs.

Learn from my experience. Ask yourself the following questions before deciding to start your own business:

- Are you emotionally and financially prepared to leave your job?
- Have you tallied up all potential business costs? Do you know how you'll cover them?
- Do you have adequate back-up funds to run the business without any profits for at least two to three years?
- Have you compiled a full list of personal expenses and examined how you would cover them each month?

- Do you have adequate funds in savings to pay for all your personal and household expenses for at least two years?
- Do you have adequate health-care coverage and/or benefits through another member of the family?
- Are you able to purchase and replace all current employee benefits for yourself and the members of your family?
- Have you thought about how you'll replace employer-sponsored life and long-term disability insurance?
- Have you considered how you'll manage your current employer-sponsored retirement funds?
- Do you have adequate reserves to pay for and finance all your costs for the potential business?
- Do you have adequate knowledge and understanding of taxation and insurance requirements for the potential business, or do you have a trusted advisor?

If you can answer "yes" to most of these questions, you should be in a good position to start your own business. But if you answered "no" too many times, postpone your new business venture until you can settle your personal affairs and come up with enough cash to fund the business.

Chapter Ten: Finances

Money as a Measurement

The paradox of our time in history is that we have tall buildings, big homes, more and more conveniences, more degrees, vaster knowledge, greater experts, and bigger and longer freeways, but less time, less common sense, smaller, broken or reconstituted families, less judgment, less wellness, and too much suffering worldwide. This is a clear indication of the fact that money can be a source of much that is positive and not just a measure of success. In essence, most of us continue to take unnecessary risks in pursuing our dreams without understanding and comprehending the true meaning of money and material goods, and the consequences of pursuing them relative to our desire to be successful, rich, and happy.

But it is also a fact that everyone has some bad luck with money and finances. It is, however, true that some do a better job in dealing with the bad luck, while others with enormous wealth have not been able to respond well in dealing with money problems and unhealthy outcomes in life. Bad things can happen to good people. Luckily, your life is a reflection of how you choose to deal with whatever comes your way regardless of your personal life, business, or career. You are ultimately in control of your own reaction and response.

This chapter discusses various aspects of financial life and the tools you need to stay on track from beginning to end.

Who Says the Future Is Bleak?

Despite all the challenges humanity faces at a time when people and governments are not on the same page, vicious minds continue to commit various crimes, including financial ones against humanity, all 7.5 billion plus of us. That is right. The majority of us wish to do the right things, like get a roof over our heads and provide the very basic needs for our families. But I do realize that the powerful and greedy are setting difficult conditions for the vulnerable majority today. I truly believe it is up to us, the people, who can and really should do everything humanly possible and acceptable to not allow mediocrity to flourish.

I am especially convinced that now, more than ever, we need to learn and grow to overcome our challenges no matter when and where, to learn about money, not because we're greedy, but rather for growth and our convenience. There will be progress in our world, but not the way things are going while relying on governments and broken systems.

Attributes of Success

Here are the qualities and attributes of successful individuals, business leaders, and entrepreneurs.

- They are always willing to learn; they become independent thinkers; and they never stop striving to become self-sufficient.
- They are open-minded and ready to apply things immediately.
- They do not procrastinate.
- They remain open to various options while moving forward.
- They don't follow the crowd.
- They are accountable and take responsibility for their actions.
- They refuse to just consume but rather they try to conserve.
- They do what they say and follow through.
- They understand the difference between growth and greed. Most people do not understand this.
- They are motivated to learn and grow, not just to make money but to improve their own and others' lives

Are you willing to join this group?

Money Realities

Let's start with some realities about money. We live in a time when illusion is a big part of people's lives; some are simply delusional and believe material will come through magically. Most of us have at some point been fooled in life. Right? The reason why we lose interest so quickly is because magic does not last and is only a delusion. We must learn to separate illusion from reality. Our lives should be ones of honesty and reality and the ability to feel and touch.

But a glimpse of magic at times is fun!

- There's an old song that says, "Money makes the world go 'round." I like to frame this a little differently and point to a bigger fact and call it not just having money but also having resources to live a comfortable life.
- If you have money, you know just how true that statement is. On the other hand, if you don't have money, the truth is just as apparent. The difference is, without money, you have to watch the "world go 'round" from the sidelines.
- As much as we'd like to think we're not ruled by materialism, we allow money to impact virtually every aspect of our lives. Money makes it possible to manage and provide our families with a comfortable lifestyle. It allows us to buy things that make our lives easier.
- Basically, money puts us in the driver's seat of our own lives, so to speak, just as much as it can put us in the driver's seat of our own car.
- When the bills are taken care of and we have things—even simple things—that bring us comfort, we are happier and possibly even more productive.

The Promise of Wealth and Dreams

The dream of the promise of wealth is an idea that continues to undermine and destabilize the goodwill of ordinary human beings. It is a fact that only a few of us reflect on how our dreams have been misled and shattered by greed, by the elusiveness of a self-centered and harmful drive for profit through an intense path of commercialization. As we seek more and more wealth in pursuit of "happiness" regardless of the consequences, social upheaval occurs in almost every country.

When confronted morally, greed is truly what separates us from our heart and its realities and attributes, eventually influencing us to become indifferent to the suffering or the lack of well-being of others. This mindset subjects our children to grow up thinking that the world is all about them as individuals, while leading them to enter adulthood with very little awareness of the lives of others or the challenges to basic survival experienced by billions around the world.

The fact is that today most dreams are driven by divisive and unrealistic ideas and emotional slogans delivered through commercials with an empty sense of pride and promise. Our dreams and aspirations instead should be inspired by true spiritual visions in line with true human values, never closing our hearts, eyes, and minds to the world's problems.

The Banking System

The banking systems around the world share many basic similarities and the majority of financial institutions in Western countries are now in much safer and sounder positions than they were prior to the financial collapse of 2008. This is due to many new and stricter regulations and lessons learned. Sadly, the really meaningful rules and regulations imposed after the 2008 collapse are once again being challenged by extreme right and special interest groups.

Here are some more facts about banking in general.

- The majority of banks offers similar personal banking products and financial business services.
- The systems are, in fact, becoming more compatible due to the availability of enhanced global technologies that enable financial institutes to offer and conduct day-to-day banking transactions around the world.
- While the world's biggest banks function internationally, there are plenty of smaller financial institutions within various countries' regions from which you can choose.
- Since banks are so competitive and tend to offer the same range of services, your main reason for choosing one over another probably will be driven by its location more than anything else.
- Banks also position themselves and try to serve people no matter where those people are. That's why it's common to find mini-branches of banks in convenience stores, grocery stores, airports, other outlets, and even in casinos.
- These small branches are not full service, meaning the number of services they offer is limited, but they can still be convenient for cashing checks, making deposits, paying bills, and carrying out other basic services.
- Another type of financial institution is the credit union. Credit unions are nonprofit; they are member-owned financial cooperatives. They generally offer the same products and services as banks, but they usually have fewer and lower fees than banks.
- In most cases, you have to qualify to be a member of a credit union.

But there are credit unions serving many different groups of people—for instance, teachers, autoworkers, universities, to name just a few—so you probably can find a credit union where you'd qualify for membership.

- A downside to credit unions is that they have far fewer branches than your friendly neighborhood bank, and they may also have shorter hours. But a lot of people love their credit unions—and, in fact, more than a third of the population in Canada belongs to one or more credit unions. So they must be doing something right.

The Functions of Banking

Banks and credit unions have two main functions.

First, they serve as a place for people, called depositors, to keep their money safe while earning more money, or interest, on deposited funds. (More on that later.)

Second, financial institutions are in the business of making money for themselves. They take the money you deposit, pay you a small amount of money expressed as a percentage for the privilege of using your money (your interest), and then make their own investments with your money as a way to grow it further. Banks are thought to be rich and powerful, but that's not always the case.

How and Where to Bank

Choosing a bank is an important step. If all goes well, you will be building a long-term relationship with that bank.

- The best option is to ask family and friends about their interaction, service, and overall experience.
- There is no better way than to find out from those who have experience with using banks.
- Research online within your community and look for the best locations closest to your home and work.

Basic Banking Products

Because of the similar product and services offered by many banks, credit unions, and financial institutions, for simplicity's sake, in this chapter I will use the term "financial institutions" from here on to refer to them all.

Financial institutions offer a variety of products and services. Let's take a look at some of the most common and basic ones.

Savings Accounts

Savings accounts are at the heart of the banking system.

- People like you entrust their paychecks, inheritance money, lemonade stand money, and other funds to banks, and in return, receive a small percentage of that money as a "reward," so to speak.
- That payment, called interest, is paid monthly or quarterly and is deposited right into your savings account. If you leave both your principal (the original deposit) and the interest in your account, you'll receive interest on both amounts when the next quarter rolls around. This is a process known as compounding interest, and over time, you can accumulate a fair amount of money.
- In some countries like the United States, most interest paid on your account is taxable. The banks will report this amount to you as well as to the country's treasury department at the end of each year. You should check with your bank to learn more about the tax consequences of earning interest in your country.
- There are other forms of savings accounts, such as Money Market Accounts (MMAs) in the US for example, which pay a higher interest rate but may require a higher balance. Most MMAs also allow you to access your funds at any time, though there may be restrictions.
- It is best to read the account disclosure carefully to maximize your savings potential while asking questions.
- Regular savings accounts usually can be started with very small deposits, although you may have to pay a fee if the balance remains low (fees are discussed later in this chapter). However, there are no limits on deposits and withdrawals.

You can access your account in several ways.

- Visit a bank branch and have a teller handle your transaction(s). This can be done inside the bank or at a drive-through window outside the bank.
- Use an Automated Teller Machine (ATM) available worldwide now for simple transactions like making deposits and withdrawals.

- Use the bank's Internet banking service. The service is free but you must set up your access in advance through the bank using your account number and a personal identification number (a PIN) assigned to you by the bank. You can usually change your PIN at the bank at your discretion.
- Use the bank's pay-by-phone system, which allows you to phone the bank, input your account number and PIN, and do most common banking transactions.

Checking Accounts

Checking accounts allow customers to make payments to other people or companies using a paper document called a check. The check provides spaces for essential information:

- the name of the payee (the person or company being paid)
- the amount of the check written in one place in numerals and in another place in words; for example, as $856.77 and as "eight hundred fifty-six and 77/100 dollars"
- your signature—you must sign the check to make it legal tender (that is, an official form of payment)
- your name, address, account number, and bank routing number (the nine digits across the bottom of the check that identify the bank) are printed on the face of the check

The majority of checking accounts also provide a debit card with the account, which you can use to purchase items and withdraw cash from your available funds.

Here are some more facts about checking accounts.

- Checking account holders are typically charged a monthly maintenance fee, especially if the account balance is below a certain amount.
- Talk to your bank to see how much you must keep on deposit to avoid monthly services fees, or find a bank that offers free checking.
- Incidentally, credit unions usually offer free checking.
- Since it's a simple matter to send direct-deposit checks to staff on your payroll via their various financial institutions, and that service is free at a credit union, you might want to think about joining and establishing a checking account at a credit union, even if you have the rest of your paycheck going to a bank.

- When you open a checking account at a bank, you'll be issued with a set of starter checks, which are generic checks with little else accept the bank's identifying information printed on them.
- Most businesses won't accept starter checks, so be sure to order a set of official checks right away. You can order them at the bank when you open your account, which tends to be expensive, or you can order them online from reputable companies for less money. However, I highly recommend ordering check blanks through the bank for potential security concerns when dealing with multiple outlets.
- Checks are numbered sequentially in the upper right corner, usually starting at number 101. Since some companies are reluctant to accept low-numbered checks, you might ask your check printer to start your checks at 301 instead. Businesses know about this trick, of course, but it still can save you some hassle when writing checks in person.
- When arranging for the printing of your checks, never have your driver's license number, Social Security number, or phone number printed on your checks. That's like issuing an invitation to a dishonest person to steal your identity and everything you've worked so hard for. If a store or other business insists on having this information before it will accept your check, write the number on the check yourself.
- Once you open a checking account, always use the check register that comes with your checks. This is the small book that has spaces to note the check number, payee, and amount of the check. Every time you write a check, you note this information in the check register, and then deduct the amount of the check from the balance in your account. It's important to know how much money you have in your account at all times so you don't spend money you don't have, which can trigger service fees (discussed later).
- You might find it easier to record checks electronically. Microsoft Office has an excel check register template you can use, plus you can find freeware check registers on the Internet. You can even get an app for your smartphone to keep track of your checks, which might be the easiest way of all to track your expenditures.
- Banks issue monthly statements for your accounts in paper form in the mail or paperless to your email account.
- When you get your bank statement, compare your expenditures and balance against the statement provided by the bank. Your figure and

the figure provided by the bank statement should balance; that is, they should be exactly the same. If they aren't, then you need to figure out what went wrong.

- And here's a tip: If the amounts don't balance, it's probably something you did, since banks use computers to do their work, and computers are rarely wrong.
- Using an electronic check register is a good way to make sure your calculations are always right.
- If you do make a mistake in your addition or subtraction, or you forget to note a transaction, you could find your account overdrawn, which means you've written checks totaling more money that you have in your account.
- If you overdraw your account, the bank will charge you an overdraft fee (known as a non-sufficient funds (NSF) fee).

Mortgages

Mortgages (home-buying products) are a bank's biggest product—and biggest moneymaker. Borrowers who wish to purchase a house, condominium, or other dwelling must qualify on the basis of income and debt in order to acquire a mortgage. You will learn more about mortgages in chapter eleven "The Big Purchases—A Home and a Car."

Overdraft Lines of Credit

Overdraft lines of credit allow customers to borrow money from the bank temporarily in case the balance in their account is insufficient to cover a check or a debit card transaction.

- If you have this overdraft protection, you'll pay a fee for the privilege of overdrawing your account, but this fee is usually far lower than an NSF fee.
- You also must repay the money as soon as possible to bring your account back into what's called "the black." It's called that because money that you don't have in your account used to be itemized in red ink.
- Talk to your banker or visit your bank's website to learn about the rules and how to sign up.

Debit Cards

Debit cards are used to access the funds in your checking account, without writing a paper check.

- Look for the word "debit" on the front of the card to differentiate it from your credit cards.
- A debit card allows you to make an electronic funds transfer from your checking account to the account of the store, restaurant, or other business you wish to pay. This is quick and easy, and works flawlessly unless you forget to note the amount of the sale in your check register.
- You could end up with an overdraft and, as stated previously, that can be very expensive. Your best bet is to keep all your debit card receipts in one place—maybe in a zippered compartment in your purse or the inside pocket of your suit coat or jacket. Then at the end of the day, gather up all of the day's receipts and carefully note them in your check register.
- When you get your debit card, you will receive a personal identification number (PIN) that you'll use to prove you're the real owner of the account. This PIN will be mailed to you separately from the card to protect your account.
- Most stores and other businesses will require you to input your PIN into a keypad when you make a debit card purchase.
- Never write down your PIN in a secret place—but especially not on the debit card itself. Select a number you can remember easily, memorize that number, and never share it with anyone else.
- Incidentally, don't choose a PIN that's too obvious, like the last four digits of your telephone number, your social identity number, your date of birth, or your address, because—were you to lose your debit card—that would make it easy for someone to guess which number to use to access your accounts.
- This is also why you shouldn't regularly carry your bank passbook or any other documents (like bank statements) with you, because they have your account number on them.
- Most banks are starting to offer smart chip cards, which come with a microchip embedded in the card. The microchip provides an additional layer of security to transactions through encryption of the information being transferred. Small purchases can be made with smart chip cards by tapping a terminal.

- Debit cards are accepted almost anywhere a credit card is accepted, including online.
- Some debit cards have only your bank's logo on the front, while others have the Visa or MasterCard logo. This allows you to use them like credit cards, in some cases, and offers you special protection if the card is lost or stolen.
- You can also use your debit card at an automatic teller machine (ATM) or an automated banking machine (ABM). You'll need your PIN to access your account. However, there is a daily limit and a monthly limit, so be sure to check with your bank first.
- Always be aware of your surroundings when you use an ATM or an ABM located outside—even machines that are located on the outside of bank buildings.
- It's always safer to use ATMs that are located inside buildings where there are a lot of people around. Likewise, you should avoid using an ATM at night, even if you can pull right up to the machine and stay in your car while you use it. You never know who is nearby waiting for an opportunity to rob you.
- Always remember that a debit card is a direct line to your checking account, and as such, should be treated the same way you treat your checking account. Enter purchases in your checking account register and reconcile the account when you get your bank statement.

Credit Cards

Credit cards are just small pieces of plastic, just like debit cards, but a credit card is a very powerful tool. The trick is whether you use that power for good—or not. A credit card is a financial instrument used to buy products and services instead of using cash. In essence, the credit card slip you sign is a promissory note—a promise that you will repay the credit card issuer for the amount of the sale.

Here is more information about credit cards.

- Banks usually issue credit cards, but there also are companies that do nothing but issue credit cards and rake in fees; examples of such companies include American Express, Visa, MasterCard, and Discover.
- Just about everyone needs to have at least one credit card. It allows you to shop or travel without carrying a lot of cash (thieves will see if you flash a big wad of cash).

- If you travel, you'll need a credit card when you check into a hotel or when you rent a car.
- Credit card companies also frequently offer buyer protection, so if something goes wrong with something you've purchased, you may be able to stop payment on the purchase until your concerns are resolved.
- Correct and timely handling of the payment for the charges you make using a credit card starts to build your credit score.
- Believe it or not, if you want to take out a mortgage and you don't have a history of paying credit cards in a timely manner, you may not qualify for that mortgage because banks want proof that you can handle credit successfully.
- Make sure to carry a card with at least three months' validity before its expiration date, to allow you to settle in your new host country where you can receive a new card.
- Inform your bank about your potential travel and your anticipated destinations. There is a good chance your purchase will be denied without warning, if it has to be processed in another country.
- You may want to validate and do a physical check-up of your card to make sure the magnetic strip on the back works properly before leaving.
- Naturally, you'll need to carry your cards with you if you wish to make purchases in stores and other venues. If the clerk has to swipe or tap it, make sure to watch carefully that it's used only for the purchase you're authorizing.
- At a gas station, make sure the card swipe is firmly attached to the gas pump, since there have been incidents where scammers have installed temporary card swipes as a way to steal card numbers and other information.
- After making a purchase, safeguard your card by placing it securely in your wallet or in a zippered compartment of your purse.
- The problem with this credit card technology is that equipment exists that allows scammers to walk within a few feet of you and capture your card's information using a Radio Frequency Identification (RFID) reader. They'll then either use your card themselves (using the ten digits of your card's account) to make purchases or sell your information to someone else who will use the card.
- Protect yourself from these scammers by putting each credit card into

an RFID-blocking sleeve, which is an inexpensive sheath that covers your card and blocks RFID signals.
- You also can purchase an RFID wallet that will protect all your cards at the same time.

Types of Credit Cards

There are several types of credit cards.

Revolving Credit Card

The first type is the revolving credit card, which gives you back your buying power whenever you pay some or all of the balance owed. This service is mainly provided by banking institutions. For example, if you have a $5,000 limit and you spend $2,000, you have just $3,000 left open to buy. But if you make a $1,000 payment, you immediately have $4,000 open for new purchases.

Store Credit Card

Stores sometimes issue their own credit cards specifically and only for purchases in their store. Occasionally, a store will partner with Visa or MasterCard and put one of those logos on their card, which means you can use the card in the store, as well as anywhere else Visa or MasterCard is accepted. The ideas behind this are marketing for the store's brand, improving customer retention, and benefiting from additional fees and interest charges.

Zero or Low-Interest Card

Zero or low-interest cards allow you to make a purchase, and then pay back the debt over a finite period of time interest-free. Stores that sell big-ticket items like furniture or electronics are among the stores that offer this type of credit. While zero or low interest cards sound like a good idea, the real long-term impact falls on consumers who are prolonging their borrowing, which inflates its cost over time. Big companies can afford to offer these services simply to acquire and target new customers for various offerings down the road.

Rewards Card

Rewards cards offer cash back or other incentives for using the card regularly. The incentives also may include merchandise or trips. But beware: This type of credit card usually has hefty annual fees to pay for the cost of offering such perqs.

Secured Credit Card

A secured credit card isn't really a credit card at all, but a way to establish credit for the first time, or to repair a poor credit history and reestablish credit. You pay a cash deposit upfront—say, three or five hundred dollars—to have the card, and that becomes your credit line. But steer clear of secured cards that charge an application fee. That fee alone can consume your entire cash deposit. You're usually better off trying for a low-limit store card instead.

Prepaid Cards

A prepaid card is an excellent tool if you are eager to shape up your budget, take care of your spending, and help you reach your financial goals. It allows for much greater flexibility about how you spend your monthly budget in advance of your income; it simply allows you to stick to a predetermined spending schedule. You can have peace of mind and be free of worrying about borrowing additional money through a traditional credit card. That way you will stick to your financial plan.

- A prepaid card allows you to deposit a set amount of money on the card and use it just like a traditional one.
- According to Consumer Financial Protection Bureau (CFPB) close to two hundred billion dollars is loaded onto prepaid cards in the United States alone each year.
- A prepaid card can provide a few additional benefits to your checking account. Prepaid debit cards can be used almost anywhere including online, to make purchases, pay bills, and get cash from an ATM or point of sale. Prepaid cards have consumer protection through major networks for loss of card, stolen card, or fraudulent transactions.
- Prepaid cards have no effect, positive or negative on an individual's credit scores.

- A prepaid card is a beneficial teaching tool for teens and children.
- A prepaid card is very convenient and provides excellent benefits as it works just like a credit or debit card while being accepted widely around the world.
- It provides access for online shopping, withdrawing cash, and travel purchases.
- You can always add more money based on need.
- You can deposit cash so that it is instantly available on your card at your local bank branch. Deposits can also be made in person through some retail stores.
- You can transfer money from your checking and savings accounts directly to your prepaid card via smartphone or computer.
- You can set direct deposit, get your paycheck, government benefits, and tax refund automatically deposited to your prepaid card also.

The Security of Prepaid Cards

Prepaid cards are secure. You will not have to worry about losing your financial information or falling victim to identity theft.

Here are some additional benefits.

- If thieves gain access to your bank account, they will be able to take whatever your available credit balance might be, whereas with a prepaid card, one has a ceiling to spending that limits your total loss.
- You will be covered against fraudulent spending or theft through your card's brand.
- The upside is the fact that, unlike a credit card, a prepaid card cannot have a negative effect on your credit rating as spending won't be reported to the major credit bureaus.
- You can enable others in your life to learn how to spend responsibly. Children can use prepaid cards as a tool for learning about online banking, money transfers, ATM usage, and saving money.
- You can authorize a sub-account such as ones for your babysitters, staff, or part-time workers for business expenses.
- There are indeed many benefits to using a prepaid card, and it might be just the tool you need to become financially sound.

Travel Credit Card Rewards Programs

Quite a few financial institutions offer travel and other benefits through a credit card to those who stay loyal to them. There are many options, so think about your travel habits before you choose a card. Do you fly often? If so, a card that lets you earn airline travel may be a good choice. But if you travel more often by car, a card that lets you earn points toward gas or hotel rooms might be right for you.

- With a travel rewards credit card, you can secure a car, a hotel room, or a flight, and you can make unexpected purchases without affecting your bank balance at home.
- With a travel rewards credit card, you can earn points for the money you spend on flights, gas, groceries, and other purchases.
- You can also earn points with some cards, based on your cell phone expenses and your charitable donations.
- Once you have enough points, you can redeem them for airline tickets, merchandise, gift cards, hotel stays, and more.
- Better yet, you may get allowances when you redeem your travel rewards points for airline tickets that can be used toward baggage fees and in-flight snacks.
- If you like to eat out while on the road you might want a card that rewards restaurant spending, but if you're more likely to prepare your own food, a card that rewards grocery purchases may be a better choice.
- Cash-back rewards are another option if you'd rather decide for yourself how to spend your rewards.
- To make the best decision for your needs, be sure you also know the interest rates, the balance transfer fees, and the annual fees for each card.
- Some cards offer additional benefits, such as travel and emergency assistance, travel accident insurance, and auto-collision-damage waivers for rental cars.
- You might even be able to get concierge services, special dining privileges, and other premium offers.

Certificates of Deposit

Regular passbook savings accounts usually don't pay much interest—in recent years, the rate has been as low as 0.05 percent. Certificates of deposit (CDs) pay a higher interest rate, but there are certain requirements to procuring them.

- To begin with, you'll be required to make a minimum deposit to set up a CD—often a thousand dollars or more. You also have to tie up your money for a set period of time. Although CDs can have a term as short as thirty days, you'll need a five- to ten-year CD to earn better rates.
- Currently, thirty-day CDs are earning just 0.25 percent on deposits of $95,000 or more.
- Just be aware that you won't be able to access your money until the CD matures, or you'll lose all the accrued interest. Still, this is also a simple way to earn a higher interest rate without paying fees.

Safe Deposit Boxes

Safe deposit boxes are literally steel boxes at the bank into which customers can place important documents and valuable belongings to keep them safe.

- It's common for people to use a safe deposit box to store things like marriage licenses, birth and death certificates, insurance policies, mortgage papers, property deeds, stock and bond certificates, jewelry, rare coins, and other valuables.
- Important immigration papers and documents, including your passport and every document you have ever received establishing your immigration status, should also go into your safe deposit box.
- A good rule of thumb for deciding what should be locked away is that if something would be hard or impossible to replace, it should go into your safe deposit box.
- Make photocopies of these important documents, including all pages of your passport, and store these copies in a safe place in your home, like in a fireproof box or safe.
- **Don't store your will in the safe deposit box.** It takes a court order to open the box after your death if no one other than you has permission to enter the box. Instead, store your will somewhere safe but accessible, and give copies to your executor and your heirs, and let them know where the original can be found.
- Don't put your green card (US) or permanent resident card (Canada) in the safe deposit box, since you're required by law to have it with you

at all times. Make a color copy of your card and store that in your safe deposit box instead.

- Safe deposit boxes are rented annually and come in different sizes. When you rent a box, you'll sign a card that will be used to verify your identity the next time you want to access the box, and you'll receive two keys. Usually, people will give one key to a trusted family member or friend, and keep the other key safely at home.
- Only you will have the keys to your box—a bank representative literally must drill a hole in the box to enter it if you lose your keys. So safeguard them carefully.

Home Equity Lines of Credit

Home equity lines of credit (HELOCs) are a product that allows a person to borrow money against your equity (your ownership value) in an existing home.

- The lender agrees to give the borrower a loan against that equity for a certain period of time; usually ten years (120 months).
- The funds usually must be used for home improvements, debt consolidation, or other major life events (including funding a college education).
- Since the home is the collateral (security) for the HELOC, it's very important that all payments are made on time. If you miss a few payments, the bank can foreclose, or take your house as payment. You never want that to happen.

See more about a HELOC in chapter eleven under "The Mortgage Process."

Banking Fees

There's an expression in English, "there's no such thing as a free lunch." This is a particularly apt expression when it comes to banking. You might think that because, in essence, you're lending your money to the bank when you make a deposit, that the bank would be very happy and grateful. After all, it recognizes your contributions to the banking system by giving you interest on your deposits. But it's a fact of life that banks are all about making money, and a significant portion of their profits is derived through fees. Following are the various types of fees you can expect to pay at a bank.

Monthly Account Fees

Smaller accounts in particular may be subject to a monthly account fee, which is a charge for maintaining your account. You might wonder exactly how much maintenance is going on if all you do is leave your money sitting quietly in your account. That's one of the big mysteries of the banking system. The good news is, it's often possible to avoid this fee if you maintain a minimum balance. This minimum balance varies by the financial institution and could be as little as $500 or as much as $5,000. Be sure to ask about this when you open your account.

Overdraft Fees

It is a very good idea to apply for overdraft protection. Everyone makes an addition error once in a while, but if you do it when adding and subtracting money in your checkbook register and you end up not having enough money to cover a check (known as being overdrawn), you'll end up paying an overdraft fee, as mentioned previously.

- These fees can be quite expensive—as much as thirty dollars or more for just one little mistake. That can really hurt, especially if the check you made the mistake on is really small.
- Worse yet, let's say you wrote four or five checks to pay your bills, and your account becomes quite overdrawn. The fees on those five checks could easily add up to $150. What's even worse is that not only will you pay a fee for being overdrawn; but, unless you have overdraft protection, the bank won't pay the money owing on the checks until your account is brought back in line through deposits or fund transfers. That can trigger late fees from the companies you're paying.
- Because overdraft fees are usually considerably lower than standard NSF fees, it's a good idea to set up overdraft protection at your bank. Alternatively, you may be able to ask your bank to set up automatic transfers from your savings to your checking account to avoid triggering overdraft fees.
- Banks make a ton of money from fees; so don't make it easier for them to collect more. Set up overdraft protection right away.

ATM Fees

ATMs are convenient, but beware, they have fees that vary from one bank to another.

- If you use a machine not owned by your bank (known as an out-of-network ATM or ABM), you may be charged a usage fee when you make a deposit or withdraw funds, plus your own bank may charge you, too.
- Typically, these charges are two to five dollars per transaction. You might even have to pay the fee if you use an ATM or ABM owned by your own bank. Before the fees are charged, you'll be given the option to cancel the transaction. So think carefully about whether you really need the cash before you withdraw it and pay all those fees.
- A better time to get cash is when you make a debit card purchase at a store, gas station, or even the post office. These places usually will debit your account for the extra amount you want (within reasonable limits) without charging you a fee. So it might be more cost-effective to drive past the bank and ask for cash back when you buy groceries or do other shopping.
- By the way, even though debit cards are accepted virtually everywhere, you still should have a certain amount of cash on hand at all times. There are some things you can't use a debit card for, such as toll crossings and possibly small purchases (under five dollars), especially at small businesses.
- In addition, studies have shown that people generally spend more than they should when they use plastic instead of cash. So you might be able to curb your spending by not using your debit card for everyday purchases and instead giving yourself a monthly allowance in cash that you are unable to exceed.

Late Fees

Banks charge late (penalty) fees whenever they receive payments after the due date. This applies to everything—payments on credit cards, loans, lines of credit, and so on. These fees can be pretty hefty.

- Buy an accordion file with pockets numbered from 1 to 31 so you can sort your bills into the appropriate pocket by due date, then make sure you pay them well in advance of the due date so you'll always avoid late fees.

- This is especially important if you mail your payments. Always put them in the mail at least seven days before the due date to make sure they arrive and are posted on time.
- Credit card companies in particular are very unforgiving when it comes to late payments.
- Alternatively, you can set up electronic bill payment at your bank so your payments are posted as designated.

Transaction Fees

Banks are fond of charging fees for basic transactions, too, including transfers, cash advances, and even direct deposits. They also may charge you for transacting business with a teller, as well as for *not* transacting business with a teller (that is, for using the ATM and the ABM, as discussed earlier). Be sure to read your bank disclosure carefully to ferret out the fee schedule, and consider switching to a bank that doesn't "fee you" to death if your own bank's charges are excessive.

By the way, as mentioned earlier, credit unions don't charge nearly as much in fees as banks do, which is another good reason to join one if you can.

Investment Basics

A section of a chapter in a book isn't enough space to cover all there is to know about investing, since the world of investing is quite complicated. So here's just an overview of the possibilities to acquaint you with the concept. Consult with an investment advisor if you need more in-depth information or you're ready to invest.

Stocks

Simply stated, a stock is a share in the ownership of a company. People buy stocks for the way their face value increases.

For example, when the online social networking company Facebook went public in 2012, its initial public offering was for 485 million shares at thirty-eight dollars each, which raised $18.4 *billion* for the founder and his associates. If you wanted to become a shareholder that day, you could have purchased one share of stock for $38, ten shares for $380, and so on. In addition to the stock price, you would have paid what's called a brokerage fee to the person (broker) or company who made the purchase for you on the stock exchange. Facebook stock as of June 19, 2017 stands at $151.42.

In fact, stock always must be purchased through established channels; the average person can't just buy a share or two directly from a company. Instead, you'll need a stockbroker, who is a professional advisor licensed to purchase securities on behalf of an investor (that would be you).

Stockbrokers

There are three types of stockbrokers: Full-Service Stockbrokers, Money Managers, and Online and Discount Brokers.

Full-Service Stockbrokers

Full-service stockbrokers are financial professionals who will meet with you to discuss your needs and help you build a balanced stock portfolio. They can advise you on which stocks look promising and which to avoid.

Money Managers

Money managers are financial pros who generally manage very large or high value portfolios and for this expertise charge high fees usually based on asset value.

Online and Discount Brokers

Online and discount brokers are basically just order-takers. You tell them what you want, and they execute the trade with no questions asked or advice offered. Alternatively, you can make your own trades with a few clicks of your mouse. This is the least expensive way to start investing because the fees are so low. For example, you can easily find an online broker who charges just $4.95 per trade (either buying or selling). You usually interact with these brokers online, or you may be able to speak to a live person by phone to make trades. Just remember that they offer absolutely no financial advice.

Watching Your Stock

Once you purchase stock, you can see how it's doing by watching the stock market indices, either online or in the financial section of some newspapers.

- In the United States, the two major stock exchanges are the Dow Jones Industrial Average (which consists of the top thirty ranking "blue chip" companies) and the Nasdaq Composite (a tech-heavy index).
- In Canada, stocks are traded on eleven different stock exchanges, including the Toronto Stock Exchange (the largest). You'll need help deciphering what the numbers mean.
- There are many more stock exchanges in Western world countries.
- Ask your broker for help, or search online for information if you're using a discount broker.
- Profits paid on stocks are known as dividends and are generated by the company from its earnings. These profits are shared among investors and may be distributed to stockholders quarterly, semi-annually, or annually.
- Naturally, the IRS or the CRA will be very interested in any profit you earn on your investments. The amount you earn must be reported on your income tax return for that year.
- Sometimes a stock is extremely popular or a company may wish to generate more income by selling more stock. In these cases, the company may decide to split its stock to create more shares. Here's what happens: the total number of shares held in the company is doubled, and the value of each share is cut in half. The newly created shares are then spread out among the existing stockholders. So if you held ten shares of stock at fifty dollars, after a stock split you would hold twenty shares at twenty-five dollars. The lower share price is then more attractive to new buyers, which ultimately (and hopefully) makes the price go up and increases the value of your stock portfolio.
- It's important to note that no matter how well-versed your broker or you are in investing strategies, it's always possible that you could lose part or all of your stock investments. It all depends on the performance of the stocks you own, which can be impacted by many factors, from economic reports to natural disasters. For this reason, it's important to watch your stocks closely and to buy or sell when the timing seems right.

- Sometimes it's smarter to sell a stock while it's dropping in value than it is to wait for it to recover.
- Avoid becoming "married" to your stocks because you like the company or because you just don't have time to study the market and move your money around. If you fall into the latter category of investors, it might be better for you to use a stockbroker who can manage your portfolio for you, or at least give you some advice about what to do. It costs more to use a broker than it does to go it alone, but if you're going to lose money on your own anyway, it makes more sense to pay for a stockbroker's help and advice.
- In the meantime, a smart investor learns how to play the stock market by reading and asking questions.
- Alternatively, you can learn a lot without risking any money by using the Investopedia stock simulator online game. When you establish your "account," you're given $100,000 in virtual cash to make virtual trades. It's a fun and educational way to learn the ins and outs of the stock market.

A Healthy Credit History

We all know that there are things in life worth having that we can't afford right away. They may include a college education for our kids, a replacement car or a home for our family. But even though we can't afford to buy these important things outright doesn't mean we can't have them. The way you get them, of course, is through credit. If you want to use credit, be sure you create a healthy credit history for yourself. Credit may be defined as borrowing power backed by financial trustworthiness.

It's fair to say that if you have never had a car loan, a cell phone, or a credit card in your name, you have very little or no credit history. This naturally makes it difficult to get a loan because of the fact that the lender—on behalf of an institution—simply does not have the information for predicting how likely it is that you will repay the amount he is considering lending you.

Establishing credit is important for each individual adult (female and male). Quite a few husbands and wives miss the opportunity to establish their own individual credit and find it extremely difficult at times of divorce and/or separation. A long-time housewife who has been responsible for managing the household's expenses may find herself without an established credit at some point.

There are some steps that may help when you're trying to establish a credit history. Establishing a new credit file takes time and patience. This isn't something that you can do overnight, and despite what you might think, there are no shortcuts to establishing good credit. Avoid making applications with places that are likely to turn you down the first time. Each time you make a credit application, it results in a hard inquiry. If potential creditors see numerous hard inquiries on your file, it could have a negative impact on future applications.

The important thing to remember when you are establishing your credit is to be patient and take your time. Make sure when you do receive credit, whether it's a loan, a credit card, or even utility bills, that you pay them on time.

This information is for educational purposes only and does not constitute legal or financial advice. You should always seek the advice of a legal or financial professional before making legal or financial decisions.

- When you borrow money, it's expected that you will repay those funds in full in a certain period of time. Depending on where you borrow the money from, you may not pay any interest (the charge for borrowing money). For instance, when the money comes from the Bank of Dad, it might be interest-free; or you may have to pay a certain percentage for the use of the money.
- That percentage is usually expressed as an annual percentage rate (APR) and can vary from a very modest amount (6 to 11 percent) to the horrific interest rates charged by credit card companies (29.9 percent or higher). There even are finance companies that advertise on television that charge the astronomical rate of 355 percent! You read that right—in financial terms, that's known as usury—they're charging an exorbitant interest rate. But loopholes in the law allow these predatory lenders to get away with it—at least for a while.
- If you stick to reputable institutions like banks and credit unions, you'll get a rate that's much fairer than that. It's then up to you to make payments in full and on time every month, which helps you to build a good credit history. That history, in turn, will make other companies trust that you will pay your debts, and they'll extend credit to you, too.
- Of course, that's where people often get into trouble. They open too many credit card accounts with high limits, spend freely, and then find they can't pay the money back (possibly because they've lost their job

or simply spent too much). If they default on their debts, or fail to pay back what they owe, they do great damage to their credit history and will find it hard, if not impossible, to obtain credit in the future, even for things they may legitimately and desperately need.

Building Your Credit Score

Lenders in the US and some other Western countries use credit scores to measure a borrower's creditworthiness. Here are some ways to build your credit score.

- A solid payment history is an excellent indicator that the loan applicant will make the mortgage payments on time. As soon as you start to consider a purchase, you need to verify your credit report and confirm there are no errors.
- Build your credit. The higher your score the better will be your opportunities to get lower interest rates and buying options. Your score affects the type of loan you can receive as well as the interest rate you will pay.
- There are many ways to build and improve your credit, the most common technique is to open, utilize, and make timely payments on a credit card.
- Taking out a mortgage on the purchase of property is a major way of building credit for many people. This is discussed in chapter eleven.
- Your payment history makes up 35 percent of your credit scores. It reflects everything from how much you pay (or don't pay) to how long your bill is overdue, so it's best to do all you can to pay your bills on time.
- It's important to keep on building your current credit. Your credit score will rely on your credit behavior. It takes into account all changes such as late charges and on-time payments.
- Using credit responsibly improves your credit history. It's important to consider your credit purchases wisely, and make sure you'll be able to afford them.
- It is helpful at times to simply pay off your existing credit; this could drive up your score.
- It's important to stay below your card limits.
- Lenders keep a tab on how well you can handle debt, and maxing out your cards may raise red flags.
- It's also a good idea not to use all of your credit at once. According to

Forbes , "the 'credit utilization ratio' should be no more than 30 percent and ideally even less." That means, try to not use more than 30 percent of your available credit at any given time.

- It's a good idea to pay more than the minimum amount due; if you can pay off the entire amount, do so.
- Another credit-scoring factor is how much debt you owe in relation to how much money you make. While minimum payments may be all you can afford in some cases, you may raise your score faster if you pay off debt and credit card bills at an accelerated rate. Plus, you'll save on interest.
- Avoid opening too many accounts at once.
- While it can be smart to use credit, stick to making the most of what you already have.
- Opening multiple accounts in rapid succession can lower your score.
- Accounts stay on your report after you close them; they don't just disappear. Therefore, you're responsible for managing any account you open.

Carrying Multiple Credit Cards

Carrying multiple credit cards is an indication that you are creating financial problems for yourself. Avoid this trap. This is a dangerous way to use credit cards. Here are some clues you might be in danger.

- Your credit card debts continue to go up while you're unable to make more than the minimum payments.
- You fall behind by the minimum payment for more than sixty days. When this happens, your credit card rate will jump up significantly, causing your financial condition to become even worse.
- You are counting on credit cards for an emergency.

The Credit-scoring System

The credit-scoring system became common during the 1980s as a way for lenders to quickly evaluate a potential borrower's creditworthiness. Today, credit scoring is used by lenders, landlords, and utility companies to evaluate your credit behavior. Your credit score is a reflection of how well you use the credit that's extended to you.

- Payments on utility bills like gas, water (a.k.a. hydro), and power are also considered in your credit score.
- In the United States, each month that you have an open credit or utility account, information about how much you pay on that account and when the payment was made (either on time or late—or not at all) are recorded.
- Your credit information is electronically recorded by one of three credit rating agency bureaus: Equifax, Experian, and Transition. In Canada, there are two credit bureaus: Equifax Canada and Transition Canada.
- When you want to borrow money for a car, a mortgage, your kid's college education, and so on, creditors will look at one or all of these credit information reports and decide whether you look like a good credit risk.
- They make this decision based on what's known as a FICO score, named for its creators, the Fair Isaac Corporation. The better your FICO score, the better the terms will be from the lender.
- FICO scores range from 300 to 850, with the higher scores being the most favorable.
- If your FICO score is too low, you won't look like a good credit risk to lenders, and you could be turned down for the loan, credit card, or mortgage you're seeking.
- Sometimes, though, the bank will relent and give you the mortgage anyway, but at a rate that's a *lot* higher than for someone with a higher score.
- Your FICO score can also be impacted by how many credit accounts you have, how much buying power you have on them, how close you are to the maximum spending limit with each account, and even how many inquiries have been made by lenders.
- And here are two more good reasons why you need to take care of your credit: Employers and auto-insurance companies both base decisions on credit scores. It may not seem fair to lose a job or pay higher auto-insurance rates because you have a lot of outstanding debt, but lenders do that all the time as a way to protect themselves. If it looks like you're too loose with your money, they won't want to take a chance on you.
- You can repair your credit history, but it takes seven years for negative information about non-payments or slow payments to drop off your credit history.

- It can take up to ten years to erase a bankruptcy (bankruptcy is discussed later in this chapter).
- It's much better to take charge of your credit and spending habits immediately, buy only the things you absolutely need, and limit the number of accounts you have.
- You could also get a credit card whose balances must be repaid in full every month, like an American Express card. These are all much more responsible ways to use credit, plus it helps you to preserve your savings in your own account, not in the account of the bank or another creditor.
- The bottom line is, you need to use credit responsibly and sparingly. Some credit is an inevitable fact of life—you'll probably need a mortgage at some point, for example—so be sure to make payments diligently and on time, and you'll preserve your good credit and your good name.

The Credit Report

There are six main components to a credit card. When you open a new account, move, or miss a payment, these components are updated with your new information:

- your profile information (name, address, birth date, and Social Security number)
- consumer statement
- account information
- employment
- inquiries
- public records

How Credit Reporting Works

In the US the leading credit rating and reporting bureaus to creditors, insurers, and others permitted by law are Transition, Equifax, and Experian, as mentioned. These companies provide reporting for the purposes of evaluating your financial responsibility.

Here is a look at how the system works.

Applying for a Credit Card

When you apply for a new credit card, the creditor requests a copy of your financial history—your credit report—from one or more of the three major credit-reporting companies.

The Creditor's Evaluation

The creditor can use your credit report, a score, and various other information you provide (such as income or debt information) to determine whether to approve your application and what rates to offer.

The Creditor's Decision

When you are issued a card, the creditor continually reports about your account to the credit reporting companies, and then updates it, including your balance and payment activity, about every thirty days.

Your Credit Profile Updating Process

The credit reporting companies update your credit report as they receive new information from creditors and lenders. Your credit profile changes based on your financial activity. The next time you apply for a credit card or loan, the process repeats.

Managing Your Credit Report

Late payments create a negative record and will generally stay on your report for up to seven years (up to ten years for certain bankruptcy information). Positive records (favorable ones) can remain on your credit report longer.

A credit report is updated in most cases every thirty days and every time your creditors report new information. However, not all creditors report to all three companies; the companies obtain their information independently, so your credit reports from Experian, Transition, and Equifax could differ from each other substantially. That's why it's important to check your three credit reports every six to twelve months to ensure that the information is accurate and up-to-date.

Understand the System

Managing your credit and maintaining a good credit history can lead to lower interest rates on major advantages such as purchases. So it is important to check your credit reports every six to twelve months or at least three months before a major purchase, in order to validate potential errors and any signs of identity theft such as unfamiliar or unauthorized transactions, multiple charges, and unauthorized inquiries.

Routine check-ups, along with paying your bills on time, keeping your credit card balances below 35 percent of their limits, and correcting any inaccuracies will help ensure your credit reports are viewed in the most favorable light.

Here are some more factors that are used to establish your credit score.

Payment History

A person who has a consistent history of making payments on time would probably be perceived as less of a risk than someone with the exact same credit profile who only has an intermittent history of on-time payments.

Outstanding Debt

Your outstanding debt is the amount of money you owe to various creditors. Reducing your outstanding debt is always in the best interest of your credit health.

Utilization

Utilization measures the amount of available credit one is using. VantageScore is a credit-scoring model launched as a joint venture by the big three credit-rating companies. VantageScore recommends keeping outstanding debt below 30 percent of credit limit.

Credit History

History again? Yep, all else being equal, someone with a longer and diversified credit history is typically seen as a less risky borrower. This fact reinforces the importance of establishing a solid foundation of good credit as early as possible.

Official Inquiries

Each time someone authorizes a lender or a business to make an official inquiry of his or her credit score in connection with borrowing money, the score typically drops a little. It is important to apply for credit in moderation.

What Does This All Mean?

This is like making good quality food! Whether you're borrowing money or baking food, what matters is what you put into the mix. When you are preparing for a major purchase make sure you check your credit scores and credit reports from all three credit reporting agencies: Transition, Equifax, and Experian. Looking at your scores and reports a few months before applying for your loan will help you get a complete picture of your credit health.

Raising Your Credit Score

There are many ways you can raise your credit score—self-improvement is a wonderful thing. Becoming a better public speaker can earn you confidence and a promotion. Going to the gym regularly can help you lose those extra pounds. And improving your credit score can save you hundreds or even thousands of dollars on life's big purchases. Improving your credit is not hard to do. It just takes time and a little knowledge about the credit-scoring system.

While each person's individual credit profile is different and can be improved in different ways, there are five basic things that everyone can do to give their credit score a boost:

1. Be Punctual

Pay all your bills on time each month. Late payments, collections, and bankruptcies have a negative effect on your credit scores.

2. Check Your Credit Report Regularly

Check your credit report regularly and take the necessary steps to remove inaccuracies. Don't let your credit health suffer due to inaccurate information.

If you find an inaccuracy on your credit report, contact the creditor associated with the account, or the credit reporting agencies to have it corrected.

3. Manage Your Debts

Keep your credit card account balances below 35 percent of your available credit limits. For instance, if you have a credit card with a $1,000 limit, you should try to keep the balance owed below $350.

4. Give Yourself Time

Time is one of the most significant factors that can improve your credit score. Establish a long history of paying your bills on time and using credit responsibly. You may also want to keep the oldest account on your credit report open in order to lengthen your period of active credit use. Long-term relationships are excellent indications of loyalty and stability. People with longer tenure with creditors have much better chances of borrowing money for major purchases as well as having access to established or new lines of credit.

Credit Report Expiration Guide

Late payments, tax liens, bankruptcies! Are you anxiously waiting for old records to be removed from your credit report? Take the initiative to check the expiration dates on the records in your report. For example, if you discover an obsolete bankruptcy from 2001 on your credit report, having it changed can boost your credit score.

Check out the following expiration guide to kick your credit management into high gear.

Charge-off Accounts

If your delinquent account is charged-off, which means the creditor has absorbed the loss already, the record will stay on your credit report for seven years.

A Delinquency in a Closed Account

A delinquency is a failure to pay back money that you've borrowed. Even if you've closed an account, if it had delinquencies, those marks will stay on your credit report for seven years from the date they were reported. If you are late with a payment, the 30- to180-day delinquencies can stay on your credit report for seven years.

Positive closed accounts (with no delinquencies or late payments) can remain on your credit report for longer than seven years, which can help your overall credit history.

Collection Accounts

Accounts sent to collection agencies will remain on your credit report for seven years from the date of the last 180-day-late payment on the original account. The record will be marked as "paid collection" on your report when you pay the full balance. If you settle with the collections agency for a reduced amount, be aware your record will state the account as "paid for less than the total due."

Hard and Soft Inquiries

An inquiry is a record of someone checking your credit information. Inquiries come in two distinct categories: (1) "hard inquiries" that occur when a business views your credit report for the purpose of approving or denying an application for credit; and (2) "soft inquiries" that occur when your credit is checked for a pre-approved marketing purpose or for account management or when you check your credit yourself. Soft inquiries will not harm your credit score.

In general, it is a good idea to minimize the number of inquiries and do not easily agree to having one just because you get it for free. Companies target customers for a variety of marketing reasons by offering free credit inquiry offers. There are also scammers who simply love to get their hands on personal and credit information.

However, if you apply for a new credit card, the creditor will check your credit and that new "hard inquiry" is listed on your credit report. These hard inquiries stay on your report for up to two years, and they can cause a slight drop in your credit score if there are too many of them.

Why Are Hard Inquiries Recorded?

Hard inquiries are recorded so that potential creditors and lenders can view how often you have applied for new credit. Potential creditors may think you are trying to spend beyond your means if there are too many hard inquiries on your credit report. You can still shop around for a loan; multiple inquiries for the same purpose in a short amount of time are commonly grouped into one less harmful inquiry session. Inquiries are also helpful for consumers because they can notify you of a potential identity thief applying for accounts in your name.

How Long Do Hard Inquiries Last?

Most hard inquiries remain on your credit report for two years from the original placement. All inquiries must stay on your credit report for at least a year. You are allowed to dispute inquiries on your credit report, but it can be difficult to prove that the inquiry is indeed inaccurate. If you are unsure of where an inquiry came from, try contacting the financial institution listed before sending off a letter of dispute.

Judgments

Most legal judgments, including small claims, civil, and child support, will remain on your credit report for seven years from the filing date.

Liens

A lien is a public record of a legal order issued against property in exchange for the purchase of real estate, cars, boats, and large office equipment. City, county, and state liens, and federal tax liens (for unpaid taxes) made at the request of creditors to collect what they are owed are especially harmful and can remain on your credit report indefinitely if unpaid. Once the lien is paid the record will remain on your credit report for seven years from the payment date.

Household Budgeting

Once you have credit cards and a mortgage and all the other things that come along with home ownership, you need a way to manage your money so you always have enough cash coming in (income) to cover the payments that are going out (expenses), as well as some extra to save. The way to do this is to establish a household budget.

- Simply stated, a budget is a snapshot of your monthly financial situation. It consists of two things: income and expenses. As long as your income from your job and your investments exceeds your expenses, you're doing fine. But when the gap between the two is too small, or your expenses are higher than your income, you will find yourself in real trouble, sooner rather than later.
- The main purpose of a budget is to figure out a way to live within your means so you never go into debt. That means you have to be disciplined enough to pay the household expenses and those credit card bills just discussed on time, and preferably, in full.
- To make sure you can do this, create a four-column budget either on paper or by using a spreadsheet program like Excel or QuickBooks. From the left, label the columns "Income," "Amount," "Expenses," and "Amount."
- In the far left column, make a list of your income, which might include wages, overtime, tips, bonuses, child support payments, pension payments, Social Security, disability, public assistance, and unemployment payments. Write in how much you receive in the next column.
- In the third column, make a list of your regular monthly expenses (such as cable, phone, utility, grocery, and other items). Finally, in the far right column, using last month's bills and receipts, note how much you spent for each line item that month.
- Once you fill in all the boxes, tally up each column.
- Ideally, the "income" column will be greater than the "expenses" column.
- If it isn't, you need to look for ways to trim your budget so you end up with a surplus of cash each month.
- Then each month after that, try to increase the amount left over further by eliminating debt or cutting expenses. This is called sticking to your budget.

Budgeting should be your life's ritual, just like religion and business. Just think about managing your life as a business until you retire. Avoid unproductive behaviors and implement best financial planning and make it a part of your daily life. This requires dynamic qualities such as discipline, candor, and honesty with yourself. It is about how you function, just like a business. Bad budgeting is just bad behavior with devastating results.

Set Realistic Budgeting Goals

All successful journeys in life begin with a clear purpose or destination in mind, so be ready to set achievable and specific plans for saving. Setting realistic budgeting and being disciplined are two keys to success. Here are some more.

Pay Yourself Back

I love this phrase: "Pay yourself back." After years of hard work, I honestly believe this is an element that I neglected to do. Be sure to pay yourself first by setting automatic deductions from your paychecks. Start with small amounts and then increase them as earnings go up and bonuses come through. A percentage of your paycheck should always go to yourself—it should go into your savings account. You will be amazed to look at your savings status within a few short years.

Track, Track, Track

One of the biggest reasons people do not succeed in saving is a lack of discipline and more importantly not tracking funds diligently. The real benefit of tracking your budget's income and expenses columns weekly and monthly is the fact that this will highlight and identify areas where you will be able to cut costs and make appropriate changes.

Frugality with Food Expenses

Food and drink are two primary areas where you can significantly improve your savings rate. Many people fail to take simple actions like packing leftovers for future meals, brewing their own coffee, or resisting the temptation of takeout menus. The long-term impact of not being frugal could mean a significant loss of savings.

Conserving Utilities

Conserving how you use your utilities is another element where you can really impact your savings rate, such as through effective and shorter showering, appropriate and healthy temperature and thermostat control in various seasons, minimizing light usage, and shutting off lights. These can really add up, so start a list while getting the entire family involved. You will be happily surprised to see your savings go up over time.

Use this table to stay connected and receive ongoing updates, discount programs, and new offerings from your utility companies.

	Service Provider	**Address**	**Phone**	**Email and Website**
Gas				
Electricity				
Water				
Trash				
Recycling				
Cable				
Television				
Internet				
Phone				
Cell phone				
Plumber				
Electrician				
Handyman				
Car Mechanic				
Tire company				
Other Service				
Other Service				

Buying in Bulk

Shopping in bulk not only helps improve your savings, but in reality adds to efficiency, ease, and saving time by avoiding multiple visits to the stores. All big retail stores offer competitive discounts and coupons to encourage consumers toward bulk-buying options. Bulk buying can be quite effective and helpful for bigger families as well as for those able to store supplies for a longer period.

Cable and Satellite Services

It is true that the telecommunications industry provides many attractive features available as different bundles. You can find many ways to enjoy movies, watch television, and keep up with the news these days without any need for expensive cable subscriptions.

Using Public Transportation

Opting for public transportation and other options such as walking or bicycling rather than driving a car not only helps your budget, it also helps your savings rate for future and provides and calls for a healthier lifestyle. The majority of people in Europe take great advantage of bikes, buses, trains, and undergrounds. In North America, commuters mainly use cars and there are not so many train and underground options. Even though buses and trains do run to and within major cities, the service is not always ideal for daily work for the majority of people. So look for carpooling and other viable options. For details please refer to chapter five.

Remitting Money

Remitting money refers to the practice of migrants sending money back home. Fortunately, we live in a time when humans and their financial services are connected around the world through mobile and other services, and so this can be accomplished in many new ways.

- You can simply remit a payment in seconds to the farthest, most remote area of the world through mobile services.
- While some countries are making good progress with this facility,

quite a few countries' financial services are still fragmented, making sending and receiving money very challenging for ordinary citizens.

- Millions of people around the globe transfer billions of dollars on a daily basis. According to the World Bank (the international organization established to control the economies of its member nations and provide loans at times of crises), almost a quarter of a billion people around the world are migrants, and they send over $600 billion in remittances annually.
- The availability of online and mobile services has really helped in reducing the cost of financial transfers throughout the world, but it also provides added benefits such as security, convenience, accessibility, speed and ease of transaction, competitive pricing, access to quality advisory services, integrity of transactions, better cash-flow management, enhanced financial planning, and inculcation of a sustainable saving habit that may boost financial security and comfort in retirement.

Best Practices for Healthy Money Management

Here are some best practices for managing your money in healthy ways. Grow your savings faster by setting up automatic deposits into your savings account. You can usually authorize either your employer or your bank to make automatic transfers once or twice a month right into your savings account.

- Increase the amount of money direct-deposited as your earnings grow, as well as when you get a raise at work, or when you get a large income tax refund.
- Try not to use the funds in your savings account for ordinary purposes. Instead, treat the account as an emergency fund, as well as a way to accumulate money for future use.
- Minimize the amount of cash you withdraw from your checking account on payday and move the rest into your savings account to maximize your earnings.
- Maintain a detailed record of your deposits and withdrawals. If your bank doesn't issue you with a passbook (and few do these days), create your own record on a spreadsheet or use a phone app to track

deposits and withdrawals. But *never* put your account number or password into the app. Hackers have figured out how to break into phone apps and could subsequently break into your bank accounts.

- Review the monthly statements sent by your bank for accuracy. If you aren't receiving statements (paper or digital) now, contact the bank.
- Sign up to use your bank's online banking system. That way, you can access your accounts 24/7 to check balances, transfer money between accounts, pay bills electronically, and more.
- Sign the back of your debit and credit cards promptly, then look at your monthly statements carefully, to make sure you know exactly how much you owe, when payments are due, and that there aren't any incorrect or fraudulent charges.
- If you do find something suspicious, call the customer service number on the back of your card immediately.
- If you report fraudulent charges in your credit card history, US federal law limits your liability to no more than fifty dollars on each card, no matter how much is charged. In Canada, it's likely that you won't be liable at all, assuming you've met your cardholder agreement.

Avoid Common Money Mistakes

It is fair to say that we are all somehow guilty of bad financial habits and when we discuss them in the open, they sound like a set of money-making mistakes. It is therefore important to establish strong discipline with a firm commitment to not make the same common money mistakes again and again.

- Never be late with your payments, no matter what the bill is for and for how much.
- Late payments inflict late fees.
- Late payments impact your credit score.
- Late payments lead to penalties and additional interest fees.
- If you skip an entire (billing) cycle, your credit card company will report the delinquency to the credit bureaus, which will hurt your rating,
- Make money budgeting and credit management part of your daily routine: wake up, brush your teeth, hit the computer, and check your account statements.

- To ensure your bills are paid on time, create calendar reminders or set up automatic payment options through your bank.

Avoid Living Beyond Your Means

Unfortunately, a growing number of people all over the world are living far beyond their means in an effort to pretend and be someone they are not. We are simply flooded with and lured by images of spectacular movie stars and models and their lavish lifestyles. Trying to impress others with expensive jewelry, clothing, and other items, some people spend more and more money year after year. Spending beyond their means continues to affect many people, particularly the younger generation. Such habits throw many into lifelong debt and unrealistic and unsustainable lifestyles. They also leave our children with a damaging and lasting impression. Just having a roof over our heads does not mean everything is okay. It is important to think and plan realistically to maintain a sustainable lifestyle with a secure future. Here are some ways to avoid these mistakes.

Establish an Emergency Fund

Establishing an emergency fund is essential. These are savings for a rainy day.

Most experts recommend setting aside at least six months of living expenses in case of job loss, sudden medical expenses, or other emergencies. Without those funds, you'll have to use high-interest credit cards or borrow money from your family.

The fund should be used for actual emergencies—the roof springs a leak or a tooth breaks—not for a designer shoe sale or a Caribbean vacation.

Set up a Separate Savings Account

I highly recommend setting up a separate savings account to minimize the temptation to raid the emergency fund savings for non-emergencies. Forget breaking into your certificates of deposits or your mutual funds; using a savings account is the best option.

If there isn't a lot of wiggle room in your budget, consider taking on extra work, selling items through online sites, or having money taken out of each paycheck by your bank through automatic deductions.

Avoid Buying on Impulse

You run into the supermarket for milk and eggs and spend fifty-five dollars on extras. Standing in line to pay for gas, you pick up a magazine and a soda. Sound familiar? You're not alone.

Research from the Wharton School at the University of Pennsylvania found that 20 percent of purchases are unplanned. If the shopping trip itself is unplanned, the rate of impulse shopping goes up to 23 percent.

The problem with buying on impulse is that it foils attempts at sticking to a budget. Avoid it by having a list.

Avoid Cashing Out Retirement Savings

It might be tempting to tap into your retirement savings to pay medical bills or credit card debt, cover living expenses or book an exotic vacation. Make sure to learn about rules, tax consequences, and the proper age at which you can start withdrawing from your retirement accounts, as there are potential penalties.

Even if it seems like cashing out your retirement savings is your only choice, it's best to consult with a financial planner to go over all of your options first.

Hire a Financial Consultant

You probably take your car to a certified mechanic when it needs a tune-up, so why not work with an expert financial consultant when it comes to getting advice for managing the cash flow it takes to pay for your auto repairs?

You have to ask yourself whether you have the time, skill, and will to handle your finances. If not, it's probably best to hire an expert. Whether you're single and just starting to save or married with a significant nest egg, it's important to work with an expert who specializes in working with clients in similar situations. There are experts who handle financial needs ranging from working with creditors to managing investment portfolios.

Start your search for a certified financial planner by asking for referrals through established financial planners such as banks and brokerage firms. Some planners are paid on commission for selling products while others are salaried or work on a fee basis, so ask before you hire. The type of compensation the planner receives will impact how much you pay and could have an effect on their advice. I highly recommend asking your local banks for availability of these services first.

Be Alert to Signs of Financial Trouble

In today's environment some people simply don't realize they're on the opposite side of reality until it's too late, when they realize that things aren't as good as they think. The fact is that some people just don't want to face up to it. In reality, the earlier you realize your challenges with debt, the better chance you have to fix them.

Here are some obvious signs you're heading for financial trouble. Be alert to them:

- arguing constantly with your spouse about money (perhaps there's not enough disposable income to finance the family's spending, or you're not on the same page about spending)
- borrowing or withdrawing from your pension plan
- carrying multiple credit cards
- counting on a bonus that may or may not arrive
- counting on credit cards for an emergency
- covering expenses with your retirement funds
- frequently paying enough to keep services flowing, but never paying balances on time and in full
- juggling bills or being late in paying your bills
- living from paycheck to paycheck
- not budgeting
- not considering savings as an expense just like any other expense
- not paying overdraft fees regularly
- not saving any money at all
- overdrawing your checking account
- paying for a new car using home equity value
- paying for a vacation through your home equity
- paying late because one is lazy (that is like throwing money away)
- paying late because you cannot afford to pay
- paying lots of non-sufficient fines for not maintaining enough to pay bills
- paying off other debts using home equity
- paying the bare minimum

- resting your plans for stability on a future payoff, such as an inheritance, a rise in the value of your home, or a big tax refund
- stressing regularly over big debts
- worrying about your bills at night and being unable to sleep because of that

Cutting Home Utility Bills

Refer to the tips in chapter three under "Managing a Household" to be sure your home utility bills are as low as you can make them.

Shopping Is Addicting

Shopping is addicting, especially for immigrants. It's easy to be dazzled by the range and availability of merchandise to buy, especially if you didn't own much in your homeland. It's also easy to fall into the trap of wanting to have more than your neighbors and friends because you want to show off. The expression for this in English is "Keeping up with the Joneses."

That happened to me, too, when I first came to the United States. I spent way more on shopping than I put aside in savings. Eventually, I realized that buying things instead of saving was having a huge impact on my well-being and the well-being of those close to me.

I recommend that you stop competing with others and stop acting as though you are rich by buying a lot of stuff. It's more important to build a solid financial life so you'll be self-sufficient and won't have to rely on anyone else or the government to come to your rescue. You're in the driver's seat and, hopefully, that seat is in a used and affordable car.

Taxation

Taxation in general is a complicated but important factor in the overall scheme of the social and financial aspects of your life. It is therefore important to learn and become knowledgeable enough about your host country's tax rules and laws to properly manage your tax obligations. While there are various forms of taxes—income, sales, fuel, property, estate, and others—it is particularly important to learn about income taxes and other tax elements depending on your job, your career, and your line of business.

Bankruptcy

The word "bankruptcy" is enough to strike fear into the heart of any responsible person. Bankruptcy, which is the state of being unable to pay one's debts, represents a personal failure; one that causes guilt and shame in most responsible people. Yet sometimes, it's the only option a person has to avoid crushing debt. Bankruptcy helps people who can no longer pay their debts get a fresh start by liquidating their assets to pay their debts or by creating a repayment plan.

Bankruptcy laws also protect financially troubled businesses and the people they owe money to. This section explains the bankruptcy process and laws. Bankruptcy laws exist in all Western countries so it's a good idea to research and learn about their rules and processes within your community.

In the US, bankruptcies under Chapters 7, 11, and 13 of Title 11 of the United States Code (the Bankruptcy Code) remain on your credit report for seven to ten years after the filing date. When you file for bankruptcy, all the accounts included should be marked as "Included in BK" and will each stay on your report for a period of seven to ten years.

Here are some facts.

- Of course, the preferred course of action is to avoid getting into a situation that would result in bankruptcy. It's important to avoid controllable situations like the reckless use of credit cards.
- Sometimes, you can be wrecked by situations beyond your control, like towering medical bills or other emergencies.
- Economic downturns that erode your ability to earn a living, deplete the equity in your home, and erase your buying power are other unavoidable situations.
- No matter what the cause, bankruptcy changes your life—and quite frankly, sometimes it changes your life for the better.
- After the initial shame and stigma of the personal failure wears off, you realize you have a chance for a new start, which can lift an enormous weight off your shoulders.

This is not a testimonial for bankruptcy; it's just a fact of life. So here are the steps involved in the US and Canada in case you must file for bankruptcy. Similar processes exist in all Western countries.

- In order to start bankruptcy proceedings, you are well advised to consult an attorney experienced with bankruptcies. They can help you decide whether you actually qualify to file for bankruptcy, whether it's the right course of action, and which type of bankruptcy to choose.

- You can file without an attorney, but it's usually better to have an experienced pro guide you through the process.
- In the United States, there are two types of bankruptcy filings. People usually choose Chapter 7 bankruptcy when they're buried in medical debt, they're unemployed and have no resources to pay their bills, or they've run their credit cards up so high that there's no possibility of repayment.
- Under Chapter 7, assets are liquidated (converted into cash). Assets may include your house, if you have any equity in it.
- The money is then divided among your creditors. Usually, they'll get far less than they're owed.
- Under Chapter 13, the court oversees the reorganization of your financial life, and you must pay your debts within three to five years.
- This might be a good choice if you want to keep your home and possessions. But it won't work if you are unemployed or don't have a way to repay debt.

Hopefully, you'll never need to file for bankruptcy. But if you ever do, you can take comfort in knowing that there's a standard process available to help you recover your life and self-esteem so you can move on to better things.

Chapter 7 (United States)	Personal Bankruptcy (Canada)
Consult a bankruptcy attorney for advice.	Contact a federally licensed trustee in bankruptcy to start the process.
Complete mandatory credit counseling.	File an "Assignment for the General Benefit of Creditors" so your creditors can no longer start or continue legal proceedings against you.
Fill out the necessary paperwork to initiate the bankruptcy.	Attend mandatory credit counseling sessions.

File the forms and a petition for bankruptcy in bankruptcy court. At this point, your creditors are required by law to stop any proceedings like lawsuits against you.	Abide by the federal government's surplus income calculation, which is a monthly net amount for a resonable living standard. You must pay the trustee 50 percent of any surplus income above that monthly net amount to benefit creditors.
Attend a meeting of creditors to discuss your debt.	Stay in touch with the trustee in case you have a means to pay off additional debt.
Complete the remaining paperwork and a financial management course.	Wait nine months for word that the bankruptcy was granted.
Wait sixty days for word that your debts have been eliminated.	
Move on and get your life and financial house in order.	Restart your financial life by being prudent and careful about future spending and debt.

Worksheets and Tables

Available Cash Assets Worksheet

Use these worksheets each month within the calendar year.

Date:	**Current Balance**	**Interest earning**	**Maturity date**	**Monthly Income**
Checking Account				
Savings Account				
Certificates of Deposit				
Other Investments				
Treasury Bills				

Stocks				
Stocks				
Stocks				
Bonds				
Bonds				
Annuities				
Total Assets				

Financial Planning Questionnaire—Basic Questions

Date:	**Answers**
Name	
Address	
Home phone	
Cell phone	
Office phone	
Occupation	
Age	
Health status	
Medications	

Financial Planning Questionnaire Follow-Up Questions

Is your mother alive?	
If not, what was the cause of her death and how old was she?	
Is your father alive?	
If not, what was the cause of his death and how old was he?	

Your financial goals	1. 2. 3.
Have you every invested in anything other than regular savings or certificates of deposit?	
Do you hold Stocks? Bonds?	
How do you feel about these investments? Stocks? Bonds?	
Year you expect to retire	
Will you receive a pension?	Y/N
Company name	
How much do you expect to receive?	
How many times have you been married?	
Are you receiving funds from an ex-spouse?	
For how many more years?	
How much?	
Will payments stop after her/his death?	
Do you pay alimony?	
Monthly amount	
Are you paying child support?	
How much?	
Are you receiving child support?	
How much?	
How long are you willing to tie up your money?	
Do you feel comfortable talking about money matters?	

Chapter Eleven: The Big Purchases—A Home and a Car

Buying a Home

There's no question that home ownership is one of the pillars of every human being's dreams everywhere. A home of our own represents comfort, security, and success. For some, it's a place to share happy times with family and friends. For others, it's a hallmark of responsibility and adulthood. In fact home buying is one of the biggest financial decisions most people make during their life.

No matter what your home means to you, it's a big step to look for that home, then sign the papers that either makes it your own, or gives you the right to live in it for a certain period of time.

While having a house is considered the ultimate in home ownership, not every immigrant is able to or wants to own a house—at least, not right away. Maybe you need time to save enough money to make the down payment, which is a partial payment toward the amount you will owe. Maybe a house is just too big for you. Maybe you can't afford the payments and still be able to send money back to the folks in your home country. Or maybe you just don't want the responsibility that comes along with a house, like lawn work, interior maintenance, property taxes, and other time-consuming tasks.

If this sounds like you, then buying a condominium instead or renting an apartment might be a better choice for you. In North America, you have plenty of different types of housing to select from, and the right one is out there, waiting for you.

The first half of this chapter explores the various types of housing that are available in North America, from modest studio apartments to grand homes situated on large pieces of property. The type of home you ultimately select will depend on your income, tolerance for debt, location, and the number of people in your household. Because the names of the various home styles are basically the same with just a few exceptions in the United States and Canada (two of the countries of the Western world), they're discussed together.

Before Committing

Once you've made the decision to find your own home, there are a number of factors to consider before you actually commit.

Location

If at all possible, you should select a home that's close to your work or to where you and others in your family want to work. That will make getting to work easier and faster, and it will give you more time to relax at the end of the day instead of sitting in traffic Also consider the community where your prospective home is located. Does it offer activities for families? Are there convenient travel routes into and out of town? Is there adequate public transportation? Are the streets safe? These are all important considerations.

Size

Depending on the living arrangements, you may need a larger home if you will be living with many people. While homes in North America are built to be single-family dwellings, it's not uncommon for more than one immigrant family to live together temporarily.

Living with family or friends comes with many benefits. You not only save on rent and other expenses, but there's the sheer joy of having their company and ongoing support.

Cost

Even though—if you decide to buy your home—you will probably take out a mortgage to pay for it and the payments will be spread out over fifteen, twenty, or thirty years, the cost of your home is still a huge factor when deciding what to buy. Work with a banker or another financial expert (for example, a mortgage broker) to determine how much you can reasonably afford, then stick to that price range when shopping. You'll find more information about how banks determine how much they'll lend you in the discussion of mortgages later in this chapter.

Remember, too, that there are many other costs associated with home ownership, from utility bills to taxes, home improvements, and more. You also have to feed your family and pay for clothing, school expenses, and other bills. You must factor in all these expenses to make sure you're financially able to handle them along with a mortgage.

Financial Stability

It's crucial that you have a stable job and savings before you buy a house, because if you miss payments due to a job loss, for example, you'll lose your house, too, and all the equity you may have built in it. This is another reason why it's a good idea to consult with a financial expert before you buy. In addition to looking at your financial situation and counseling you about whether you can manage all the costs associated with home ownership, a financial expert can help you draw up a budget and help you develop a plan that will allow you to support your family for a minimum of six months if you lose your job and your income.

Buying Rather than Renting

If you plan to be in your home for more than five years, conventional financial wisdom holds that it's better to buy rather than rent an apartment, house, condo, or townhouse. Although it's possible to rent a condo or a townhouse, it's much more common for people to buy these types of homes. You can buy a condo or a townhouse with cash, of course, but you're much more likely to need a mortgage, which allows you to pay for the house using money from a lending institution like a bank and paying the money back over time. As with a house, you can make improvements or redecorate a condo or townhouse only if you own it. It's "hands off" for people who lease or rent.

- Buying a home is a matter of qualifying for and obtaining a mortgage from a bank or another financial institution, signing papers, and making monthly mortgage payments.
- Investing in a home and building equity in potential tax-protected assets instead of paying rent year after year is a reliable and proven path to building wealth over the long term.

- Buying is an investment in your future.
- If you make significant payments—that is, payments above the cost of the regular mortgage—you'll build equity in your house faster as long as the housing market remains strong.
- Your home's value will rise in a strong housing market and may go down in a weak housing market.
- You'll own the house and property outright once the mortgage is paid off. If you sell the house before it's paid off, you may get the equity back, based on local market conditions.
- You will also have to pay property taxes, utility bills, and other household expenses.
- Mortgage interest rates, property taxes, insurance, and maintenance costs tend to be high. You can get a federal income tax deduction for mortgage interest and property tax; you cannot recover the cost of insurance and home maintenance.
- You're free to do any redecorating, remodeling, landscaping, or other beautification work you wish, though some of the work may require permission from your city planners first.
- The outside work may include cutting the lawn, weeding, trimming bushes, caring for trees, maintaining retaining walls, and so on.
- If you buy into a subdivision that has a homeowners' association, you'll be required to pay a monthly or annual homeowner's fee, which usually covers landscaping around the entrance to the subdivision, snow removal, and other beautification and maintenance projects.
- You don't have to deal with landlords or leasing agents, though you may have to deal with city planners and a homeowners' association.
- Home ownership gives you the opportunity to become a part of a community made up of local schools and shops while creating a support system of friends.
- Your investment in your home also plays a major role in the community you choose to live in.
- Immigrants in general throughout the world are gaining in homeownership, which is a very positive development and very likely to increase their contribution to a country's economy.
- Studies indicate foreign-born homeowners are much more likely than foreign-born renters to amass home equity and wealth and spend more.

Renting Rather than Buying

Both buying and renting have advantages and disadvantages—pros and cons. The cons against buying may lead you to consider the pros of renting—to rent rather than buy. There are a lot of fees associated with mortgages, and it's not worth paying them unless you plan to stay in the house for several years.

Be sure to not allow yourself and your family to be trapped in the cruel prison of poverty. America and quite a few other Western countries have faced stagnating and failing incomes and this has led to the bottom falling out of the housing market, which is incredibly hard for people who still have years of a mortgage to pay off.

Of course, if you don't have enough money for a down payment or you just prefer having the freedom to move on to another place when you're ready, then renting might be the better choice for you in many ways.

- You have to qualify for a mortgage based on three factors—your income, debt level, and credit score. You may be unable to settle on your dream home if any one of the three factors is out of line.
- If you don't have sparkling credit or you just aren't ready to buy yet, you still can get into a home of your own by leasing it. With a lease, you're committing to a long-term contract to stay in the house and make the lease payments.
- You have to commit to renting for a certain length of time when you sign a lease—a rental agreement—usually at least a year; more commonly, three years. It's easier to break a lease (although not recommended) than it is to sell a house and get out of your mortgage.
- Renters have the flexibility to contract for either months or years, allowing them to test out an area before committing to a long-term contract or buying a permanent home.
- When you rent, you're planning to stay for a shorter period of time, say, thirty days. A rental agreement does renew automatically at the end of the rental period if you give written notice that you wish to stay. Renting can be the way to go if you're not ready to buy but need a place to live right away.
- If you're considering an apartment, then the choice is easier. With very few exceptions (there are exceptions in New York City, for instance), apartments are rented rather than purchased.

- When you rent, your money goes to your landlord—you never see it again.
- Figure out exactly what percent of your income goes toward rent in order to find a place you can afford.
- Rent payments are usually due on the first of the month, and you're likely to have to pay the first and last rent payment when you agree to take the apartment and sign on the dotted line.
- You will also have to pay a security deposit, which is used to pay for any damage to the apartment above normal wear and tear (such as gouges in the walls or flooring). The deposit also covers key replacement, painting, carpet cleaning, and other services necessary to prepare the apartment for the next tenant.
- The landlord should have the apartment freshly painted and cleaned before you move in.
- As a resident, you're usually not allowed to paint, wallpaper, hang pictures, or otherwise alter the living space—inside or outside—in any way. Because you don't own the apartment, you will call the building superintendent (or perhaps the landlord) when repairs are needed on the plumbing, appliances, and so on.
- Apartments come either unfurnished or furnished. If the latter, then you're stuck with whatever furnishings are in the place, no matter how much you hate them.
- The only thing you can do with furniture you don't like would be to store it in an offsite storage unit, then bring it back before you move. (But hands off the draperies—you're stuck with them.)
- Do let your landlord know that you're moving his furniture out if you choose to do so. The landlord is prohibited by law from entering your apartment once you've moved in, but he or she could get very upset seeing the furniture on the way out the door.
- Some apartments come with all utilities included in the monthly rent payment. Others may require you to pay for electricity, water (hydro), and gas or heating oil. You are responsible for your own landline phone, cable television, and Internet service bills.
- Pets are often not allowed in apartments, but there are exceptions. So if you're bringing Fido or Fluffy, be sure to ask if she's welcome.
- Most landlords also won't allow you to have long-term guests. If you are expecting someone from your home country to come for a long

visit, be sure to check your lease first, because if there's a clause prohibiting guests, you could lose your lease due to noncompliance.

- Some apartments also may have a nonsmoking policy. If you or a family member smokes, be sure to ask before you make any commitments.
- Just as with buying a home, renting also gives you the opportunity to become a part of a community made up of local schools and shops while creating a support system of friends; often rental accommodation is actually situated nearer efficient transportation and shopping than houses for purchase are.
- Finally, when it's time to move, it's customary to give at least a month's notice before you actually move out.

Dwellings

Apartments

Apartments are called different names in other countries—digs, a flat, lodgings, a suite, a tenement, and a bedsitter. This type of dwelling is a group of rooms that together form a single residence. You'll find many apartments located in a single building or in an apartment complex, from as few as a dozen to as many as a couple of hundred. There are three styles of apartments: the low-rise apartment, which is located in a building of fewer than four floors; the mid-rise apartment, which is usually no more than four to six floors high and may have usable outdoor space (like a garden) around it; and the high-rise apartment, which in addition to being in tall building of six stories or more, may have special amenities like a front lobby, excellent views, a fitness room, and even retail space on the ground floor. The number of rooms in an apartment depends on the square footage of the building it's in.

There are several types of apartments.

Efficiency Apartment, Bachelor Apartment, and Studio

The small apartment that combines the living room, bedroom, and kitchen into a single room is variously called an efficiency apartment, a bachelor apartment, and a studio.

Convertible Apartment

The convertible apartment is a studio-style apartment that's large enough to be subdivided into different rooms—walls can be permanent or can be temporary structures like screens.

Loft

Similar to a convertible apartment, a loft is an open space in a converted commercial or industrial building. A loft usually features architectural details like high ceilings, concrete floors and posts, and exposed pipes and ductwork. These types of dwellings often are found in urban settings and can be very large.

Basement or Garage Apartment

Located in—you guessed it—the basement or over the top of a garage, these can be very basic one-room living quarters or beautifully appointed multi-room homes.

A Duplex

A duplex is an apartment with two levels connected by an interior stairway.

One-, Two-, and Three-Bedroom Apartments

As the names imply, the one-, two-, and three-bedroom apartments have up to three bedrooms, along with a living room, bathroom(s), and kitchen.

Classic Sixes and Classic Sevens

The classic sixes and classic sevens comprise a type of apartment found in older, renovated buildings, in cosmopolitan cities like New York and Boston. They're high-end and expensive, with multiple bedrooms (two in a classic six and three in a classic seven), a spacious living area, a formal dining room, and a kitchen. There's also a small room off the kitchen known as the "maid's room," which back in the day was intended for the homeowners' live-in staff but it makes a great office or playroom for the kids today. The buildings that house classic sixes and sevens usually have spacious lobbies and a doorman to welcome you home.

Co-operative Living and Cohousing

Co-operative living happens when three or more people who are unrelated decide to live together and share a common residential dwelling. Generally, in these co-operatives, people occupy a single dwelling such as a big house with each person or couple having a private area including a bedroom and a bathroom. Other common areas include shared dining room, kitchen, living room, and outdoor spaces. Cohousing brings separate private homes together around such shared community spaces as kitchen, dining, and recreational areas.

Condominiums

A condominium (a.k.a. " a condo") is a style of home common mostly to North America. Condos are grouped together in a building in the same way apartments are, and may be low-, medium-, or high-rise style. Everything within the living space of a condo and an apartment—fixtures, flooring, walls, balcony (if you're lucky), and more—is owned by the resident (unless he is renting). The major difference is that a condominium is run jointly by one management company working on behalf of the strata council, and the strata council comprises individual condo owners chosen to represent all the owners. Whereas the interior of a condo belongs to the individual owner, the rest of the condo—the lobby, corridors, roof, basement, garage, and grounds—belong to everyone jointly. This ultimately means that a condominium is a business owned by everyone living in the building.

The strata council creates rules about how you decorate elements of your home seen by passersby. Meanwhile city planners want to know about structural alterations you want to make to the interior space. As a result, you must do some research before you decorate or alter the space. You also may be allowed to have pets (as long as you clean up after them).

Condos may come with an underground parkade, a shared outside garage, or individual protected spaces known as carports. A carport is basically a canopy under which you park your vehicle to protect it from the elements. There's also usually a common area where mail is deposited into individual mailboxes, and there may be other shared amenities like tennis courts, walking trails, parks, children's play equipment, and an activity center.

Along with your monthly mortgage payment, you must pay a monthly association fee to live in a condo. This fee covers outside services like lawn care, snow removal, exterior painting, and roof repairs, and easily can amount to hundreds of dollars a month. But if you don't want to take care of that pesky outdoor stuff, then a condo can be a good choice for you and your family. You'll also be responsible for real estate property taxes, as well as interior repairs.

Since you actually own the condo, if you're going to be away for a long period of time, you can rent it to another person if you wish and your strata council gives you permission. Just make sure you check with the condo regulations for restrictions. There may be a cap on the number of condos that can be leased in your building.

Detached Condominiums

Detached condominiums are single-family homes that are located within a cluster of other similar homes. The owners leave the exterior maintenance to a condo association. These types of homes usually have small (or no) yards because they're placed very close together. Style-wise, they can be anything from a modest bungalow (discussed later) to a very large luxury home. Because they tend to be located in or near affluent communities, detached condos allow you to enjoy a good neighborhood and a high standard of living at a lower price than a house.

Townhouse

Similar to a condo, a townhouse consists of one house in a row of identical homes with shared walls. The difference is that townhouses generally don't have shared common areas. As a result, there's no homeowner association, so the townhouse owner is responsible for all interior and exterior repairs, as well as the annual real estate property taxes.

Single-Family Homes

As the name implies, these types of homes are meant to house one family, although depending on the home and the number of rooms, they could house a *lot* of family members. There are dozens of types of single-family homes.

Some of the most common include the following.

A Rancher

Also known as a rambler or a California ranch house, the rancher is a single-story, rectangular-shaped home. It often has a very plain exterior and an uncluttered layout. Sizes run from modest one-thousand-square-foot homes to dwellings of three thousand square feet or more. Ranchers commonly have two or three bedrooms, a bath-and-a-half, a living room, and an eat-in kitchen. Depending on its location, a rancher may have an unfinished basement (usually in the Midwest); otherwise, they're built on a foundation known as a slab. Ranchers also can have an attached or detached garage or a carport. They're usually found in subdivisions in urban areas.

A Split-Level Home

Commonly called a tri-level home, a split-level house has staggered floors, meaning the main floor, which has the entryway, is halfway between the upper and lower floors. The main floor usually has the common areas like the living room, kitchen, dining room, and family room. One set of stairs will lead to the upper level, where you'll find two or three bedrooms; a second set of stairs will lead to the basement, which is usually finished (that is, completed like the rest of the house) for use as a den, office, or laundry room. The garage may be attached or detached. Like ranchers, split-level homes are generally found in subdivisions in urban communities.

A Manufactured Home

A manufactured home is built very much like a normal single-family home, except that it's assembled in pieces in a factory, then transported to the home site. (You may have heard this type of home referred to as a mobile home, but that term is outdated.) A manufactured home may be placed on a slab, a crawl space, or a basement on private property that you own, or it might be positioned in a manufactured home community on land that is owned by someone else. If you don't own the land, you'll pay rent to the community. If you do own the land, you'll pay property taxes. In addition, there's always the possibility that your state will charge you a property tax on the home itself. Check with your region's treasury department or bureau of taxation for information.

Manufactured homes can be very basic, with just a few rooms, or can have many rooms with upscale features like vaulted ceilings, fireplaces, crown moldings, and more. What makes them very appealing is that they can cost 25 percent to 30 percent less than a site-built home, according to MSN Money.

A Carriage House

A carriage (or coach) house is actually more like a studio apartment than a house, but since it's a freestanding building, it's discussed here. Originally designed to house a horse-drawn carriage, a carriage house is a building that has since been converted into residential space. Carriage houses are usually quite charming and are usually found as an outbuilding on the grounds of an estate or a very large home. They can be very small (enough to originally house one or two horses) or very large (enough for a whole stable). Naturally, the horses don't come with the carriage house anymore!

A Bungalow

This is a small, single story or one-and-a-half-story home common in many small communities across North America.

A Craftsman

Also known as the American Craftsman (and once sold as a kit by Sears, which still sells Craftsman Tools), this is a small, vintage home with wide porches anchored by columns. Natural materials like wood, stone, and brick were used in the construction of this type of home. They're common in older neighborhoods in North America, especially in the Midwest.

A Shotgun

This is a modest home commonly found in the American South. It's a narrow, rectangular structure that features three to five rooms in a row with no hallways. The whole building usually is no more than twelve feet wide and has a doorway at each end of the house.

A Saltbox

Very common in Northeastern United States, a saltbox is a wood-frame house that has two stories in the front and one in the back. Some companies still build this style of home, but you're more likely to find it in the older parts of a town.

A Multiple-Family Home

The most common type of multiple-family home is the duplex, which is a single building divided by a common vertical wall into two separate side-by-side residences, each with its own entrance and separate ownership. In some areas, the two units are on top of each other (upstairs and down). It's also possible to find triplexes, which have three side-by-side residences. New duplexes and triplexes are more common in Canada, since the United States is more a land of single-family homes. But if you want one in the US, you can still find them in the older parts of many towns.

Working with a Realtor

The easiest way to find a new place to live is to use a realtor. This business professional will help you prequalify for a mortgage so you know exactly how much house you can afford. He or she also will locate homes in your price range and target area that have the features you want. You then will visit each property personally for an inspection to determine whether it meets your needs.

- Realtors charge a commission for their expertise. The average commission rate is 6 percent, although it can be higher or lower depending on where you live. This commission is split between your realtor and the realtor who represents the seller. Because realtors are independent contractors, you may be able to negotiate the fee. It never hurts to ask.
- Alternatively, you can look for and negotiate a home sale on your own. However, even a native English speaker will find it difficult to decipher the terms and other legalese in a real estate sales contract. It's usually a better idea not to do this on your own and instead to pay the commission and work with a professional.
- To indicate your interest in a home, you'll submit an offer through your

realtor. If you really want the home, you should offer at least 90 percent of the asking price, if not the full price. If you're a gambler and want to get a really good deal, you can offer less, but don't be surprised if your first, second—or fifth—offer is rejected. If you offer too little, you run the risk of offending the seller, which could scuttle the deal. Your realtor will be the go-between for all the negotiations and counteroffers.

- If you've been prequalified for a mortgage, you can now approach the bank to get the paperwork started. Within three days of applying for the loan, your lender is required by law to provide you with a Good Faith Estimate, which gives the purchase price of the home, the interest rate, and an accounting of all the fees you'll be required to pay at closing.
- These fees, which are required by your bank and local government, can be truly mind-boggling and may include a loan origination fee (for processing your paperwork), an appraisal fee, a survey fee, title insurance, an escrow deposit (to be held for property taxes and private mortgage insurance), and plenty of others.
- These fees are nonnegotiable, although you may be able to get the seller to pay them for you if they are especially motivated to sell. As mentioned earlier, it never hurts to ask.
- Keep in mind, too, that these fees are just an estimate—they may be higher or lower at closing time, so don't write a check until you get there.

Real Estate Inventory

Whether you're considering buying a new home or you wish to remain in the same place, it's a good idea to take stock of your real estate holdings so you can see at a glance exactly what you have. Answer the following questions as a starting point:

Date__________________

Question	Response
Do you rent or own your home?	
What is the current value of the home you own?	

When did you purchase your home?	
What was its purchase price?	
Do you have records of all the improvements you've made to your home?	
If so, where do you keep those records?	
What is your current mortgage balance?	
What is the interest rate?	
Do you have a home equity line of credit on your home?	
What is its interest rate?	
How long do you plan to stay in your current home?	
When do you plan to pay off your mortgage?	
What are your plans for selling this home?	
Are you interested in buying an additional property, or do you own another one already?	
If yes, what is the value of this second piece of property?	
Do you have or plan to invest in commercial property as a source of income?	
What price range are you considering?	
What type of property are you considering?	

The Mortgage Process

A mortgage is a loan secured by property or real estate such as a home. With a mortgage, the lender (a bank or another financial institution) gets a promise in writing from the borrower to make monthly payments until the mortgage amount is repaid, usually within fifteen, twenty, or thirty years.

It's important to note that although people are said to be "homeowners" while they're making payments, technically, the bank is the actual owner of the home. If you as the borrower default—you stop making payments on the mortgage—the bank can swoop in, claim the home, and evict you and your family. This is the last thing you want to happen as a homeowner. That's why it's important to have a stable income and a consultation with a financial advisor to make sure you're in a position to make mortgage payments regularly and faithfully. In the discussion of mortgages that follows, it's assumed that you have the means to make mortgage payments and cover all the other expenses associated with home ownership.

- You may prefer to rent while you save money for a larger down payment that will lower your monthly mortgage payment. But you have to understand that homeownership may provide many benefits, including building equity and providing a tax deduction based on interest paid.
- As a homebuyer, you need to ask yourself how much capital you have to accumulate to afford buying a home. A solid rule of thumb is to not spend more than a third of your gross salary (commissions, bonuses, alimony, child support, pension, Social Security, interest, and dividends) to buy a home.
- You should not consider buying until the house is ready. Some houses and apartments may need remodeling to make them into the living space you prefer. Another option to consider is buying a lot—a piece of land—and building your dream home to your exact preferences and specifications.
- You will most probably be asked to provide mortgage pre-approval from your bank when you make an offer to buy a piece of property. Mortgage pre-approval is issued for a specific loan amount based on a number of factors that include your credit score, income, debt, employment history, insurance, and current mortgage rates.
- Having pre-approval greatly increases the likelihood that a buyer will

obtain a final loan approval. But it's important to know that a pre-approval is temporary and usually good for only ninety days.

- Putting a larger down payment into your new mortgage loan saves you money on the principal and the interest, and on private mortgage insurance payments.
- For example, if the down payment is at least 20 percent of the purchase price, you will be able to eliminate mortgage insurance (required by most lenders), which will save you even more money.

Calculate Your Mortgage First

Buying a new home can be a complicated process and everyone's situation is obviously different. However, the following material provides some information you need to begin and get on the right track. Calculate your mortgage first so you are prepared.

Here's a table that shows how much the term of a loan impacts the amount of money you must pay over the life of a $200,000 loan at a fixed interest rate of 5 percent.

Exploring a $200,000 Mortgage Loan Based on a 5% Interest Rate (Short-term payment and interest rates are traditionally lower than 30-year mortgage rates)			
Term	**Monthly payment (principal and interest)**	**Total loan amount at end of loan term**	**Total interest amount**
30 years	$1,073.64	$386,510.00	$185,511.00
20 years	$1,319.91	$316,778.00	$116,778.00
15 years	$1,581.59	$284,685.00	$84,685.00
10 years	$2,121.31	$254,964.00	$54,964.00
5 years	$3,794.23	$226,455.00	$26,455.00

It's important to know there is a real upside to paying into a shorter mortgage term. The vast majority of lenders allow additional and multiple payments toward thirty-year mortgages without restrictions. It is a good idea to direct additional available funds toward your monthly mortgage payment despite the thirty-year amortization schedule and so reduce the life of your loan to a shorter term. You certainly have the option to renegotiate your mortgage term with a solid payment record.

Types of Mortgages

Looking for the right mortgage is the important first step in the home-buying process. Banks and mortgage brokers provide various options that will alter your overall costs and the interest rate you'll pay for the life of your loan. The various types of mortgages include the following.

Government Loans

Both the United States and Canada have government loan programs for their citizens that are insured by their respective Federal Housing Administrations (FHAs). In addition, the Veterans Benefits Administration in both countries offers loans for military veterans. Such programs usually require minimal down payments (3.5 percent in the United States, 5 percent in Canada for FHA; zero and up for veterans loans). These are great options for people with low incomes or less than perfect credit, as well as for those who can't qualify for private mortgage insurance. Talk to your mortgage banker about your options.

Fixed Rate Mortgages

A fixed-rate mortgage has a guaranteed interest rate during the entire life of the mortgage, which means your payment (including principal and interest) will not change during the loan term. This can help you manage your payments better because you always know exactly how much you must pay. Typically, banks offer terms of thirty, fifteen, ten, and five years.

Adjustable-Rate Mortgages

Adjustable-Rate Mortgages (ARMs) in the US are known as Variable Interest Rate Mortgages in Canada: With this type of loan, your interest rate may fluctuate based on the movement of financial indices. The benefit of such loans is the lower initial interest rate, which in turn will help you buy a bigger or more expensive home. In addition, if interest rates decrease, the adjustable mortgage rate will decrease as well. However, the rate is just as likely to increase, which can make your monthly payment increase. Make sure to agree to a maximum cap (how much it can rise to). If you're not much for risk, you should avoid an ARM.

Combination Rate Mortgages

Canada makes available a Combination Rate Mortgage. This type of mortgage helps you manage your interest, yet it allows you to take advantage of short- and long-term rates while having a stable principal and interest rate.

Keep a Lid on Mortgage Costs

While it's exciting to think about having your own home and the freedom that comes with it, keep a lid on mortgage costs—don't ever take on a larger mortgage payment than you reasonably can afford. Your banker actually will have a lot to say about how much buying power you have. He or she will consider your debt-to-income ratio, which is a comparison between the amounts of money you earn versus your debts, including your prospective mortgage payment, as well as your car payment(s), credit card debt, and household expenses. Typically, the guideline is 33 percent and 38 percent (shown as "33/38"), where your housing costs total no more than 33 percent of your monthly gross (before taxes) income, and your monthly consumer debt is no more than 38 percent. You may be turned down for a mortgage if the sum of this ratio is too high. There are exceptions. In the United States, for example, the qualifying ratio is 29/41 for an FHA loan; for a US Veterans Benefits Administration loan, the upper limit of the consumer debt load is the only figure that counts—no higher than 41 percent.

Even if you don't meet these requirements, there's still hope. If you can come up with a large down payment or your credit is A-1, these ratios may be flexible. Your banker will determine whether you qualify.

It's always a good idea to get prequalified for a mortgage before you start shopping for property. This indicates to the sellers that you're a serious buyer and prevents you from looking at homes that are out of your price range.

Reverse Mortgage

What is a "reverse mortgage"? It is also called a home equity line of credit (HELOC) and is mentioned under "Basic Banking Products" in chapter ten.

It is every potential retiree's hope to end up with a pot of gold at the end of a professional career. It is quite possible that answer may come in the form of the equity you built up in the value of your home. It is possible to use your earned value in the form of cash in a reverse manner to accommodate your needs.

The Mortgage Closing Process

Once the home sale has been negotiated, your banker will get to work finalizing the details of your mortgage. The process culminates in a loan closing at your bank. You can expect to sign a lot of documents, then turn over a check to cover the closing costs, which typically amount to 2 percent to 5 percent of the purchase price. Once the mortgage papers are signed, the fees are paid, the hands are shaken, and the keys are passed over, you're a homeowner. Congratulations!

Atta's Lessons on Owning a Home

Even as a single young man, I knew how important it was to own a home. In fact, not having a home to call my own was one of my biggest concerns and nightmares when I immigrated to the United States. But even though I worked in a bank and dealt with financial matters related to home ownership all the time, I made the huge mistake of not investing soon enough in a home. Instead, I spent way too much money on rent and possessions for a good ten years instead of investing in real estate.

Eventually I was able to buy my first home, but it happened at the time when home prices had risen significantly. With a little more planning earlier, I could have owned a comfortable home and had enough left over for other real estate investment opportunities.

Many immigrants fall victim to the same kind of situation. Home ownership and real estate investment should be prime priorities for everyone. Invest wisely, and then put yourself on an accelerated payoff plan so you can own your home in a maximum of ten or fifteen years. Being a homeowner for thirty to forty years, during which you pay tons of mortgage money to banks and lenders, is not really home ownership, but home "renter ship." You want the property to be yours free and clear of any debt as soon as possible. Learn about what it takes to own your home and put a plan in place to make it happen.

Buying a Car

Driving in Your New Country

The adult population growth in the world's largest cities is causing many people to own their own cars in order to get around. Also the sprawling vastness of North America is why most citizens tend to own their own transportation rather than rely on public transportation. This leads to a lack of public transportation infrastructure and cities jammed with traffic. Whereas European cities and some big cities like Mexico City, New York City, Los Angeles, and Toronto have busy subway, cable car, and bus systems, many of them do not. So, if you're a North American resident, you're much more likely to eventually drive yourself around in your own vehicle.

Obtaining a Driver's License

Obtaining a driver's license is extremely difficult for a variety of reasons. For those who don't speak the host country's language, a translator is needed, and they are never easy to come by. Also, the driver must be literate in order to pass a written exam. Here are some of the details involved in getting a driver's license.

- The laws regarding the licensing age for driving passenger vehicles vary by states and countries from as young as sixteen to up to twenty-one and older.
- Make sure to find out exactly what the age limit and other requirements are. In US for example, you must be sixteen years old to operate a motor vehicle and must have a certain number of hours of training and behind-the-wheel experience before you can take your test, but that may differ by state.
- There are various types of driver's licenses based on the kind of driving you do, including a standard operator's license; a chauffeur's license (if you drive a bus or other commercial vehicle); a commercial driver's license, which is issued to truck drivers and long-distance haulers of vehicles such as eighteen-wheelers; and others. In order to drive a motorcycle in some states, you must have a driver's license plus a motorcycle endorsement. See dmv.org for more information by state.
- You qualify for these types of licenses usually by taking both a written

and a road test, and completing a vision screening. You must also take an alcohol and drug test. Check with your local licensing authority for details.

- Some countries offer what's known as an enhanced driver's license, which is identification that allows you to cross countries by land or water without a passport. An enhanced license is less expensive and much smaller than a passport; it's the size of a standard driver's license and will fit into your wallet.
- Some countries and their cities offer educational materials and tests in languages other than English. You may be able to print them directly from the websites of the secretary of state or the department of motor vehicles, or you may have to visit these offices in person. Go online or call your local office for information. In the southern and western states of the US, Spanish is commonly spoken as a second language so you may be able to get forms in Spanish. In Canada, French and English are the official languages, so forms are available in both languages.
- Don't be nervous if you can't understand everything the examiner says. If you study your instructional materials well and practice before the test, you should do fine.
- Large families (of two adults and more than two children) with only one car to share often have challenges getting children to school as well as adults to work. This puts the entire family at a big disadvantage and it's incredibly difficult to fit in all the additional commitments such as language schools and medical requirements.
- Statistics show that new drivers are involved in the most accidents across North America, and not surprisingly, young drivers, especially those aged sixteen to nineteen years old, have higher traffic accident rates than any other group.
- Inexperience is a big part of the problem among this age group, but recklessness and alcohol also figure significantly into the statistics. So it's no surprise that both new and younger drivers pay more in auto-insurance premiums. Look for more information in chapter thirteen on insurance.

SIGNAGE

Signage varies from one country to the next. Even if you come from a country where drivers use left-hand drive cars down the right side of the road, you will still find it challenging to get around in a country that's new to you, such as the US.

- To begin with, signage on traffic signs in some countries tends to be wordier than you're used to seeing in other countries.
- While you will see some of the standard passenger and pedestrian symbols used around the world—symbols like an airplane to signify an airport or a railcar to indicate a nearby railroad station—you're just as likely to see "Sea-Tac Airport" or "Grand Central Station" and a bunch of accompanying information on a sign instead of the symbol. This can be confusing if you're trying to drive and read the signs as you navigate your way around.
- In addition, in some parts of North America and Europe, both English and native languages share the same sign. If you don't know either one or you have only a passable vocabulary, you can get a real dose of culture shock when you try to drive anywhere; this can make you nervous behind the wheel and, therefore, a danger to yourself and others.
- Sometimes, street names are posted on relatively small signs about ten feet above the roadway surface. It can be hard to catch the names if you're traveling at high speed or if you're not in the lane closest to the sign, not to mention that some cities and states have very colorful and confusing street names. Just try to find Kuilei Street in Honolulu, Hawaii, for example, when all the streets around it are named Kahoaloha, Kapaakea, Kapiolani, Kaipuu, Kaaha, and Kamoku! Or try navigating the streets of Miami, where SE 1st Street intersects SE 1st Avenue.
- If you're planning to drive in an unfamiliar city, always study a map before you set off or get driving directions from your local auto club, MapQuest.com, Google maps, or your GPS.

Road Construction

Residents of North America and Europe who have a sense of humor believe that there are only two seasons: winter and construction. The fact is, though, that you may find orange construction barrels blocking off the lanes of large and small highways alike at any time of the year. Driving around barrels while trying to figure out where you're going can be challenging, especially during rush hour or when the weather is bad. Listen to the local radio traffic report before you set off so you can find an alternate route, or check the local auto club website or a national traffic condition website.

Avoid Distracted Driving

According to the US National Highway Traffic Safety Administration, crashes caused by distracted driving killed 3,300 people and injured 387,000 people in a recent year.

- Distracted driving includes doing things behind the wheel in addition to driving, including talking on a cell phone, texting, eating, drinking, putting on makeup, shaving, reading a map, adjusting the radio, programming a GPS device, and many other activities.
- Whenever you drive, concentrate on driving only. Pull over to make a phone call, send a text, and consult a map, and do your grooming at home. It's the best way to stay safe on the road and protect others around you, too.
- Take a driver's training class. Even if you've driven in your home country, the rules in all Western countries are different from what you're used to. Look for an instructor-led driver's training class at the local high school or community college, or sign up at a driving school to learn the rules of the road.

Automobiles, Trucks, and Sport Utility Vehicles

If there's one thing that defines America and some European countries, it's the car culture—you will see automobiles, trucks, and sport utility vehicles (SUVs) everywhere. There are also numerous motor vehicle companies in North America.

- The largest domestic companies in both the United States and Canada include General Motors, Ford, and Chrysler, while the biggest foreign car companies are Toyota, Honda, Volkswagen, and Kia. But this is by no means a complete list of the manufacturers—German, British, Swedish, and Korean automakers, among others, all have a market presence throughout the world.
- The car companies build passenger cars, trucks (both for city and rural

use), minivans, and SUVs. The type of vehicle you buy will depend on how many people will ride in it and the purpose for which it's used. For example, if you're commuting to work around those construction barrels mentioned earlier, you might prefer a sedan. If you will be carrying a lot of cargo, a truck may be a better choice. If you have a large family and need many seats, a minivan or SUV could be your best choice.

Determining Your Budget

It is important that you carefully calculate what you can afford before you begin browsing new or used cars, by determining your budget—what you are willing to pay.

- Prepare for costs beyond just the sticker price displays. If you plan to buy a new car, its basic invoice cost might not include the features or accessories that you want most.
- Don't forget to factor in some of the following costs when budgeting for your vehicle purchase:
  * the cost of a car insurance policy or changes to your existing one
  * change (increases or decrease) in your fuel budget for the new vehicle
  * the trade-in value of the vehicle you want to sell, if you have one

Whether to Buy or Lease a Car

Leasing a vehicle in the past was reserved for corporate customers buying luxury cars, but it has now found its way into almost every aspect of the car industry as a viable option. In reality, it is similar to financing an outright purchase in a lot of ways. In buying a car, your loan value is based on the entire cost of the vehicle; leasing is based on the depreciation of the car that will occur during the lease term, which will be for a specific number of years. At the end of the lease, you simply return the car to the dealership. Be sure to ask for additional service and other benefits while considering this option.

A Car to Meet Your Requirements

Once you have set your budget and are ready to find a car that meets your requirements or to replace the car you have, it's time to think about what you'd like. Here are some proven and common points to consider regarding what is important to you.

Fuel Efficiency

Smaller cars with alternative fuel sources are ideal. Some countries provide excellent discounts and benefits for purchasing energy-efficient cars.

Capacity

Figure out exactly how many people will be driving in this car. Stay away from driving in big cars if you don't require their big capacity, because they are more expensive to drive.

Safety

Safety is an important element and priority for many. Research and pay attention to crash test results, rollover safety, recalls for similar models, potential for blind spots, and the level of impact protection.

Performance

Rapid acceleration, super-responsive steering, and a turbo-charged engine are often attractive to buyers with an eye on vehicle performance.

Appearance and Style

The look, design, and color of the car may be important to you and should be considered.

Used versus New Vehicle

Spend some time considering whether a new or a used vehicle might be the better investment for you.

New Vehicles

New vehicles can be ordered to your exact specifications, have never been in an accident, will be under a warranty, and may require less in terms of maintenance and repairs for the first few years. If you're in the market for your first vehicle, you have numerous purchase options these days. Dealers in new cars usually have the biggest car lot in town, filled with all types of shiny vehicles in brilliant colors.

- You'll pay the most for a new vehicle, of course, but it can be worth the money because you get to select the vehicle options you really want.
- You will get a new car warranty that usually runs for a few years or a certain number of miles. This type of basic warranty is known as bumper-to-bumper coverage, meaning major components in the electrical, fuel, air conditioning, and audio systems, as well as the vehicle sensors, are covered.
- You may also get powertrain coverage for the engine and transmission. A powertrain warranty typically runs ten years or 100,000 miles, whichever comes first.
- You're also likely to be offered an extended warranty at an additional cost. This is a supplemental warranty contract that begins at the end of the basic warranty included with your new vehicle. The warranty usually runs several years and has a deductible.
- Coverage varies from one automaker to another, so be sure to ask specific questions about what's covered. The extended warranty can be expensive, but since it's transferable to a new owner when you sell the vehicle that becomes a positive selling point when you're ready to part with your "ride."
- Dealers offer their own auto financing, but you can choose to finance through your own bank or credit union instead. You'll find information about financing further down. And, of course, cash is also gladly accepted when you buy your vehicle.
- It's worth noting that American automakers have worked hard to catch up to imported vehicles in terms of quality and durability. For example, North American vehicles have finishes that resist rust and parts that are engineered to last a long time. So you can buy a domestic vehicle with confidence.

Used Vehicles

Used vehicles may be lower in price than new ones—they avoid quick depreciation after purchase, and they often include lower associated costs like insurance and registration. Used vehicles represent some of the best values for your money.

- A new vehicle automatically depreciates—loses its value—as soon as you drive it off the lot. That can amount to big bucks. According to bankrate.com, the basic rule is that a vehicle loses 10 to 20 percent of its value each year.
- When you purchase a used vehicle, the previous owner has absorbed some significant depreciation already, which means you get a better deal. In fact, CNNMoney estimates that if you purchase a three-year-old vehicle, you could save as much as 30 to 40 percent over the cost of a new one.
- You can buy a used vehicle from many sources, including used-car dealerships (which typically have the *second* largest car lot in town). While most used-car dealerships are independently owned, chain dealerships do exist. One national chain to investigate is CarMax Inc.
- When you buy from an established used-car dealer, you can be assured that the vehicle has been inspected and cleaned thoroughly, especially if the dealer sells "certified" used cars. The dealers that are backed by vehicle manufacturers sell newer used cars (usually less than three years old) that have passed a series of inspections before being certified. Once a car passes certification, the manufacturer adds a new warranty of up to twelve months or more. Furthermore, these used vehicles can be financed.
- One way to check whether the vehicle you've chosen is sound and reliable before you sign on the dotted line is to order a Carfax or AutoCheck vehicle history report. The reports tell you things such as whether the car has ever been in an accident or sustained other major damage from floodwaters or hail.
- These reports also will tell you whether the vehicle has a "lemon history," which means there are indications that the vehicle has problems too severe for it to operate properly. These reports also verify the last reported mileage and estimate how many miles the vehicle has been driven annually, which will give you an idea of how much wear and tear there has been on the engine and other components.
- According to CNNMoney's website, about one in ten of the cars in the Carfax and AutoCheck databases has had some kind of service

problem, so it's a good idea to order a report before you buy. Make sure you have the Vehicle Identification Number (VIN), which is usually listed on a metal plate just inside the windshield, before you go to carfax.com or autochek.com to get your report.

Other Used Car Sources

Naturally, an established used-car dealer has overheads and has to pass on those costs to its customers. So if you're really looking for a bargain on a used car, consider one of these sellers instead.

A Private Seller: A private seller is someone who is selling his or her own vehicle. If you ever see a lone car or other vehicle sitting in a parking lot with a "for sale" sign in the window, then you know you're dealing with a private seller. Vehicles of all kinds are also sold by private sellers through newspaper-classified sections and on Craigslist.

Online Sellers: Dealers commonly use online resources like autotrader.com and cars.com to spread the word about their inventories to a wider market. Just enter your ZIP code on either site, and you'll get a selection of cars within ten miles or more of your home. These sites are just like classified ad sections in the newspaper, but you'll get a lot more details about the vehicle there than you will in the newspaper.

EBay Motors: While some private sellers do sell their cars through eBay Motors, you're more likely to encounter used-car dealers in this online marketplace. There is some risk purchasing something this expensive sight unseen, plus you have to make your own arrangements to pick up the vehicle you've won. Even so, you can get some serious deals. Check out the site at www.ebay.com/motors.

Buyer Beware

It's "buyer beware" when it comes to buying a car. Are you not sure if the price the seller is asking is fair? Here's some advice.

- Check edmunds.com and Kelley Blue Book (kbb.com) in the US. Your bank or credit union will also have a copy of the blue book.
- These free services will tell you the going price for vehicles of nearly almost every make, model, and year, both new and used. It's a good way to make sure you're not paying too much for the car or other vehicle of your dreams.
- Once you find the used vehicle you want, have a mechanic inspect it

before you buy it. You can expect to pay about a hundred dollars for an inspection. Used cars and other vehicles are sold "as is," meaning what you see is what you get. If you accept a vehicle without checking it out, then find out it has major problems, you're stuck because there are no refunds or adjustments with an "as is" purchase.

- You have a little more protection if you buy your used vehicle from eBay Motors. It offers purchase protection on every vehicle, which covers odometer rollback problems, missing titles, and other issues. EBay Motors also has paired with SGS Automotive, a national inspection and testing company, to offer independent third-party vehicle inspections for just a hundred dollars. For more information about vehicle protection, go to ebay.com/motors and look for the Vehicle Purchase Protection Warranty.
- If a private seller refuses to allow you to have the vehicle inspected, walk away. It's possible that the seller is hiding something—maybe shoddy repairs, evidence of significant damage from a crash, odometer rollback, or some other safety hazard.
- It's also possible to plug radiator or oil leaks temporarily, conceal body damage with a putty product known as "bonds," or otherwise hide things the seller doesn't want you to see until you've handed over the cash and it's too late to complain.
- And incidentally, used-vehicle dealers won't allow you to have an independent inspection, but that's not because they're hiding something. Dealers generally have their own in-house inspection and repair teams, so if the dealership has a good reputation and/or sells certified used cars, you should be able to trust its integrity. But there's no reason why you can't bring your own mechanic with you when you buy the vehicle to give it a quick once-over.

Atta's Lesson on Buying a Car

When I was a child in Afghanistan, I walked almost four miles to and from school each weekday. I certainly did not enjoy the walk during cold winter and hot summer days. So it was a happy day in my junior year of high school when my father bought me a bicycle. Fortunately, I was able to rely on public transportation for almost four years to and from work after arriving in the United States. I'll admit, though, I was tempted—just like millions of other immigrants are—to buy a fancy car. But I was determined to not fall into debt and three years after arriving in the United States, I finally settled for an old Ford Maverick, which cost me $700.

Over the years, I have seen many people spend money on fancy cars and pay thousands of dollars in interest charges on those purchases when they could have used public transportation instead. It's your choice, but think about it. You can save a lot of money taking the bus, train, or subway; or by walking or riding a bike—and the physical activity is good for your health. If that's not possible, at least consider buying a used rather than a new vehicle, and make sure it's a fuel-efficient model. By avoiding the competition trap, you'll save money.

Auto Financing

Buying a vehicle can be a big decision and a very important part of buying a new car is organizing the auto financing.

- Consider auto financing with the auto dealerships that is selling you your car.
- Visit your bank for more information on auto loans and financing options.
- Whether you're buying new or used, be sure to compare several auto loans first.
- Take action before applying in order to secure the best possible interest rate.

Refinancing

If you're paying a high interest rate or payoff seems too far away, you might benefit from refinancing your auto loan at some point.

- Things might be different for you or the market since your initial auto loan. These changes may allow you to refinance at a lower interest rate, which means lower payments.
- Refinancing changes the terms of your loan and transfers your vehicle's title from one lender to another.
- The new terms can be beneficial for you and could save you money.
- Here are some reasons why a loan refinance might work for you:

Your Credit Score Has Increased

If your credit score is higher than it was when you first bought your car, refinancing could be a smart choice. A higher credit score could make you less of a risk to lenders, so they may be willing to offer you lower rates. Refinancing can make a difference even with just a minor increase to your score.

Interest Rates Have Shifted

The rates themselves may have also shifted a lot since you purchased your car. If they were high at the start of the agreement but have since lowered, refinancing could save you a significant amount. Decreasing your interest rate by as little as 1 percent may be enough of a reason to change lenders. For example, if you borrow $25,000 on a fifty-month loan term with 4.7 percent interest, dropping down to 3.7 percent would save you about $135 per year.

To Shorten the Length of Your Loan

If you have a long-term loan, such as a seventy-two-month loan, it can make sense to reduce the loan duration. Refinancing to a shorter loan may bring the overall interest cost of the loan down.

Potential Disadvantages to Refinancing

Refinancing carries few risks, but it's not always the best choice. Take care to avoid these potential pitfalls.

Prepayment Penalties

Check to see whether your current loan will issue a penalty for prepayment. In this case, refinancing could actually cost you more money.

Extended Loan Life

Avoid any refinancing that will extend the life of your loan. While extending could reduce your monthly payments, it may cost you more interest over the long term.

Refinancing your auto loan can be a great way to save. As refinancing isn't right for all situations, it's good to review the pros and cons and all your options carefully.

How to Winterize Your Car

Prepping your car to handle the coldest months, especially if you live in a northern climate, is a great way to extend the life of your car and help keep you safe. Both frigid and extremely hot temperatures can put wear and tear on your car. You really don't have to pay too much money to get through winter if you do the following.

Check Oil Regularly

- Check the level of oil in your engine regularly and get an oil change before the coldest months arrive to avoid having to do it in cold temperatures, especially if you are doing it yourself.
- Use lower viscosity (thinner) oil that circulates better in below-freezing temperatures. Ask your mechanic what type of oil is good for your car in the winter.

Keep Your Engine Cool

Keeping your engine cool is very important.

- Blasting your heater while driving can heat up your engine. You need coolant to keep things working evenly.
- Check your coolant for color and levels. Look at your manual or do some online research to determine how often it should be flushed and replaced.
- Coolant needs to be mixed with water before being put into the vehicle (unless you purchase it pre-mixed—check your coolant bottle!).
- Make sure you're using the recommended ratios. It's really simple. Do it yourself once and you'll feel confident doing it from then on.

A Healthy Battery

Working with a healthy battery is essential.

- An outdated battery or one that cannot keep its charge could come back to haunt you if it's not tended to in advance. Give the battery a once-over for cracks, misaligned cables, or anything else that may raise a red flag.

- You'll also want to read your battery's charge level using a hydrometer. These are usually built into your battery, but if not, you can buy a handheld one. The charge level should read at a minimum of 12.2 volts for you to feel confident about the battery's ability to withstand winter weather.

Tires

Pay attention to what separates you from the road—your tires—particularly in icy climates.

- Most cars are already equipped with all-season tires. If yours is, all you'll need to do is check their pressure.
- All tires have a recommended PSI (pounds per square inch) level printed on them. Find yours and fill them with air to that level.
- Because air constricts in cold weather, your tire pressure will naturally reduce as the temperatures drop, so make sure your tires are always properly inflated.

Wiper Solution

Winter provides plenty of obstacles for clear vision. Make sure your windshield wiper solution is full and contains a deicer. A clear line of sight helps keep everyone safe.

Jumper Cables

Be sure keep a set of jumper cables in your car, so that, if your battery dies due to cold weather, a jump from another car's battery can rescue it. Having a set of jumper cables in your trunk can be an easy fix when you or someone else needs it.

An Emergency Kit

Keep an emergency kit of these essentials in your car, just in case:

- a flashlight
- a jack
- a reliable spare tire
- a small tool box
- a snow brush
- an extra pair of gloves
- an ice scraper
- blankets
- washer fluid

Chapter Twelve: Preparing for Your Retirement

Retirement and Pensions

While human beings continue to form and grow, when wives and husbands plan to make a living, have children, and talk about buying a home, many unfortunately neglect to discuss their finances and their futures. In light of today's challenging economic uncertainties and an eroding lack of focus on future planning, a large majority of workers globally are simply unable to retire with enough income to live on independently and with dignity. Citizens of European countries are probably the least vulnerable when it comes to retirement, thanks to the establishment and strength of solid retirement and pension programs. But even members of those societies could be returning to a time when a growing number of seniors who want to live independently without burdening their children will lack the financial resources to do so.

When most people think about retirement planning, they think of retirement accounts and scrimping and saving now so they'll have enough money to live on later. This can be a challenge for people who are in the "sandwich years"—the time when they're paying college tuition for and otherwise supporting one or more children, and at the same time helping and caring for aging parents with their costly medical needs. But while the savings part of retirement planning certainly is of paramount importance, there are other issues you'll face when retirement age comes along.

In this chapter, you'll read about the savings issues, resources, and decisions you'll have to make when you finally decide to say goodbye to your work life. After all, you want to ensure your golden years—a.k.a. your retirement years—don't end up being made out of lead instead of gold.

THE REALITY

There are many disturbing facts describing the fiscal reality for retirees.

- Thirty percent of private industry workers with access to a defined contribution plan (such as a 401(k) plan) do not participate.
- The average American spends twenty years in retirement.
- The situation isn't any better in Canada. Statistics Canada says that just 24 percent of eligible tax filers contributed to a Registered Retirement Savings Plan (an RRSP) account, a type of retirement account, in a recent year. In addition, they're saving only 4 percent of their personal disposable income.
- Financial experts in both the United States and Canada estimate that people will need 70 percent of their preretirement income—or up to 90 percent for low-income earners—to maintain their standard of living when they do finally retire.
- On the other hand, Fidelity Investments recommends having a minimum of eight times your salary in various savings vehicles before moving into retirement.
- Either way you look at it, that's a scary figure considering the low levels of savings among baby boomers in the Western world. But the good news is, by saving and cutting expenses now, you can at least improve your chances of having money to support yourself after retirement.
- In general, the majority of today's seniors are at significant economic risk—some living in poverty or close to it, and many others are just one economic shock away from having trouble meeting their basic needs.
- It's fair to say that tomorrow's seniors are likely to be in worse financial shape than today's.
- Current elder year and retirement programs in certain Western countries provide a comfortable financial foundation for the twenty years after retirement, but the elders' benefits are far from adequate by themselves. Indeed, they are modest by virtually any measure.
- In the US, for example, Social Security's retirement benefits average just $15,571 per retiree a year. This does not come close to replacing a large enough percentage of wages to allow workers to maintain their standard of living once wages are gone.

- Social Security's benefits are also extremely low by international standards, ranking near the bottom when measured against the old-age benefits provided by other developed countries.
- As the world recovers from the Great Recession that affected the first two decades of the new millennium, wealthy households are recovering faster than low-income ones, whose incomes have stagnated or declined since the crash.
- The inability to pay for their mortgages and the ultimate loss of their homes has crippled thousands of homeowners for the decade since 2007, and these effects continue to impact the American economy.

Retirement Strategies

It's crucial to plan for your "golden years" so you have as many years as possible to save the funds you'll need for a comfortable retirement. Here are some tips to get you started.

- Begin your preparation for your "golden years" first by learning and gathering as much as information as possible within your environment. Find out exactly what type of retirement plans will become available at the time you wish to retire.
- Start your research by connecting and exchanging information with established members of your family, your community, and professionals.
- Find a financial advisor you can trust. This can be a registered investment advisor at a brokerage firm or an independent financial planner. If you choose the latter, it's usually best to work with a certified financial planner (CFP), since he or she has specialized training in personal finance.
- Ask relatives, friends, and coworkers for referrals, or contact your bank or attorney for leads, then check references.
- A financial professional from your bank can help you review your readiness for retirement and what may occur throughout the rest of your life.
- Take the advice of your financial advisor. Naturally, you may not always agree with what he or she proposes. But if you knew everything there was to know about finances, you wouldn't need financial guidance. So listen carefully and make rational decisions based on the advice you receive.

- Start with small investments if that's all you can afford to set aside. Over time, even small balances grow nicely due to interest compounding, which means interest is paid on the interest that has been added to the original capital. Depending on the rate of interest, compounding can result in some serious increases in your savings.
- Increase the amount you invest when your income goes up. In fact, when you get a raise, consider putting the entire extra amount right into savings.
- Pay yourself first. When your paycheck comes in, make sure a set amount flows right back out into your investment accounts. If you wait until after you've paid your bills, taken that trip to Paris, or otherwise earmarked those funds, you'll find that there's nothing left at the end of the month and you won't save anything. Set up recurring electronic transfers from your account right to your investment accounts to guarantee that saving is always ongoing.
- Diversify your financial holdings. While 401(k) plans and IRAs in the United States and RRSPs in Canada are safe investments, you may be able to grow your retirement money faster by investing in the stock market, buying municipal bonds, and making other investments. Just be aware that not all investments have a guaranteed rate of return, which is another reason why it's good to diversify.
- It is also a good idea to diversify your financial holdings through different companies. Many people have lost significant lifetime investments, for instance during the 2007-08 financial turmoil when some firms got completely wiped out. The old saying to not put all your eggs in one basket should apply to not putting all your investments through one firm. It's important to research and look for sound and safe institutions for investment purposes.
- Never cash out a 401(k) when you change jobs. Instead, preserve your retirement assets by leaving them in your previous employer's plan, or rolling over (transferring) the funds into a new account or the plan offered by your new employer, if that's an option. Always transfer funds directly to the new financial institution to stay on the IRS's good side.

The Cost of Health Care

Factoring health-care costs into your budget is an extremely important part of retirement planning. According to the latest retiree health-care cost estimate in the US, a sixty-five-year-old couple in 2017 will need an average of $260,000 to cover medical expenses throughout retirement. This is up from $245,000 in 2015. Monthly health insurance premiums are on the rise and may cost $1,500 to $2,000 a month per person. This is the reason why many in the US are deciding to continue working in order to take advantage of company benefits.

Covering Expenses

In partnership with government-sponsored income and health-care expenses, it is important to develop two budgets:

- basic expenses (phone, utilities, mortgage payments, property taxes, and any other fixed expenses)
- discretionary spending (money, eating out, doting on grandkids, entertainment, and travel)

Once that is done, it is time to determine whether you have more than enough money to retire at an earlier age just for fun, or if you need to develop a plan to raise more income.

Retirement Ages Are Rising

Retirement ages are on the rise throughout the world due to the fact that people are living longer. Here are some current official retirement ages.

- The full retirement age in the United States is sixty-six for people born after 1938, or sixty-seven for people born after 1957, although it's possible to start claiming reduced Social Security benefits beginning at age sixty-two.
- In Canada, the retirement age is sixty-five. Generally speaking, retirement is voluntary, although there are exceptions.
- In France, the average retirement age is 59.5 years and the state pension payment begins aged sixty.
- In Greece, the average retirement age is sixty and the state pension payment begins aged sixty for women and sixty-five for men.
- In Italy, the average retirement age is 60.5 years and the state pension payment begins aged sixty for women and sixty-five for men.
- In Germany, the average retirement age is sixty-two years and the state pension payment begins aged sixty-five

- In Australia, the average retirement age is rising and though the state pension age is 65.5 years for men and women, that age is also on the rise, legislated by the government.

There is also a significant shortfall in savings for government-supported pensions and other retirement plans worldwide. Other factors contributing to the rising retirement age are the impact of the recent financial collapse and an inadequate level of retirement savings and planning by individuals.

If you're in this position, you may end up holding on to your full-time job for many years past the official retirement age—perhaps as late as age seventy or beyond. That's fine as long as you're physically able, but it's not unusual for people in their sixties to start experiencing health problems, which makes working difficult, if not impossible. So you may find yourself in a position where you have to retire to attend to your own or your spouse's health-care needs. If that day comes, but you still need a paycheck to make ends meet, you might consider taking a part-time job instead. Just keep in mind that landing a job is not necessarily a sure thing, and, in fact, can be more difficult as you age. Alternatively, you might start your own business. This is an especially good option if you have a skill from your work life that can be parlayed into self-employment.

The bottom line is, it might be wiser to retire later rather than sooner so you have more time to save and otherwise prepare financially. A paper presented recently at the Alzheimer's Association International Conference suggested that the risk of getting dementia decreased by more than 3 percent for every year worked past retirement age. It's something to think about.

Here are some important points to consider before deciding to retire.

- Are you financially ready to retire?
- You may have prepared a rough estimate of your projected retirement planning in the past. As your retirement vision gets closer, it is important to put a solid but realistic plan together on paper. Pension plans, Social Security payouts, and other asset values constantly change. Are you confident about being able to carry 70 to 80 percent of your current income during retirement?
- Take a good look at your spending and get real about how your spending will change based on your answers to what and where you are going to retire.
- Are you ready to consolidate all your assets in order to retire?
- Are you debt free? This is a really important question to answer before

thinking about retiring. It is not a good idea to retire unless you are free of debt, including credit-card debt; also you need to be current and able to keep up with monthly HELOC payments.

- Do you have or do you anticipate receiving adequate insurance coverage? This is important not only for health, but for home, car, and other valuables.

Retirement Funding Options

In addition to accruing savings from a full-time job or other sources, planning for your financial future is key to a solvent retirement. Here are some of the sources of income you may have already or could establish to build a retirement nest egg.

Company-Sponsored Pension

It wasn't so long ago that the majority of employers, large and small, offered a company-sponsored pension to reward employees who stayed with the company for a set number of years. Those who met the length of stay requirement—most often a minimum of five years—were said to be vested in the company's retirement plan. But in the United States and several other Western countries, at least, all that changed after the collapse of the financial systems in 2007-08, leading to a phaseout or total elimination of pension benefits by many companies.

The number of company-sponsored pension plans in North America is falling faster than the rate it is falling in European countries. This elimination of pension plans leaves almost two-thirds of the people without a pension and makes them responsible for saving for their retirement in other ways. As a result, if you have a company-sponsored pension, you're one of the fortunate few. It may be a good idea to hold onto your present job longer for that reason alone.

There are two types of pension plans.

- In the defined benefit plan, the employer contributes a set amount each month to an employee retirement fund that is managed by a plan administrator.
- In the defined contribution benefit plan, the employees make investment decisions about the money in their own retirement account. In

effect, this puts the onus on the employee to make the right investment decisions, something they might not be qualified to do.

- If your retirement plan is set up so your employer will match your contribution, by all means maximize the amount you contribute, if at all possible, so your money will grow twice as fast.

Social Security in the United States

Social Security is a government-run system that serves as a source of income for retirees and disabled Americans. It also serves as a source of income for the beneficiary of a retiree who dies. However, it is not intended to be the primary source of income—it is intended to supplement a person's own savings and investments.

According to pewresearch.org, 166 million Americans paid into Social Security in 2014; and according to the Social Security Administration, approximately 62 million people received monthly benefits in 2017 of approximately $955 billion.

Social Security has a retirement estimator you can use to get a general idea of how much you might receive in benefits after you retire (ssa.gov/estimator). The amount of Social Security you receive is calculated on your lifetime earnings. Social Security uses the thirty-five years of your life in which you earned the most money as the basis for this calculation. The actual calculation is based on your age at retirement, your income, and factors such as military service, railroad employment, or benefits earned on work for which you were not required to pay Social Security tax. The resulting figure is the amount you would receive if you were to wait until your full retirement age to start collecting. That could be sixty-five, sixty-six, or sixty-seven, depending on the year you were born.

It's possible to start collecting Social Security as early as age sixty-two. However, if you do start collecting early, your benefits will be reduced by a fraction of a percent for each month you collect before your full retirement age—and you never recover the lost benefit amount. To maximize your benefits, you should defer collecting as long as possible. You may defer applying for benefits until as late as age seventy.

Another thing that can reduce your benefit amount is if you have a pension for work you did that was not covered by Social Security. Federal civil service jobs as well as some jobs at the state and local level (such as law enforcement jobs) may fall into this category. However, federal and state civil service jobs in most Western countries provide workers with a pension and other attractive benefits and these compensate that reduction.

Continuing to work while you are collecting Social Security benefits may also reduce your benefit amount. In 2016, Americans were allowed to earn $15,120 in gross employment wages or net self-employment wages and still earn the full benefit amount. Any income earned above that amount reduces benefits by a dollar for every two dollars earned.

Although many people don't pay federal income tax on their Social Security benefits, you may have to if you have substantial taxable income like wages, self-employment income, interest, and dividends on investments. Generally speaking, however, if your Social Security benefits are your only source of income, you won't have to pay income taxes on them.

Although you can apply in person at any Social Security office, it's easier to apply online at ssa.gov/planners/about.htm. The entire process takes about fifteen minutes. If you are within three months of age sixty-five, you can apply for Social Security and Medicare at the same time.

Medicare (US)

This is the US government's health insurance program for people age sixty-five and older. It helps with the cost of medical care but doesn't cover everything. You can also go to medical.gov and download a booklet that should answer all your questions.

Employer-Sponsored Retirement Savings Plans (US)

Larger companies generally offer tax-deferred retirement savings plans to help you save for retirement. A 401(k) plan, or defined-contribution benefit account, is the most common type of retirement plan; a 403(b) plan is for people in public education, health professions, and the ministry. Some companies will contribute to or match the amount of money you contribute to your account, which helps your savings grow faster.

Retirement Programs

In order to provide clarity and respect for the technicality of various retirement programs, I am going to provide an overview of programs separately for US, Canada, and Europe.

United States

United States—Individual Retirement Arrangements

The US has a wide range of financial instruments to help you save for retirement, but it is a really good idea to utilize more than one plan. Good retirement is not comprised of a single product or asset but a package of income sources structured to meet your goals. It is a good idea to start your research through your local bank and more importantly spend dedicate significant time before investing. There are also many national and local firms that offer advice.

United States 401(k) Plans

A 401(k) plan is a type of profit sharing that allows employees to contribute a certain amount of their earnings for long-term growth.

- In some cases, employers contribute to employees' accounts in lieu of contributions to a traditional pension plan.
- The amount you contribute annually is excluded from your taxable income, thus reducing the amount of tax you'll pay on your annual tax return, but the distributions are fully taxable when you start making withdrawals after retirement.
- 401(k) plans should be considered hands-off savings vehicles. But if you really must tap into your account to cover an emergency situation, it's almost always better to see if your employer offers a loan option so you don't have to take a hardship distribution.
- If you borrow against your 401(k), you can repay the funds over time just like you would a bank loan; you won't have to pay taxes on the funds you took out as long as the full amount of the loan is repaid.
- If you take a hardship withdrawal, you're liable for income taxes on the distribution and you can't replace the money in your account.

There are other types of accounts created for general purposes that you can still use to save for your retirement, although they may not have the same tax advantages. Consult your tax consultant for the tax ramification in your situation.

CANADA

In addition to providing all Canadians with Old Age Security and working Canadians with the Canada Pension Plan, Canada offers several incentives for its residents to save money for their retirement.

CANADA—REGISTERED RETIREMENT SAVINGS PLAN

The Canada Revenue Agency (CRA) offers Canadians a retirement savings plan that can reduce annual income tax and work toward a retirement fund—the Registered Retirement Savings Plan (RRSP). The allowed RRSP contribution amounts have risen from $11,500 in 1990 to over $26,000 in 2018. Despite the ease of using this savings vehicle, many Canadians fail to take advantage of it.

CANADA—TAX-FREE SAVINGS ACCOUNT

Touted as an easy way to save for both short- and long-term goals, the Tax-Free Savings Account (TFSA) enables Canadians to save tax-free money throughout their lifetime. If you start at age eighteen, the magic of compounding can really make the dollars in your account add up. The annual TFSA dollar limits are low—$5,500 in 2017, for example—and contributions are not tax-free. But the income earned and withdrawals are usually tax-free. There are restrictions. For more information, see the CRA website at cra-arc.gc.ca/tfsa/.

CANADA—POOLED REGISTERED PENSION PLAN

The Pooled Registered Pension Plan (PRPP) is a large-scale, low-cost deferred income plan that was established in 2013 for both employed and self-employed people who don't have an employer-sponsored pension plan. Funds are pooled with those of other qualified individuals across the country, which results in greater investment opportunities at lower administrative costs, according to the CRA. The fund is also portable, meaning it moves with you when you change jobs.

- It's possible that your employer will establish a PRPP to which you can contribute. But if you're going solo, you can open your own PRPP account at a financial institution like a bank.
- The amount you can contribute annually depends on your unused RRSP contribution room (discussed above). Because PRPP contributions are tax-deductible, direct withdrawals are taxable.
- At the time this book was published, PRPPs were available only to employees "whose employment falls under federal jurisdiction, including banking and inter-provincial transportation, and Canadians who are employed or self-employed in the Yukon, Northwest Territories and Nunavut," according to the CRA.
- However, it's expected that more provincial governments will enact PRPP legislation, making plans available to more people. Check with the CRA or your financial institution to find out where things stand in your province. In the meantime, you can find more information about this savings vehicle if you search for "tax" at cra-arc.gc.ca.

EUROPE

European countries in general have more established and better funded retirement plans than North America has, but with the three similar pillars:

- state-provided systems
- employment-related plans
- individual retirement savings

STATE-PROVIDED SYSTEMS

State-provided systems vary from country to country across Europe. Switzerland for example targets each person at about 30 percent of final salary. Italy on the other hand targets about 80 percent of salary. Quite a few European countries too are in dire need of reforms. It's fair to say the changes and reforms within European markets will certainly force more and more people into second and third pillar options.

Employment-Related Plans

Defined benefit and defined contribution arrangements can be found pretty much all over Europe. Designs and utilization of these programs vary, based on social norms and historical factors.

Individual Retirement Savings

Europeans have invested roughly 830 billion Euros in individual retirement savings plans. In general, European countries' retirement savings plans benefit from favorable tax treatments for personal savings as well as a more equity-oriented culture in which people prefer more ownership of their home and other personal assets. Personal savings plans ratios are lower in Germany and the Netherlands due to very strong employment-related systems and fewer equity-oriented plans. Residents of France and Italy rely on state systems heavily.

While changes and reforms are certainly on the way in Europe due to changes within the labor market, aging, and the influx of migrants, it is highly recommended that Europeans accelerate their rate of saving within their retirement plans.

Other Retirement Tactics

Maximizing the amount you contribute to retirement accounts is a reliable and sensible way to build retirement equity. But there are other things you can do to prepare yourself for retirement.

Adopt the 4 Percent Withdrawal Habit

Financial experts say that you will help to stretch your savings farther and prevent you from running out of money by withdrawing just 4 percent from your retirement savings for living expenses in your first year of retirement, then adding just 3 percent to that figure every year to cover the cost of inflation. This assumes, of course, that you have a good-sized nest egg to begin with. If your retirement savings are more modest, you'll need a different strategy.

Cut Spending

You may have had a great time gleefully buying whatever you wanted while you were employed. But now that you're facing retirement, it's time to put the brakes on nonessential spending. You don't have to save every nickel from now on, but if you spend wisely, you'll have more money to pay your household bills, buy groceries, and enjoy life for a longer period of time. In addition, you should make a budget and stick to it so you don't overspend.

Pay Down Debt

Consumer debt is more like consumer *death*—the only ones thriving are the credit card companies. High interest charges erode your savings and, worse yet, if all you pay every month is the minimum balance, it literally can take you a decade to pay off even small debts. So if possible, use some of your savings to pay off your high interest credit cards. The 1.5 percent return you'll get on money parked in the bank is no match for the 18 percent or more you're paying on revolving debt. Pay down your debt or pay it off and you'll keep more of your money in the long run.

Convert Nondeductible Debt into Deductible Debt

Convert your nondeductible debt into deductible debt. In the United States, the only deductible debt you have is your mortgage. So if you have a lot of unsecured loans or credit card debts, consider getting a second mortgage or line of credit and using those funds to pay off higher interest debts. But if you do this, you absolutely must cut up the credit cards, close your other revolving credit accounts, and resist opening new accounts. If you don't, you run the risk of racking up charges all over again, and you'll be even farther behind than before.

The majority of Western countries offer deductible interest options or benefits so it is important to research and learn about these benefits within your local communities.

Downsize Your Life

Downsize your life by cutting your expenses ruthlessly.

- Reduce your cellular phone bill by dropping data plans and take advantage of free calling options offered by your email provider. Google, Yahoo, and Facebook offer excellent free calling options around the world.
- Drop the premium channels and videos on demand from your cable service.
- Borrow best-selling videos from the library rather than buy them, or buy Kindle versions, which generally are 25 percent or so less expensive.
- Watch movies online through your laptop by signing up for Netflix, which is most probably cheaper than buying cable packages.
- Lease a smaller car when your current lease expires, or buy a well-maintained used car.
- Physically downsize your possessions by purging your home of things you don't use or wear anymore.
- Sell new and gently used items in a garage sale or on eBay or Craigslist (where you'll earn a little pocket money), and then donate the rest.

Downsize Your Home

If you're now an empty nester (meaning the children have all moved out), you probably don't need that four bedroom house anymore—not to mention, you probably don't want to clean and otherwise maintain such a leviathan anyway. Find a smaller home more suited to your smaller family. In fact, you may even find that renting an apartment or condo is a better choice for you now. If you free up all the money you used to sink into a big mortgage and taxes, and invest your income from selling your big house, you can save more money while having enough disposable income for living expenses.

Move to a City with a Lower Cost of Living

Moving to a city with a lower cost of living can be a good option for reducing costs, although the emotional cost of leaving family and friends behind may not be worth the savings. But if this is a viable option, start your search on the

Internet. You can find enough information related to the cost of living in major cities to make an informed decision.

Reassess Your Retirement Dreams

Maybe you had big plans to travel or build a new house when you retired. But you may find that these dreams are no longer as tempting. Now's the time to reassess them. Quiet afternoons spent reading, volunteering at a hospital, picking up a new pastime, or visiting friends may hold more appeal. Consider what's really important to you now and adjust your dreams.

Working during Retirement

Ahh, retirement! Leaning back in the lounge chair, sipping on coffee, tea, or an iced tea, and planning the next visit with the grandkids—right?

This might sound like the ideal day for some people when they reach their country's magical retirement age. It is probably everyone's wish to retire early, but the important questions should always be, "What am I going to do in order to create a fulfilling retirement? And what is the most effective way to transition from work to retirement?"

Also, for the majority of wishful others, full retirement at the official retirement age isn't a viable option. But more often than not, people are retiring later because they simply haven't saved enough to retire comfortably. It may be worthwhile to consider working during your retirement.

Sometimes the choice of time to retire is driven by personal or family medical issues; sometimes a need to relocate may force retirement. Many people in Western countries continue to work not just for financial reasons but for the fact that they enjoy working and volunteering their time to serve their communities, while attending to some lifelong hobbies as well. Still others may not find their vocation until late in life.

Reasons to Keep Working

There are lots of reasons to keep working even in your golden years. Working part-time after retirement age is always an option, especially if it can help delay taking your government or other sponsored benefits.

- Many people may want to retire from their career, but take up part time work to sustain their living expenses.
- Some simply try to remain socially active or try to find something engaging to do while they wait for a younger spouse to reach retirement age.
- Others may determine that their financial savings may not be enough to cover expenses, especially if they're not yet eligible for medical and other coverage.
- People generally start finalizing their retirement plans when they reach fifty-five to sixty. If you haven't done so already, that is a good time to meet with a financial planner to help strategize the different financial scenarios.
- This is the time to start thinking and planning regarding health-care costs, Social Security payments and taxes, income taxes, and retirement savings withdrawals.
- Discussion will often have to include if you want (or need) to only partially retire. Below are some discussion items a future retiree will want to discuss.

Start Your Own Business

If you have a skill from your former profession that can be spun off into a freelance or consulting job, consider using it to create a business of your own. Project management, writing, graphic design, website development, and bookkeeping are just some of the skills you can use to keep busy, earn some cash, and feel needed.

Work Part-Time

Many people retire, then find they're completely bored. Think about it—if you're in reasonably good health, you probably can expect to live another twenty to thirty years in retirement. How much golfing can you reasonably do in the next two decades, or how many years of reruns can you watch on the Sci-Fi channel?

Part-time work doing something you enjoy can keep you energized and revitalized. It doesn't have to be a professional job. If you'd enjoy greeting people at Wal-Mart or serving Egg McMuffins at the drive-thru window, then that's better than sitting at home with nothing to do.

And of course, some part-time jobs come with health-care benefits that are much appreciated in retirement. If that's not an option, at the very least you can use your earnings to help cover the cost of the health-care benefits you are probably now paying yourself.

Working While Collecting Benefits

In the United States, there is no requirement that a person has to collect Social Security at sixty-two (which is the earliest qualifying age). In fact, the monthly payments received at age sixty-two are only 70 percent of the full retirement amount. People who retire from a career early and take a part-time position may find they can delay taking Social Security until full retirement age because of the income they bring home with their job. People should also keep in mind that Social Security income can be taxable, which can influence their plans.

Taxes

It is extremely important to learn about your earned income, government benefits, and withdrawals from retirement accounts and required minimum distributions from your personal plans at the appropriate age. This information can help you to complete your financial planning picture—but how will your financials affect your tax bracket?

- If you decide to work part time in retirement, there is a possibility it will affect your tax bracket. Knowing one way or the other may help you determine what types of income to use—Social Security, retirement accounts, or other investments.
- Advances in health care help many people feel younger and more energized when they reach retirement age in Western countries. It's giving them options to continue working at their career if they wish, to retire and take on a new part-time job, or to retire fully and spend the time working on hobbies and visiting with family.
- If you're starting to plan your life after retirement, be sure to work with a financial advisor to help develop a written plan that will best match your interests while serving you financially.

Elder Abuse

At a time when our population is aging and our world suffering from failures of humanity to adequately protect its vulnerable, it should not be a surprise that elder abuse is becoming a more significant issue. In the meantime, you may be surprised to learn how prevalent the problem has become.

- In the US alone, it is estimated that more than two million Americans fall victim to elder abuse, neglect, or exploitation each year. This reflects only the reported cases. Some experts believe the problem may be far more significant.
- You may think of abuse as being physical in nature; a more commonly occurring form involves the abuse of an elderly person's financial resources.
- As parents reach their elder years, they may rely on the support of others—their children, other family members, neighbors, caregivers, and financial advisors—to help them manage their money. In cases like these, elderly individuals put their trust in the hands of someone else—a relative or professional—with the belief that the person making financial decisions will be working in their best interests.
- Unfortunately in some cases it doesn't work out that way and people become unwitting victims of those they trust. In fact, billions of dollars get lost each year as a result of elder abuse issues.
- Women are quite often the victims, but it happens to elderly men as well.

Examples of Financial Elder Abuse

Currently, there are many examples of financial abuse in evidence:

- outright theft of money belonging to the elderly person
- using the elderly person's credit cards to make purchases for personal needs
- borrowing against the value of the older person's home as a way to access money
- misusing a power of attorney control that has been granted
- phone and email scams that rely on an elder's lack of awareness of new technologies

Best Practices to Avoid Financial Elder Abuse

An awareness of the potential for financial abuse is a big first step.

- Open and honest communication between parties involved in any financial relationship is critical.
- As retirees grow older, they should try to retain as much control as possible over their financial lives.
- On a day-to-day basis, retirees who are capable should continue to write and sign their own checks, open and send their own mail and emails, set up direct deposit for any payments received (like state pensions and annuity payouts).
- Seniors should set voicemail to screen phone calls (as a way to avoid unwanted or deceptive solicitors), and do their best to keep track of all their money and possessions.
- Planning is also a very important part of making sure you and your loved ones are protected from potential abuse.

Other Steps to Avoid Elder Abuse

As an elder or as someone offering support to an elder, there are steps you can take to avoid elder abuse.

- Make sure that you have updated your will and any other important documentation, such as advanced health directives, trusts, and powers of attorney.
- Assign a person you trust as your power of attorney. Make sure you are able to communicate well with that individual and are confident that they will continue to carry out your wishes if you become incapable of making important decisions for yourself later in life.
- Review all beneficiary designations for retirement accounts, bank accounts, and insurance policies to make sure the designations are current.

Atta's Advice on Growing Older

There's an expression that growing older isn't for the faint of heart. Most of the time, we only think about the physical limitations that come with advanced age, but for immigrants, it goes much deeper than that. Think of it this way. People in their native, secure environment can carry on and plan for retirement with relative ease. But it's a totally different ball game for immigrants who may have to leave their native countries during middle age or even their senior years and start life over in a brand-new environment without any financial security. It can be very scary.

The answer is to plan for the future, which can be difficult if you're starting a new life from scratch. I know this from firsthand experience. When I first came to the United States, I talked to the financial consultant at my bank right away about the various retirement fund options available to me, even though this was at a time when I was struggling financially because I was also trying to rescue my big family from refugee conditions. I became convinced it was a good idea to not wait to plan for the future and I started by making the minimum possible automatic deductions.

I strongly promote the idea of saving and planning for retirement early. Refugees and immigrants in particular are actually at a bigger disadvantage due to starting new life and work in their host countries later than those born in the country. It is also unwise to count on retirement support from the government due to the same reason of not being able to contribute to pension and other retirement plans early enough. It's up to us to fund our retirement years on our own.

Chapter Thirteen: Insurance

Insurance As Protection

Insurance is the fair transfer of the risk of a loss from one entity to another in exchange for payment. Insurance can have several positive effects on society through the way that it changes who bears the cost of losses and damage. On the one hand, it can increase fraud; on the other, it can help individuals and societies prepare for disasters and ease unpredictable effects both on households and society.

Insurance can influence the probability of losses through moral hazard (insurance fraud and preventive steps by the insurance company), policy provisions requiring certain types of maintenance, and possible discounts for loss-mitigation efforts. Insurance in general is a subject that is increasing in importance in today's environment.

You may want to learn some basic terminologies used in insurance before you read this chapter. The terms are listed in Appendix C.

Some Types of Insurance

Property Insurance

Property insurance provides protection for physical property (buildings and exterior structures) against such risks as fire, theft, or weather damage. This may include specialized forms of insurance such as fire insurance, flood insurance, earthquake insurance, and home insurance.

Home Insurance

Also commonly called hazard insurance or homeowners insurance, home insurance provides coverage for damage or destruction of the policyholder's home. In some geographical areas, the policy may exclude certain types of risks such as flood or earthquake that require additional coverage. Maintenance-related issues are typically the homeowner's responsibility. The policy may include inventory, or this can be bought under a separate policy, especially for people who rent housing. In some countries, insurers offer a package that may include liability and legal responsibility for injuries and property damage caused by members of the household, including pets.

Health Insurance

Health insurance policies cover the cost of medical treatments. In the same way that medical insurance works, dental insurance protects policyholders against dental costs. In the US and Canada, dental insurance is often part of an employer's benefits package, along with health insurance. Please refer to the section on health care in chapter seven for details and explanations.

Flexible Spending Account

A flexible spending account (FSA) is a type of voluntary savings account set up by your employer that will help you save money on your income taxes. Each pay period, you can contribute the dollar amount you specify from your paycheck into the FSA. These funds then can be used to pay for qualified expenses like medical or dependent care costs. Because the funds are deducted from your pay before taxes, in essence you're getting a tax deduction on your medical costs. It's a great plan, but it does have a catch: If you don't spend all the money before December 31, you'll lose it. So if you decide to contribute to an FSA, make sure you calculate the amount of money you think you'll use every year very carefully, then divide that amount by the number of paychecks you'll get in the next year. Have that amount withheld from your paycheck.

Other Types of Insurance (United States)

Some employers offer various other types of insurance as perqs you may find helpful as an additional way to protect your family's finances. They include life insurance (sometimes up to the full amount of your annual salary, plus you may be able to extend coverage to your spouse and children), accidental death or dismemberment insurance, short- and long-term disability insurance (which replaces part of your income if you're too ill or injured to work), and long-term care insurance. You generally have to pay premiums to get this coverage, but often, the rates you'll pay are lower than what you'd pay if you bought the policies on your own. You'll have the option of paying with pre- or after-tax funds. Be sure to weigh the tax consequences carefully before you make a decision.

Liability Insurance

Liability insurance is a very broad set of insurances that cover legal claims against the insured. Many types of insurance include an aspect of liability coverage. For example, a homeowner's insurance policy will normally include liability coverage that protects the insured in the event of a claim brought by someone who slips and falls on the insured's property. Also automobile insurance includes an aspect of liability insurance against the harm that a crashing car can cause to others' lives, health, or property.

The protection offered by a liability insurance policy is twofold: (1) a legal defense in the event of a lawsuit commenced against the policyholder; and (2) payment on behalf of the insured with respect to a settlement or court verdict.

Liability policies typically cover only the negligence of the insured, and will not apply to results of willful or intentional acts by the insured.

Environmental Liability Insurance

This protects businesses from bodily injury, property damage, and cleanup costs caused by any harmful chemical material.

Casualty Insurance

Casualty insurance insures against accidents, not necessarily tied to any specific property. It is a broad line of insurance included in a number of other insurance types, including auto, workers compensation, and some liability insurances.

Atta's Advice on Insurance

While looking for a good insurance company, survey at least two or three family members and friends with extensive (minimum five years' relationship) with an insurance company. Pay attention to the following:

- competitive prices
- convenient access
- exceptional claim handling
- financial strength and integrity
- around-the-clock service
- personalized service from a company you can trust

Life Insurance

Life Insurance refers to a policy that pays benefits to a named beneficiary or beneficiaries when someone dies. The most common reason for purchasing life insurance is to provide money and protection for spouse and/or children. You need to do your homework and learn as to the type and amount of insurance to buy depending on various individual conditions.

Life insurance provides a monetary benefit to a deceased person's family or another designated beneficiary, and may specifically provide for income to an insured person's family for burial, funeral, and other final expenses. Life insurance policies often allow the option of having the proceeds paid to the beneficiary as a lump sum cash payment or as an annuity (see below). In some regions of the Western world, a person cannot purchase a life insurance policy on another person without their knowledge.

Here are a few important facts about life insurance.

- Most employers provide various levels of life insurance. You can also elect supplemental life insurance coverage for one, two, three, four, five, or six times your pay for yourself.
- You can also elect life insurance coverage for your spouse or partner.
- You can elect life insurance for your children if they are at least fifteen days old and qualify as dependent children under the flexible benefits program.

Questions to Ask

The first question to ask about life insurance is why protecting yourself and your family against the unexpected is critical.

You're working hard for your money and you'd like your family to enjoy the fruits of your labor throughout the coming years. Preparing for your family's future, however, means more than investing appropriately in order to achieve the right combination of growth and stability for your goals and your time horizon. For many people, it also involves purchasing the right amount of life insurance during their working years.

Life insurance can help impact and potentially eliminate the financial impact on your loved ones in the event of your death. With a life insurance policy, your family can use the proceeds to help replace lost income, eliminate debt, pay for college, keep a business afloat, or address other financial needs and goals while they adjust to a new life without you.

Life Insurance Provisions

A life insurance policy provides a payment in the event of your death that can help protect your family's lifestyle in the absence of your earning power.

- Many people have financial goals they are trying to meet with hard-earned income such as paying off a mortgage, putting a child through college, or supporting an elderly parent.
- Life insurance can help support your family goals.
- When you purchase a life insurance policy, you're buying a contract with the issuing insurance company. The issuing insurance company guarantees that upon your death, it will pay a preset amount to your beneficiaries.
- The guarantee is subject to the insurance company's claims-paying ability. The proceeds are typically free from income taxes. Be sure to ask for details through your insurance company.
- The insurance company pays your beneficiaries directly, so they receive the funds without delays and expenses.
- Depending on the size of your estate, benefits from a life insurance policy may be subject to estate tax. Again, it's very important to review and understand the details.

Best Times to Insure

You might wonder, "When are the best times to buy life insurance?" The answer is, "As soon as someone else is depending on your income." The fact is many people can benefit by having life insurance. When someone else is depending on your income, there's generally a need for life insurance.

- You may already have life insurance coverage through your employer. Find out.
- Even so, it's usually a good idea to consider purchasing additional coverage independently, because policies you buy outside an employer's plan are transferable, meaning your coverage continues even if you lose or leave your job.
- Your employer's coverage may not meet your financial obligations to adequately protect your family.

It is very important to review your need for life insurance whenever a major life event occurs. Consider the following events and the ways in which life insurance might help protect your family.

- You buy a new home.
- You purchase or make major home improvements.
- You want to protect your mortgage or home equity obligations in the event of your death.
- You plan to marry. An upcoming wedding should prompt you to review your entire financial situation, including your income needs, debt, and other liabilities, and to add a layer of protection for both spouses.
- Your family expands through the birth or adoption of a child. A life insurance policy can provide protection for your family's increased income needs as well as any debt you may have taken on, including college expenses.
- You take on a new job. A term insurance policy can replace any group coverage you may have had from a former employer, and allow you to increase your coverage amount in accordance with your new salary.
- If one spouse is staying home to care for children in the family, it is important to have life insurance for both spouses: the primary wage earner and the stay-at-home parent. If the spouse who stays home were to die prematurely, in addition to being a devastating loss, it would be a huge financial strain on the family and it might impact the working spouse's ability to continue making the same income.

- Term life insurance can cover future college expenses, funeral and estate expenses, and even business ownership needs.
- Small businesses may wish to consider purchasing life insurance policies for key individuals, such as the owner or a top employee, to help prevent financial distress if either were to die.
- While considering life insurance, keep in mind that you'll generally have to provide "evidence of insurability." This means that before an insurer issues a policy, the company will typically require the person to undergo a basic medical screening, often scheduled at your home or workplace.
- Generally speaking, the better your overall health, the lower your premium will be. Many factors contribute to the price you will pay for insurance, such as your age and your health. Low blood pressure and low cholesterol along with a healthy body weight will typically lead to a lower price.
- It's usually easier and less expensive to buy life insurance in your twenties and thirties than in your forties, fifties, sixties, and so on. Sometimes health issues arise later in life that can make insurance difficult or costly to obtain.

Life Insurance Coverage Amount

There are several ways to go about determining how much life insurance coverage you need. One common method is to buy coverage equal to five to ten times your annual salary plus bonuses. For example, if you make $50,000 annually, you'd buy a policy between $250,000 and $500,000.

Other options are as follows.

- It depends on your financial situation such as the capital you've already accumulated, the liabilities you've accrued, and the specific costs you'd like your family to be covered for in the future.
- It is important to know that the amount of insurance you need is tied to the annual income you would need to replace in the event of a premature death.
- If you can afford to retire—which means you no longer need to work to support yourself and your family—then you may no longer need life insurance. However, most people who are in their working years aren't in a position to afford to retire and they need coverage.

- When purchasing term life insurance, you'll also have to determine how long you'd like to have the coverage in place. One common rule is to use the number of years you have until you can comfortably afford to retire. You may, however, want to consider other scenarios, such as the number of years until all your children complete college, or how much it would cost to replace your income for ten years.
- One of the major benefits of term life insurance is its ability to protect your assets at an affordable price. Take care to avoid buying a policy with premiums you may not be able to afford in the future.
- It's a good idea to buy a smaller policy with premiums you can comfortably afford now than to buy a bigger policy that you have to let expire because you can't pay the premiums.
- As you progress in life, you will likely accrue greater financial responsibilities for your loved ones. Term life insurance can provide the money they need to help meet their expenses and maintain their standard of living.

Cost Calculation

Generally your coverage options are calculated as multiples of your base salary on the cut-off date mainly in September, rounded up to the next even thousand dollars. Depending on the amount of coverage you elect, you may be required to complete an application and submit proof of good health before coverage takes effect. Enrollment worksheets usually provide good coverage options.

Financial Planning Questionnaire—Basic Questions

The next two forms are identical with the "Financial Planning Questionnaire—Basic Questions" and "Financial Planning Questionnaire Follow-Up Questions" in chapter ten.

Date:	**Answers**
Name	
Address	

Home phone	
Cell phone	
Office phone	
Occupation	
Age	
Health status	
Medications	

Financial Planning Questionnaire Follow-Up Questions

Is your mother alive?	
If not, what was the cause of her death and how old was she?	
Is your father alive?	
If not, what was the cause of his death and how old was he?	
You financial goals	1. 2. 3.
Have you ever invested in anything other than regular savings or certificates of deposit?	
Do you hold Stocks? Bonds?	
How do you feel about these investments? Stocks? Bonds?	
Year you expect to retire	
Will you receive a pension?	

Company name	
How much do you expect to receive?	
How many times have you been married?	
Are you receiving funds from an ex-spouse?	
For how many more years?	
How much?	
Will payments stop after her/his death?	
Do you pay alimony?	
Monthly amount	
Are you paying child support?	
How much?	
Are you receiving child support?	
How much?	
How long are you willing to tie up your money?	
Do you feel comfortable talking about money matters?	

Life Insurance Worksheets

Use these worksheets to log additional details about the life insurance policies you carry.

	Life (Whole)
Company name	
Name of insured policy holder	
Monthly premium payment	
Face value	
Beneficiaries	
Maturity date	

	Life (Term)
Company name	
Name of insured policy holder	
Monthly premium payment	
Face value	
Beneficiaries	
Maturity date	

Types of Life Insurance Policies

Term Life Insurance

A term life insurance policy covers a specific period of time, such as ten or twenty years. At the end of that period, you normally stop paying premiums and your coverage ceases.

If you die while the policy is in effect, the insurance pays your beneficiaries the face value of the policy. When the term expires, so does the coverage. Term life insurance policies are less expensive than permanent insurances. Term insurance allows you to gain access to life insurance with a lot less money than you'd need if you were trying to buy the same amount of permanent insurance.

Permanent Life Insurance

A permanent life insurance policy covers you until your death, regardless of age as long as premium payments are up to date.

- Permanent life insurance generally includes an investment component along with the insurance policy, and generally carries higher premiums as a result.
- Permanent insurance is commonly used for wealth transfer and estate planning purposes.
- Permanent life insurance cannot be cancelled as long as premium payments continue to be made.

An Annuity

An annuity is a form of insurance that provides payments and is generally classified as insurance because it is issued by insurance companies, it is regulated as though it were insurance, and it requires the same kinds of actuarial and investment management expertise that life insurance requires. It refers to a sum of insurance money that is paid out annually.

The Annuity Clause

The annuity clause refers to part of a policy that allows for the establishment of a monthly or quarterly payment to the subscriber instead of a lump-sum payment.

Burial Insurance

Burial insurance is a very old type of life insurance, which is paid out upon death to cover final expenses, such as the cost of a funeral. It is more commonly included with life insurance these days.

Whole Life Insurance

Whole life insurance is a more expensive option but is a fixed coverage amount with an established payment plan during the life of the policy.

Universal Life Insurance

With a better policy, universal life insurance combines the benefits of both fixed and whole life. Be sure to read the details of the benefits and features carefully.

Variable Life Insurance

Variable life insurance is a policy where cash reserves are held in various investments. The investment return is therefore tied to market performance.

Variable Universal Life Insurance

Variable universal life insurance is a policy that combines the benefits of flexible premium payments and coverage with the investment opportunities and risks of variable life insurance.

Single Premium Life Insurance

Single premium life insurance is a type that requires you to pay for the policy upfront. Upfront payments vary from $5,000 to $10,000 or more a year depending on your age and other requirements of the policy.

Survivorship Life Insurance

Survivorship life insurance is a policy that insures two lives jointly. No proceeds are distributed when just one person dies. Benefits become available only when the second person dies.

Supplemental Life Insurance

Some employers only provide term life insurance to their employees and in most cases this is not enough to provide for adequate coverage in the case of death or the loss of wages. It is therefore advisable to look into the option of purchasing supplemental life insurance. Whether you need life insurance depends on your personal financial situation. A general rule of thumb suggests that 60 to 80 percent of the spendable income lost when a breadwinner dies is required to maintain a comparable standard of living. Consider how long the replacement income would have to last, taking into account the age of the dependents.

When selecting coverage amounts, consider these questions.

- Do I need life insurance or additional life insurance coverage for myself?
- Would my spouse need to replace part of my income if I were to die before retiring?
- Would my family need continued financial support if I were to die before retirement age?
- What financial obligations would my family then have? (Consider mortgage or rent, daily living expenses, college or school bills, car payments, insurance needs, and other obligations.)
- What financial resources are available to my survivors? (Be sure to consider all potential sources of income, such as other insurances, Social Security, retirement plans (such as a 401(k) plan), an individual

retirement arrangement, and any other assets that could provide financial resources.)

- Do I need life insurance coverage for my children? What expenses would I incur if one of my children were to die? (Consider how you would pay those expenses.)

AUTO INSURANCE

Auto insurance, also known as car insurance and motor insurance, is insurance obtained for cars, trucks, motorcycles, and other road vehicles. Its primary use is to provide financial protection against physical damage and/or bodily injury resulting from traffic accidents and collisions, and against liability that may occur as a result.

The specific terms of vehicle insurance vary with legal regulations in each country and region. Vehicle insurance may additionally offer financial protection against theft of the vehicle and possible damage to the vehicle sustained as a result of an accident other than traffic collision.

Coverage typically includes the following:

- property coverage for damage to or theft of the car
- liability coverage for the legal responsibility to others for bodily injury or property damage
- medical coverage for the cost of treating injuries, rehabilitation, and sometimes lost wages and funeral expenses

Most countries, such as the United Kingdom, require drivers to buy some, but not all, of this coverage. In the US, drivers have the option to buy any of the above policies. However, if a car is used as collateral for a loan, the lender usually requires specific coverage.

AUTO-INSURANCE POLICY COVERAGES

Insurance policies cover the following people and items:

- you, your spouse, and any other person using the car with your consent
- all cars registered under you, your spouse, and children living in the same household
- a car being used temporarily while your car is being repaired or serviced (This is called a substitute car. A temporary substitute car cannot belong to you or your spouse.)

- a car you and your spouse acquire that either replaces your car or is an added car (This is called a "newly acquired car.")

Insurance policies have other rules they follow.

- Most insurance companies will provide coverage for a new or used newly acquired car for up to fourteen days after you take possession of that car. This extension of coverage applies for your new or used car whether it replaces an existing car or is an additional car in your household. You will be required to purchase insurance policy beyond fourteen days.
- Most insurance companies are able to cover rented and borrowed cars for twenty-one consecutive days.
- Relatives living with the first person named on your policy are also covered while using an insured car. However, you must inform your insurance agent about how to include those who obtain a driver's license after the policy is written.
- You can also purchase an additional endorsement to extend liability and medical-payment coverage to cover you while you use a car that is owned by your employer or rented or borrowed for more than twenty-one consecutive days.

Types of Auto-Insurance Coverage

Liability

Auto-insurance coverage has a liability to pay for damages due to bodily and property damage to others for which you are responsible. If you are sued, it also pays for your defense and court costs. Medical expenses, pain and suffering, and lost wages are some examples of bodily injury damages. Property damage includes damage to property and the loss of its use.

Insurance Limit

No one can ever tell the most you would have to pay if you were to cause an accident. Consider how you would pay damages that would exceed your insurance limit. The higher your limits, the more likely it is that insurance will be able to pay all of the damages for you.

Medical Payments

This coverage pays medical and funeral expenses for bodily injury sustained by a covered person in a car accident. A health-care provider must treat that bodily injury within one year after the accident. Check with your insurance for details.

Uninsured Motor Vehicle Coverage

Uninsured motor vehicle coverage pays for bodily injury when an insured is injured in a car accident caused by another person who does not have any liability insurance or who has liability insurance, but whose limits are less than the limits you chose for this coverage.

Uninsured Motor Vehicle Property Damage Coverage

This pays for property damage to your car if it is damaged in a car accident caused by an uninsured driver. If you have collision coverage, your insurance will pay damages up to the amount of your collision coverage.

You might ask yourself, "Why should I buy uninsured motor vehicle coverage?" The answer is it allows you to decide how much coverage is available to pay your damages. Without uninsured motor vehicle coverage, you must rely on whatever liability limits are carried by the other driver to pay your damages. This policy also covers property damage.

Comprehensive Coverage

This type of coverage pays for a covered car that is stolen or damaged by causes other than a collision. For example, damage caused by fire, wind, hail, flood, earthquake, theft, vandalism, or hitting a bird or animal would be covered. Comprehensive coverage will also pay for substitute transportation expenses (check with insurance for the limits). Payments will begin when you tell your insurance company of the loss.

Collision Coverage

This coverage pays for a covered car that is damaged by collision with another object or by upset of the car.

Emergency Road Services Coverage

This auto insurance normally pays the fair cost for the following emergency services for your car:

- mechanical labor for up to one hour in most cases
- towing to a nearby place where repairs can be made
- towing the car out if it is stuck on or next to a public road
- delivery of gas, oil, battery, and change of tire, but not the cost of such items
- locksmith labor, usually up to one hour

Car Rental and Travel Coverage

Car rental coverage pays for some of the expenses of insuring a rented car. Check with your insurance company for details and choose the amount you wish to cover.

Travel Expenses Coverage

Travel expenses insurance pays up to a certain amount when your car is not drivable as a result of a loss that occurs more than a certain number of miles from home. Items covered are meals, lodging, and transportation home or on to your destination plus the return trip to pick up your car.

Rental Car Coverage

Rental car coverage pays for a certain amount that you choose in advance if you have an accident in a rental car. Check with your insurance agent for options and details on programs offered.

Death, Disbursement, and Loss of Sight Coverage

Death, disbursement, and loss of sight coverage pays if the covered person dies as a result of injuries sustained in a car accident. Limits vary.

Loss of Earnings Coverage

This coverage pays for lost earnings as a result of a car accident if a covered person is, as a consequence of the car accident, unable to do their usual work or any other work.

Auto-Insurance Discount Programs

Safe Driving Discount

This discount is available to customers who agree to share certain driving information and have an eligible vehicle. The premium savings will be used on the actual usage of your vehicle. The less your vehicle is driven, and in some cases the more safely your vehicle is driven, the more you can save.

Loyalty Discount

If a household has insured a private passenger vehicle with an insurance company, in order to reward its loyal auto policyholders, insurance companies provide discounts on bodily injury and property damage liability, medical payments, comprehensive, collision, and uninsured motor vehicle coverage.

Vehicle Safety Discounts

Insurance companies provide discounts for certain types and makes of cars depending on safety and other specifications. Check with your insurance company for details.

Good Student Discount

Some insurance companies provide discounts for married and unmarried male and female drivers with less than nine years' driving experience. They must have at least a B or equivalent grade average their previous school term.

Other Discount Options

Check with your insurance company for other discounts, such as Mature Driver Improvement Course Discount, Safety Education Discount for

Inexperienced Drivers, and Lower Rates for policyholders with thirty-four to fifty-eight years of driving experience.

Atta's Lesson—A Real Story About Insurance

A former refugee and successful professional passed away at age fifty-four due to a massive heart attack, which left behind a wife and three kids. He however had purchased a life insurance contract that resulted in a healthy payment to his family, which paid off a mortgage as well as his children's education.

Chapter Fourteen: Legalities and Citizenship

Equality under the Law

The laws of some countries often favor some immigrants over other immigrants. Chinese and Japanese immigrants, for example, were on the receiving end of very restrictive laws in the United States between 1924 to 1965. In general, thousands of similar forced movements of refugees throughout history, separated only by time and place, had the same goals in mind—simply to try to find a safe place to live out their lives with their families.

It is extremely important to understand that human beings, no matter where they are, should be equal under the law. First-generation immigrants have historically found it challenging to question authority, their elders, their own values, and their religious beliefs. But children who grow up in their new environments learn the values and principles practiced there.

The majority of Western world societies have freedom of speech, freedom of press, and under the rule of law can question any authority and speak up when needed. Generations continue to pass on this value system to the next generations of this cycle of the great experiment.

It is therefore important to be aware of what would happen if we really were to do something bad against the rules and laws of the host country. Committing crimes decreases opportunities for all refugees and immigrants, destroying their image and the future of the person who is committing a crime. I believe you will be taking part in the decrease of refugee crime rates by becoming someone who is aware of laws and principals, and that is indeed a great service.

When you think back over your life, the memories that probably come to mind first are closely tied to your loved ones. For example, your marriage would be one of those memorable life events, as would the birth of your children, joyous birthday and anniversary celebrations, and the deaths of treasured loved ones. These are milestones you remember.

There's no question that your family is your most precious "possession." So it should make sense that you need to make plans and take the appropriate steps to protect both your loved ones—and yourself—as you travel through this life. For this reason, this last chapter covers the various legal matters you should consider and documents you should have drawn up, either now or in the immediate future. Many of these legal matters require the services of a lawyer, but the time and expense is worth it to protect those closest to you. Please also note that this chapter provides just a general overview of various legal matters. Seek the services of an attorney experienced in the legal area you're interested in to make sure you get the latest and most accurate counsel for your situation in your host country.

Important Legal Terms and Documents

Almost everyone needs the services of an attorney once in a while, for instance to set up a trust, review legal documents, or even change one's name to simplify its spelling. Immigrants do that all the time to fit into their new country better. So if your employer offers a legal services plan, you might want to sign up. The per-pay cost is usually fairly low. Here are some of the important legal terms and documents you will need to know to be prepared.

A Will

A will is a written document—signed and witnessed—that indicates how your property will be distributed at the time of your death. You can change it and add to it at any time during your lifetime. It also allows you to appoint a guardian for your minor children.

- Your estate consists of various assets, from money you have in cash, stocks, bonds, and other financial instruments, to any personal possessions you have.
- It also states your wishes concerning any minor children (under the age of eighteen) you have.
- The term for when a person dies without a will is "intestate." If you are married and you die intestate, your estate usually will go to your spouse, or possibly to your spouse and your children, depending on where you live.
- While this may be fine with you now, you must consider that your

spouse and children could die at the same time as you. It's much better to draw up a will that states exactly where you want your estate to go than to leave it to chance.

- If you are not married when you die and you die intestate, the state where you live will determine where your estate will go.
- According to legalzoom.com in the US, the state will distribute your estate to the following people in this order: your children, or if they are not alive, their children; your parents; your brothers and sisters or, if they are not alive, their children; your grandparents or, if they are not alive, their children (that is, your uncles and aunts); the children of your deceased spouse (assuming they are not your direct offspring); any relatives of your deceased spouse.
- If there are absolutely no heirs, then the state where you live acquires your assets.

There are several types of wills.

- The testamentary will is the most common, and consists of a document that is drawn up by an attorney, and then signed in front of witnesses.
- The second type is a holographic will, which is a written document signed without witnesses. The problem with this type of will is that it rarely holds up in court, which is where your estate will end up. The result could be challenges to the will and fights over how your estate should be divided.
- Finally, the oral will is given in front of witnesses, but like a holographic will, it doesn't stand up in court very well.

As a result, you should spend some time thinking about how you want your estate divided.

- Make a list of every asset you own, including anything that's stored in a safe deposit box, any family heirlooms, and anything else you'd like to go to a particular person.
- Then seek the assistance of an attorney to record your wishes.
- After you've signed the will in the presence of witnesses, your attorney will take care of having it filed correctly.
- You'll receive a copy of your will after it has been executed (signed). Store it in a safe place but not in your safe deposit box.
- You should give a copy of the will to the executor of your estate, who is the person you select to carry out your wishes after your death.
- Make sure all your loved ones know where the original is stored.

- It's possible that you may wish to change your will after it has been executed. All you have to do is write a new will to replace the old one, or have your attorney make a change, known as a "codicil," to amend the previous will.

A Living Will

This type of will—a living will—has nothing to do with your assets. It's also known as a power of attorney for health care (not to be confused with a power of attorney for personal care, discussed below). It's a way to indicate the type of medical care you wish to have if you are unable to speak for yourself by becoming ill, incapacitated, or mentally incompetent and unable to communicate your wishes about the medical treatment you consent to receive. The advance directive usually covers such issues as whether you wish to be kept alive by artificial means (resuscitative intervention) in the case of a catastrophic cardiac event or brain injury. You might indicate that you want everything possible done for you medically.

You don't have to name anyone to look after you when you have an advance directive. Rather, you just need to sign and date an advance directive form, have it witnessed by two people not related to you, then give copies to your spouse, family, doctor, and other trusted individuals. You can search for "A Living Will" or "Advance Health Care Directive" forms online.

Advance Directive Patient Advocate

Another document you should have to let medical professionals know who is authorized to speak—to advocate—for your care if you are unable to do so yourself is the advance directive patient advocate form. This person is known as your advocate or proxy, and the document authorizes the appointment of this person of your choice to act on your behalf and make medical decisions concerning your care, custody, and treatment. Your named patient advocate must be at least eighteen years old and of sound mind (that is, mentally capable).

You may designate an additional person to act as your advocate in case the first is unable to do so. Additionally, you'll indicate specific instructions regarding care you wish and don't wish to receive. This will include the "do not resuscitate" (DNR) order you may have given in your living will. Finally, you'll indicate any other special instructions you may have, including religious requests (for example, allowing medical care provided only by a person of a specific gender), and instructions regarding anatomical gifts (organ donation).

The advance directive should be signed, witnessed, and stored in a safe place until it is needed. Make sure several people know where to find it.

A Living Trust

A living trust provides lifetime and after-death property management. If you are serving as your own trustee of the living trust of your property, the living trust legal document—the instrument—will provide for a successor upon your death or incapacity. Court intervention is not required. Livings trusts also are used to manage property. If a person is disabled by accident or illness, the successor trustee can manage the trust property. As a result, the expense, publicity, and inconvenience of a court-supervised distribution of your estate can be avoided.

With adequate protective provisions, your assets can also be protected against your beneficiaries' creditors through the living trust. The primary drawback for many people is the loss of ownership and control over the assets once they have been transferred to the trust.

The assets become the property of the trust. Any assets not funded into the trust properly remain vulnerable to creditors and lawsuits. An irrevocable trust also lessens possible tax liabilities for those who will benefit from the assets in your trust.

If a living trust is properly written and funded you can do the following:

- avoid probate on your assets
- bequeath your assets to the person or persons of your choice by establishing a trust fund
- control what happens to your property after you are gone
- plan for the possibility of your own incapacity
- use it for any size of estate and prevent your financial affairs from becoming a matter of public record

Trust Funds

Trust funds are not just financial tools for the wealthy; they're a good way for you, the grantor, to leave a legacy to someone you love. Trust funds are legal entities that are usually established for minor children (including grandchildren) who are inexperienced with handling money. However, you can set up a trust for anyone, including a charitable organization. Trusts can even be set up to take care of a beloved pet after your death. A financial institution manages the trust, and the proceeds avoid probate court upon your death.

There are two types of trusts.

- The living trust is set up by the grantor while he or she is still alive.
- An after-death trust is established through the terms of a will after the death of the grantor.
- Living trusts can be designated as revocable (able to be changed) or irrevocable (unable to be changed).
- Both types of living trusts have tax shelter benefits, but irrevocable trusts are the most advantageous.
- Grantors typically set up a revocable living trust to benefit a charitable organization.
- As the grantor, you have the right to tailor the trust at any time to meet the needs of the person named to receive it (the beneficiary).
- To set up a trust, determine how to transfer your assets into it, and change the trust as you see fit, engaging the services of an experienced estate and trust attorney.

A Power of Attorney

If a situation arises where you need someone to act legally on your behalf, then you can give that person the power of attorney (POA) over your affairs. You might do this for a number of reasons. For instance, maybe you need to return to your homeland for an extended period of time and would be unable to take care of your financial affairs and other responsibilities from afar. If you're in the military, you could be deployed for a long period of time and need assistance. Or maybe you're facing treatment for a serious illness. All these situations, among others, may warrant the creation of a POA.

- A POA is a written legal document, but it doesn't have to go through a court. Rather, you'll draw up the document (use a state-specific template found online or ask your attorney for one), have it signed by two adult witnesses not related to you, and then have it notarized.
- Keep the original copy in a safe place, and give a copy to the person

who will see to your affairs. Be sure to include language in the POA stating that a copy is acceptable when presented.

- The POA becomes valid as soon as you sign it, and the person who acts on your behalf is called the "attorney-in-fact." However, he or she does *not* have to be an attorney—that is, a lawyer—to be your proxy.
- You don't lose control over your own affairs when you have a POA agreement, and you can revoke it (take it back) any time you wish.
- You also can give POA rights to more than one person, but be careful, they'll all have access to your bank accounts and other financial matters.

Other Types of Powers of Attorney

Besides the general POA described above, other types of POAs include these:

Durable POA

This continues indefinitely rather than ending when you recover or otherwise retake control of your affairs. Some individuals do this so it's not necessary for their family to establish a conservatorship if the individual in question becomes incapacitated at a later date. Any of the POAs mentioned in this section can be made durable, if you wish.

Health-Care Limited POA

This gives the attorney-in-fact permission to make health-care decisions for the grantor, including terminating care and life support. For this reason, some grantors amend the POA to prevent his or her representative from having this power. Incidentally, the health-care limited POA is different from an advance directive patient advocate (discussed earlier) because it doesn't grant any financial rights to the person who administers it.

Limited POA

This gives the agent the authority to handle certain transactions on your behalf for a set period of time. This could include tasks like check writing, managing savings account deposits, entering a safe deposit box, or buying and selling real estate, to name just a few. It's entirely up to you which rights you wish to grant and the length of time for which these rights are in effect.

Conservatorships

Sometimes the people in your life need someone to advocate on their behalf to ensure their good health, safety, and security. In those cases, it may be necessary to establish a conservatorship, which is a legal arrangement that puts someone in charge of handling another person's day-to-day affairs while that person is incapacitated (due to an illness or an accident, for example) or unable to handle matters by themself (due to dementia, for example). The person in charge is known as a conservator and is entrusted with the right to make legal decisions on the incapacitated person's behalf.

- Things a personal conservator may handle include arranging for care and a living space, being in charge of personal and medical care, and making sure the person eats and takes medication.
- An estate conservator is given the right to handle financial matters and make financial decisions.
- To establish a conservatorship, a petition must be filed at probate court and contain relevant facts regarding the needs for a conservatorship. A court investigator will speak to the prospective conservator, after which a hearing will be held to select a conservator.
- A conservator is usually a family member, although a friend or financial professional may also be appointed. You may need an attorney if there are any disputes about who should be named the conservator. The conservatorship lasts as long as the person needs it, or until his or her death.
- There are two basic types of personal conservatorship: (1) the general probate conservatorship (or guardianship in some states, regardless of the age of the person), which is for adults who are unable to tend to their own needs, as discussed previously; (2) the second type is the limited probate conservatorship, which is set up to care for a developmentally disabled person.
- Another type of probate conservatorship is the mental health conservatorship. This is set up for a person who is so gravely disabled by a severe psychiatric disorder that he or she is unable to handle day-to-day activities. These disorders may include (but are not limited to) bipolar disorder, clinical depression, obsessive-compulsive disorder, and schizophrenia.

For additional information about conservatorships, contact a conservatorship attorney.

Guardianship of a Minor and of an Adult

Guardianship is an arrangement to protect someone who is unable to protect himself from abuse and exploitation. In this type of arrangement, a person (the "guardian") is designated to look after the needs of another individual (the "ward").

There are two types of guardianship: guardianship of the person (to handle personal care, living arrangements, and health care), and guardianship of the estate (to handle finances, manage investments, and so on). Typically, the same person fulfills both roles. A court oversees the establishment and administration of a guardianship, and an investigator will visit the ward and gather information about the guardian. If approved, the guardian is required to provide an annual accounting of income and expenses to the court. The guardian usually is a spouse, family member, or other responsible adult, but if no one is available to assume the role, a judge may designate a person or an organization instead. Alternatively, a trust company may be appointed to look after the financial needs of the person.

An adult may apply to act as the guardian for a child under the age of majority who does not have or is unaccompanied by his or her parents. This includes children under the age of majority who are refugees and others who migrate to study. In addition, a parent or parents who can no longer care for their minor children may request a guardianship. The guardian makes decisions related to the health and safety of the ward, much as he or she would do for a minor child, although it's possible to be named a guardian for a mentally or physically incapacitated adult.

The court usually first tries to place such children in the home of a close relative. If that's not possible or if the child's parents reside in his or her country of origin, the child becomes the ward of a children's aid society until the court makes a placement that is in the best interests of the child. However, the minor child is consulted and is allowed to express his or her opinion about the proposed living arrangements.

Sometimes, it's necessary to legally name a person to look after the welfare of an adult (usually elderly) who has become physically or mentally incapacitated. If he or she hasn't named an attorney for personal care or property (as discussed earlier), the court can be petitioned to create an adult guardianship to care for that person.

An Executor

An executor is a person or institution who executes the terms and responsibilities of a will. Being named the executor of someone's estate is a matter of pride and honor, but it's also a lot of work and requires a substantial time commitment. Therefore, when you're considering who to name as the executor of your estate, ask yourself these questions.

- Will the person I've chosen have enough time to take on the task, especially on top of his or her other work and family commitments?
- Is he or she organized enough to prepare the required documents and records accurately and completely?
- Does he or she have the patience, temperament, and tact necessary to deal with the people involved in the estate, as well as to handle all the hassles and frustrations inherent with diverse legal and financial matters?

Due Process

Due process refers to a legal requirement exercised and respected in Western world countries. It balances power between the laws of a country and the rights of an individual.

Citizenship

Becoming a Citizen

The vast majority of the Western world and other progressive countries offer many freedoms and benefits that you may not have had in your homeland. At some point in your residency, you may decide that you wish to become a citizen of one of these countries. Naturally, there are specific requirements you must meet and processes you must follow on the road to citizenship, so it is your responsibility to search out, learn, and follow the specific instructions and guidelines for your host country.

For example, the US provides a pathway to citizenship for its immigrants. After twelve months, refugees who are admitted are required to apply for a green card, giving them the status of legal permanent residency.

The Top Ten Immigration Nations

Moving and settling down in a new country can be a truly exciting experience, but it's important to know the immigration rules and laws that differ from one country to the next. Here is a list of the top ten countries where immigrants can settle with ease. The choice is once again linked to your personal conditions and priorities.

1. Canada
2. United States
3. Germany
4. Singapore
5. Australia
6. United Arab Emirates
7. Brazil
8. New Zealand
9. Norway
10. Argentina

Over time, these rankings change. Here's a quite different list from www.standard.net in July 2017.

1. Sweden
2. Canada
3. Switzerland
4. Australia
5. Germany
6. Norway
7. United States
8. Netherlands
9. Finaland
10. Denmark

The Value of Citizenship

As a result of mass migrations and the flow of refugees in recent years, quite a few Western countries are turning into immigrant nations. Canada is becoming the world's most immigration-friendly nation in the world. America in particular has an incredibly bright history of immigrant success. In fact, the sculptor of the State of Liberty famously inscribed its base with words from a poem by Emma Lazarus: "Give me your tired, your poor, your huddled masses yearning to breathe free." The inscription has come to mean that people of all ethnicities, nationalities, race, color, and age are welcome here. Their contributions are valued and they contribute much toward making America a great place to live and raise a family.

When you make that momentous decision to seek citizenship in your host country, you'll join the ranks of many famous people—and the not so famous—who have walked along that path and added to its rich heritage. It fact, applying to become the citizen of your new homeland is one of the most important decisions you'll make in your lifetime.

Rights and Benefits of Citizenship

Citizenship comes with a number of rights and benefits:

- access to public assistance and other resources
- eligibility for employment
- protection from deportation or expulsion from the country against your will
- the ability to obtain citizenship for your children who were born abroad
- the ability to sponsor your family members who wish to join you
- the right to hold an elected office
- the right to public education, scholarships, and grants
- the right to travel with the passport of your host nation
- the right to vote, which allows you to have a voice in your government

Responsibilities of Citizenship

Becoming a citizen of any country should be considered a privilege but along with citizenship come responsibilities. We should agree to manage our human responsibilities regardless of our location. You'll swear to these conditions of citizenship when you take the oath that makes you a citizen. Here are some of the responsibilities and privileges you will agree to:

- to give up all prior allegiance to any other nation or sovereignty
- to get a job, take care of your family, and work hard in keeping with your abilities
- to protect and enjoy your new country's heritage and environment
- to register and vote in elections (The right to vote comes with a responsibility to vote in federal, state, provincial, territorial, and local elections.)
- to support and defend the constitution and the laws of the country
- to swear allegiance to your host country

Eligibility Requirements for Citizenship

It is fair to say that the eligibility to become a citizen of your host country will fall within these requirements but make sure you research and learn about the specifics for your country:

- be a person of good moral character, attached to the principles of the constitution of the country
- be a resident of the host country for a specific period of time
- be able to read, write, and speak some basics in your host country's language
- be eighteen or older at the time of filing
- be well-disposed to the good order and happiness of the country during all relevant periods under the law
- have knowledge and an understanding of that country's history and government
- have permanent resident status
- reside continuously within the country from the date of application for naturalization up to the time of naturalization

Dual Citizenship

Some host countries allow you to be a citizen of your host country and your home country at the same time. Also known as "dual nationality," dual citizenship means you owe allegiance to both countries, you must obey the laws of both countries, and you can carry the passport of both countries. Under certain countries' laws, you may not be required to choose one nationality over the other. However, your host country government may not encourage dual nationality because it can cause problems. For example, claims of the host country on dual nationals may conflict with a home country's laws. It may also limit the host country government's ability to provide assistance if you need help while you are abroad.

Once you become a country's citizen, you must use that country's passport to leave or enter the country. Your native country may also require you to use its passport to enter or leave, so be sure to check the requirements before traveling.

The Naturalization Test

Most naturalization applicants to the US are required to take a test on language and civics (history and government). The language test covers speaking, reading, and writing skills, while the civics test has a hundred questions. During your naturalization interview, you'll be asked up to ten questions from the civics questions list, and you must answer at least six correctly to pass. It's a good idea to look for free citizenship resources that will help you study for the test.

The Oath Ceremony

Once you've passed the test, the final step in the naturalization process is the oath ceremony. During this ceremony, you will take the Oath of Allegiance, which is your promise to the government and the people of the host country that you will do the following:

- support and defend the constitution of the host country
- support, defend, and obey its laws
- swear allegiance to the host country
- serve the country, if required, in times of war or national emergency (you may be allowed to serve in the military or help military efforts in some capacity)
- give up any prior allegiances to other countries

While not a legal requirement, being a citizen also means being tolerant of others.

The Citizenship Ceremony

If you pass the citizenship test and fulfill all other requirements of citizenship, you'll receive an invitation to attend a citizenship ceremony. All adults and children aged fourteen and up may be required to attend this ceremony and take the oath of citizenship.

Atta's Lesson on Citizenship

Next to the dream of making it to North America, the desire to become a citizen is every immigrant's goal. I remember getting great advice from a member of the church that sponsored me. He told me to work on becoming not just a citizen but also a "great citizen," someone who respects and obeys the laws and rules of his adopted country, gets engaged in the community, and lives up to his civic responsibilities and duties.

I took his advice to heart. I learned about US history, the Constitution, the various branches of the government, voting, and various local and federal laws. This knowledge, this sense of responsibility, and these privileges enabled me to become an empowered citizen and something to truly uphold when I became an American citizen.

I am a firm believer that it is every immigrant's job to take personal responsibility and proactively transform himself or herself into a productive member of society who makes a difference in others' lives. I hope you'll do this, too.

Appendix A: Stress Survival Skills for Refugees and Immigrants

by Judith Trustone, author of the *Global Kindness Revolution: How Together We Can Heal Violence, Racism and Meanness*

Kindness at Noon for Refugees and Immigrants

When Atta Arghandiwal invited me to contribute my work to this book, he thought it might provide comfort and healing for you, especially the Refugee and Immigrant reader and others touched by trauma. If this is just too strange or woo-woo for you, just skip this appendix.

I've been a humanitarian and social change agent for forty-five years and have developed some practical, lighthearted approaches to reducing stress, including the very popular "Chocolate Meditation and Other Delights." Throughout my decades-long counseling and teaching career, I've come to recognize the power of visualization, Healing Circles and, more recently, "Kindness at Noon for Refugees and Immigrants, Everywhere, Every Day," which I'll describe in a minute. Theories like **String Theory in the New Physics, now give us new ways to understand how energies work in our lives.**

For far too many of you, your journey to your new home may have been fraught with violence and fear, whether you left home in terror or in a high level of doubt and anxiety, following a decision based on the turmoil in your once-peaceful land. In response, many of you may be suffering Post Traumatic Stress Disorder (PTSD), which is described in chapter seven. Seeking treatment for PTSD can be frustrating, but if you educate yourself and do what you can while seeking help, your suffering may ease a bit. Observe your children closely for symptoms that might explain any unusual behavior. If you can go online, check publications like the magazine *Psychology Today* for their lists of symptoms and referrals for therapists in the US and other Western world countries.

Seeking mental health counseling can be difficult, especially for men whose culture, like America's, pressures them to always be strong and to never cry or seem weak. The current redefining of both femininity and masculinity is a major change in the West and it is causing a lot of upheaval, as traditional roles for both men and women are changing, and it can be difficult adapting to these changes. Only a man who is secure within himself can be open to seeking mental health care; but even if he is not ready to seek help for himself, he will surely see that his family gets necessary treatment once he recognizes their trauma and their need for help.

Mindfulness Meditation

Perhaps in your homeland you've already heard of or been exposed to Mindfulness Meditation. This simple technique and lifestyle influence is practiced in schools, businesses, community centers, and organizations throughout the planet. Twenty-five hundred years ago, the Buddha predicted that the technique he taught, Vipassana Meditation, would resurface in the West. Today there are hundreds of Vipassana meditation centers around the world where they offer one-, three-, and ten-day silent retreats. You only need to give what you can afford. Sitting in silence for ten days along with others from different religions and also from atheistic backgrounds is incredibly healing. However, especially at the beginning of your new life, it's hard to get away for long periods. In that case, look for a Vipassana Meditation Center that's near you (www.dhamma.org) and try to get at least a day of the non-denominational-though-Buddhist-style soothing balm of silence as you learn to focus your mind. Too busy? Add this to your list of goals.

Mindfulness evolved from Vipassana (meaning "to see things as they really are"). It is an easier, more Westernized version that can be practiced everywhere. The prevalence of Mindfulness has set the stage for acceptance of Vibrational Medicine (recommended by Atta Arghandiwal along with Vibrational Social Change in chapter eight). Now people have become more open to change and to accept the new physics and String Theory, which tells us there are eleven dimensions of reality in any given moment; thus there are eleven different pathways to communication and healing.

Skepticism is appropriate but keep an open mind.

Here is the link to learn about using Mindfulness in the treatment for PTSD. www.ptsd.va.gov/public/treatment/therapy-med/mindful-ptsd.asp.

The mental focus and strength these practices offer prepares you to joyfully join our "Kindness at Noon (KAN) for Everyone, Everyday, Everywhere." If you like the experience and can envision the power in sharing it with many others, you can find a page of simple instructions about how to do the Kindness at Noon Technique on both www.trustonekindness.com and www.attamoves.com. For now, a longer version follows.

The KAN Technique is your first and most important non-medical tool to reduce your stress, help you heal, and strengthen you to achieve your goals on an energetic dimension of which you may be so far unaware.

Participate in five breaths and one thought of Kindness every day at noon with over three billion others and encourage all around you to join in. Your life will definitely change for the better and healthier. Be sure to join others around the planet at noon, but by all means also use KAN as often as you can, and mention it to others to try. Use the KAN Technique in interpersonal conflicts, even behind bars, or to reduce tension and enhance joy. Atta and I give out the flyers and talk about Kindness at Noon whenever we can. Try it!

The Global Kindness Revolution Invites You to Join Kindness at Noon for Refugees and Immigrants Everyone, Everywhere, Everyday

When you want to do something to help diminish violence and hatred, especially toward Immigrants and Refugees, the KAN Technique is one simple yet powerful thing you can do. And you can join the expanding Vibrational Social Change energy field, helping it grow stronger and more disciplined, and join in sending the Light of Kindness, especially to those you've left behind.

So many of us have heavy hearts as we watch the inhumane policies and hatred of refugees and immigrants spewing globally, from fear-mongering politicians and manipulated citizens who are victims of ignorance and fear.

Do we think these refugees wanted to flee their homes with only what they could carry? Their lives threatened? What would you do in their place? Could you integrate into communities where you're forced to go, let's say maybe into a village in a foreign country where they don't speak English, where you don't know the language or customs and your education and skills mean nothing? Where despite having a PhD, you can only work as a janitor? Or you're someone who watches what's happening to refugees and immigrants with horror, mothers and children fleeing rape and murder, being rounded up and jailed or deported, not knowing what we can do to help them and to try to change it.

While Kindness at Noon, the KAN Technique, is only a first, tiny step, this is something anyone can do, anytime, anywhere. It costs nothing, needs no special training, and will actually make participants healthier and feel more empowered and connected to our common humanity regardless of belief systems. You can hold onto all your beliefs, still hate your neighbor if you must (but maybe not so much), and still experience strong, spiritual growth. The KAN TECHNIQUE will organize our KIND MINDS against the anti-immigrant MEAN MINDS at an energetic or vibrational level; this is the new, unexplored frontier when it comes to **Vibrational Social Change**. Since scientists now claim there are eleven simultaneous dimensions going on in any given moment, so we now understand what's happening when we think of someone we haven't talked with in a while and the phone rings and it's them. It's just a matter of coordinating the common intention of KINDNESS with our aligned minds, and neutralizing the vibration of violence and fear that holds us and our planet in its grip.

For more information, research Vibrational Medicine and Energetic Medicine such as acupuncture and its evolution. We're at the starting point in thinking about and considering "**Vibrational Social Change**" in terms of energetic change. Don't immediately dismiss this as folks first did in reaction to the concept of Vibrational Medicine such as yoga, which twenty years later is now acceptable, but which was once considered "The work of the devil."

Obviously, once you give the KAN TECHNIQUE a try and see how good you feel afterward, you can do it as many times a day as you wish, helping to leverage your mind in common with others seeking a kinder world. Catholics and other denominations already ring the Angelus bell at noon, which you will hear if you are near a church. Islam issues five calls for prayer each day, with alerts on smartphones. Listen for these reminders. So half the world is already tuned in; they just need to turn the dial a tiny bit on their prayer wheels to include the KAN TECHNIQUE. Prayer takes place on a vibrational or energetic level. The KAN TECHNIQUE is one addiction that would be terrific to cultivate. You don't even have to get out of bed! Here's all you have to do.

Kindness at Noon

For Everyone, Everywhere, Everyday

* Set your device for noon.
* Pause and center yourself ....
* Take a slow, deep breath into your jaw, letting it relax ....
* Take another breath into your armpits, relaxing your neck ....
* Now take a slow breath into your belly, relaxing your back ....
* This time breathe into your bottom, allowing your lower back and torso to spread out and relax ....
* Take a final breath into your knees and, as you exhale, imagine you're releasing any fear and anger from your feet ....
* Now you're ready to send your Light of Kindness to Refugees and Immigrants everywhere, and to everyone else, creating a Wave of gentle Kindness that sweeps the Earth daily, like a gentle Wind of Light, time zone by time zone.
* That's it. Every day. Everywhere. Over and over and over, creating more and more Light as darkness is lightened, numbers growing by the millions as you encourage others to join us, just a little over three billion is all we need to change the world. Or do it and say nothing. Just do it ....
* Notice how you feel ....

You don't have to just wait for noon or for others. Obviously you can do the KAN TECHNIQUE as often as you wish. Many are exploring other uses for the TECHNIQUE, some with grumpy spouses, cranky kids, or trouble getting out of bed themselves. (You can do KAN from bed). When there's tension and conflict between people, try the KAN TECHNIQUE, pausing for five breaths before reacting. Even behind bars, people are exploring the KAN TECHNIQUE instead of escalating to violence. At work, try filling the workspace and wrap your coworkers with the Light of Kindness from your KIND MIND before beginning a meeting or in any situation, especially if things start to get tense.

If on days when your Mean Mind takes over, and you feel overwhelmed or sorry for yourself, pause, do the KAN TECHNIQUE keeping refugees and immigrants and others in your Kind Mind, and send out your Light of Kindness from your heart. Start a Gratitude List and keep adding to it.

Now that you have the idea, here are some fun, effective **Stress Survival Skills** that will make all the waiting you have to do in this new life more tolerable, no matter where you are. Have fun, let your imagination soar free, and observe how your body feels as you let go. Remember what my mother used to say, "Everything is temporary!"

Kind Mind versus Mean Mind

As we've evolved into being "civilized," though there are days when that's doubtful, we still retain vestiges of our primitive "lizard" brains that get us into a lot of trouble. Our task in these turbulent times is taming our MEAN MINDS, containing them while we nourish KIND MIND activities, such as welcoming Refugees and Immigrants into "Community Kindness Circles." If you go to YouTube and search for my name—Judith Trustone—you'll find my documentary, "How to Create a Kindness Circle." This is the second most important tool you need for successful integration into your new community; a Community Kindness Circle couldn't be a nicer entry to your new world.

I hope any agencies you're dealing with have implemented or plan to implement "Community Kindness Circles" to welcome you. Perhaps you can inspire someone in charge to watch the video and start one. During the more than four decades I've been leading Healing Circles for a wide range of populations, I've always wondered about the powerful experiences; what made them so powerful? Now, without the need for words, String Theory helps us understand the energy blending that happens when we connect our hands and maybe our hearts too. Again, it's very simple and easy, though there may be initial awkwardness at first.

How to Create a Community Kindness Circle

* Sit in a circle in chairs, close to one another, knee to knee, and link hands ....
* Imagine deep in the center of the Earth is a giant ball of Earthlight ....

* With your inhale, draw the universal Earthlight up through the many layers of the Earth, into your feet, slowly drawing it up to your heart, where it swirls around, and lights up your compassion ….
* Now imagine the Web of Life surrounding the Earth and all of us dangling by a slender thread of Light, connected to the Web and to each other, so that whatever happens to one affects all by vibrating ….
* Draw down the Light from humanity's Web of Life, swirling through our heads into our hearts where it blends with the Earthlight ….
* Now imagine yourself as a balloon, filled with bubbles of Light that are healing you, clearing you, and filling you with your KIND MIND's Light of Kindness as you, in silence, send it out your right hand into the left hand of the person next to you ….
* As this happens, the person holding your left hand focuses their KIND MIND and sends you the Light of Kindness from their right hand into you, brightening your own Light ….
* Now you can envision bringing anyone you wish, living or dead, into the Circle of Light ….
* Maybe you have some unfinished business you need to express softly or you just need to feel or seek forgiveness … let it out, softly ….
* The Circle can expand like a carpet unrolling in every direction, lighting its path with the Light of Kindness ….
* Focus the Light especially toward Refugees, Immigrants … those in hospitals and those behind bars ... those born and sold into slavery … and all those seeking a kinder, more just, and peaceful world ….
* If you're in an expansive mood you can zap the sun, moon, and stars with your Light of Kindness—appreciate, feel your connection to the Universe ….
* Now roll the carpet of Light back to your Circle … making your Light even brighter ….
* Fill yourself with a deep, slow breath ….
* Notice how you feel, what you experienced ….
* Give thanks ….
* Open your eyes, and slowly, at your own pace, while being gentle with yourself, share feedback or choose "pass" when it's your turn to speak.….

That's it!

Notice how you feel.

Oh, My Aching Feet

Nothing feels better than a foot massage to reduce stress no matter how amateur you may feel that you are. It's the gentle touching that's important. Of course a good foot washing is the way to begin; the one receiving the massage can do it or you can incorporate it into a sacred ritual like when Pope Francis washed the feet of prisoners, just as Jesus did.

Remember the elders whose feet are so sore. Or in pairs, sit facing each other on a sofa, feet in each other's laps. Maybe arrange an exchange with a friend. Or treat yourself to a foot reflexology session.

Teach children how to do it.

Oh, My Aching Back! A back massage is soothing no matter your age.

Learning massage and foot reflexology can be good career paths for Refugees and Immigrants as training is short and verbal language skills aren't as important as strong, educated hands. Too often touch is limited to sex, and those without partners, like many elderly, only get minimally touched by health-care providers.

After World War II, there were many infants and children in orphanages. Though they were fed well and kept clean, they still died. Doctors decided they suffered from "marasmus" or the lack of touch. We are tribal, and we depend on our connections with others, or we die, especially babies and the elders.

Mindfulness Exercises

Here are some fun visualizations—mindfulness exercises like **The Chocolate Meditation and Other Delights** —to fill time while waiting in life's endless lines. You can do them alone or with others. These suggestions will surely inspire some fantastic visualizations that could provide you with fresh ideas, entertainment, and connections for a more successful future. You can do the **Chocolate Meditation** while standing on the bus, standing in most lines, though do keep your eyes open while you do it in public places. When you are at home or in a safe space, you can lower your eyelids.

The Chocolate Meditation

Imagine that up in the sky is a beautiful goddess figure sitting next to a vat of warm chocolate, just the perfect temperature for your skin.

She dips into the warm vat with a golden dipper, which she slowly tips down onto the top of your head; the chocolate slowly oozes across the top … slowly, in slow motion ….

Then it goes down your ears and eyes … your mouth …. Go ahead, have a lick …. Then it slides over the back of your head … the sweet warmth relaxing your tight head … rolling down your neck … across your shoulders … and down your sides … across your back … smoothing, soothing … down your belly … your torso … down your knees and out your feet … draining away whatever you need to release …. Now either open or close your eyes and the chocolate that encases you in healing relaxation is gone without a trace or maybe it leaves just a lingering taste of chocolate in your mouth. Enjoy!

Becoming a Warrior of Light

Get spiritually dressed for psychic protection in the morning in addition to practicing your religious or cultural customs. Given the negativity coming at you at times from some mean-minded people, this technique is also protective; you are putting on your psychic armor as you become a Warrior of Light. It is quick and simple; you can train yourself to do it while brushing your teeth. Never forget who you really are.

- Do your Five Breath Clearing, at in the KAN technique ….
- Draw up the Earthlight, the fire ….
- Then draw the Light of Kindness down from the Web of Life ….
- Draw it in to mingle with the Earthlight that is within and all around you ….
- You are wrapped in this hybrid Light, which is more than the sum of its parts ….
- Maintain and continue repairing and replacing parts of the visualization … parts of yourself ….

Wherever you are, picture yourself wrapped in a glowing egg of Light ….

Have a good day, a wonderful joyful, healthy successful life, and may you always be in beauty no matter what the challenges!!

Appendix B: Financial Terms

401(k): a US employer-sponsored retirement plan
Amortization: the process of paying off a debt (often a loan or mortgage) over time through regular installment payments
Annual Percentage Rate (APR): the interest rate charged on a loan, credit card, or other financial instrument plus all fees
Asset: something you own, including possessions and investments
Average daily balance: a method used to calculate finance charges on an account
Balloon payment: a huge sum due at the end of a brief loan term (such as a mortgage); usually set up so payments are as low as possible
Bankruptcy: a legal state in which a person or company is unable to repay debt
Broker: a person or company licensed to sell financial investments like stocks, bonds, and mutual funds
Buy down: process of paying an amount to a mortgage lender or the lender of another loan to obtain a lower rate and to lower payments
Buyer's agent: a licensed real estate agent who represents home buyers
Cash advance: money withdrawn against an account
Closing costs: the amount charged to close a mortgage loan, which includes numerous fees, as well as property taxes and escrow amounts
Credit report: a document that show a person's credit purchase and repayment history
Credit score: a rating given by scoring agencies to reflect an individual's use of credit over time
Debit card: a card used to withdraw funds directly from an individual's checking or savings account in a financial institution
Default: failure to repay a loan, like a mortgage
Delinquency: the state of being late on two or more payments to a financial institution
Depreciation: progressive decrease in an item's value over time

Dividend: a payment paid to stockholders as a return on their investment

Down payment: a cash payment required by a lender at the time of the borrower closing a loan

Escrow: a fund held by a third party to collect funds due from a home buyer for another party such as a mortgage insurance provider, or for a property tax collector such as a government agency

Finance charge: the interest fee on a revolving charge account

Financial planner: an individual who helps you manage your finances and investments

Fraud: a criminal act intended to result in financial gain for the criminal

Good faith estimate (GFE): a preliminary report listing the loan terms, costs, and fees for a new mortgage

Gross income: income before taxes are taken out

Home inspection: a visual evaluation and inspection of a property either by a bank representative or a private inspector hired by the potential buyer to determine a property's overall condition so the soundness of the building can be established and a price can be set

Homeowner's insurance: a type of insurance that reimburses a homeowner for property damage due to theft, fire, liability, and disasters

Individual Retirement Account (IRA): a personal retirement account funded with pre-tax funds

Interest rate: the cost to borrow money for a loan; expressed as a percentage

Loan origination fee: the amount charged by lenders and brokers to originate a mortgage

Minimum payment: the lowest amount of money that must be repaid on a credit account

Mortgage insurance: insurance that protects a mortgage company against loss in case the homeowner defaults on the mortgage

Net income: income remaining after income taxes and other deductions have been deducted

Net worth: overall value of assets minus the amount owed (a.k.a. liabilities)

Online banking: a system that allows people to use the Internet to conduct banking transactions

Origination fee: a fee for processing a mortgage

Point: 1 percent of the principal amount of a mortgage; also referred to as a discount point

Principal loan balance: the mortgage loan amount, not including interest
Rate lock: a fixed-rate guarantee for a limited period of time
Realtor: a person licensed to sell real estate on behalf of a qualified buyer
Secured credit card: a credit card backed with collateral; used to rebuild credit
Seller's agent: the real estate professional who represents the seller of a property
Settlement costs: the fees associated with selling or purchasing a home or other large purchase
Stock: a share of a publicly traded company
Transaction fee: a fee charged to the user of a financial service

Appendix C: Insurance Terms

Accidental Loss: Any event that triggers a loss that is outside the control of the beneficiary of the insurance. The loss should be real, in the sense that it results from an event for which there are real records and/or witnesses.

Adjuster: The term "adjuster" refers to someone within an insurance company who investigates each claim, usually in close cooperation with the insured, to determine whether coverage is available under the terms of the insurance contract. If coverage is available, the adjuster lets the insured know the reasonable monetary value of the claim, and he or she authorizes payment.

Claims: Claims are demand by the insured person for the amount due subsequent to the loss suffered. They may be filed by the insured directly with the insurer or through brokers or agents. The insurer may require that the claim be filed in writing, through phone, or online. Insurance company claims departments employ a large number of claims adjusters supported by a staff of records management and data entry clerks. Incoming claims are classified based on severity and are assigned to adjusters whose settlement authority varies with their knowledge and experience.

Indemnity: The insurance company indemnifies, or compensates, the insured in the case of certain losses only up to the insured's coverage.

Insurability: This is about the risk level to which the insurance company can insure a person or an item.

Insurance Carrier: The company selling the insurance is the insurance carrier.

Insurance Contract: The insured receives a contract also called the insurance policy; it details the conditions and circumstances under which the insured will be financially compensated.

Insured: The person or entity buying the insurance policy is known as the insured.

Insurer: The company selling the insurance is also known as the insurer.

Loss: The loss is the event against which the insured insures himself. It may occur at a known time, in a known place, and from a known cause. A clear example is the death of an insured person who held a life insurance policy.

Mitigation: This is a process of research, negotiation, and exchanges between all parties to appease the situation. In the case of a loss or a casualty, the asset owner must attempt to keep the loss to a minimum, as she would do were the asset not insured.

Policyholder: The insured person, party, or entity buying the insurance policy is also known as the policyholder.

Premium: The amount of money paid for a certain amount of insurance coverage is called the premium.

Reimbursement: This is about the process of payment to the policyholder or to a third party on behalf of the policyholder.

Risk Management: This is the process of appraising the item or person to be insured to determine its value. It also refers to controlling the risk to all parties.

About the Author

Atta Arghandiwal was born in Afghanistan but has spent over half his life in the West. He left his home shortly after the Soviet invasion and became a refugee in Germany. He immigrated to the United States in December 1981. Two weeks after his arrival in the United States, he started work as a bank teller, building a successful twenty-eight-year career and earning the status of senior vice president and regional manager.

With deep passion for his heritage, Arghandiwal published his first book, the award-winning memoir *Lost Decency: The Untold Afghan Story*. Through *Lost Decency* he shares his own turbulent journey to the West as well as stories about other people of Afghanistan as they escaped their war-torn country. *Lost Decency* spans a history of fifty years in order to increase general awareness about the political upheaval in Afghanistan and the innocent people who have been caught in chaos.

In 2014, Arghandiwal tended to his lifelong dream of writing *Immigrant Success Planning: A Family Resource Guide*. Now in 2017, he takes this dream to the next step by writing a family and community comprehensive resource guide *The Self-Sufficient Global Citizen: Guide for Responsible Families and Communities* to help refugees and migrants build successful lives within Western countries.

As a keynote motivational speaker, financial services professional, and humanitarian, Arghandiwal shares his best practices for practical life journeys through thought-provoking, heart-warming, and inspiring real-life stories and insights as an immigrant.

Specialties: Keynote and motivational speaking on Refugees and Immigrants, Afghanistan issues, banking, leadership, talent development, and management in service industries.

To learn more about Atta Arghandiwal, please visit attamoves.com.

Also by Atta Arghandiwal

Lost Decency: The Untold Afghan Story. This Benjamin Franklin award-winning memoir describes the turbulent history of Afghanistan's last fifty-plus years in order to increase awareness about the upheaval of the millions of innocent people caught in political chaos.

Immigrant Success Planning: A Family Resource Guide is a comprehensive resource guide for immigrants to North America

As a keynote motivational speaker and former refugee, Arghandiwal, shares life journey's best practices through inspirational real stories, insight, and experience as a successful immigrant.

To learn more about the author please visit www.attamoves.com.

CPSIA information can be obtained
at www.ICGtesting.com
Printed in the USA
BVHW04s1201010918
525693BV00001B/1/P

9 780997 887020